Modernist Approaches to English Fiction

Edited by
Neeru Tandon

ATLANTIC
PUBLISHERS & DISTRIBUTORS (P) LTD

Published by

ATLANTIC

PUBLISHERS & DISTRIBUTORS (P) LTD

7/22, Ansari Road, Darya Ganj, New Delhi-110002
Phones : +91-11-40775252, 40775214, 23273880, 23275880
Fax : +91-11-23285873
Web : www.atlanticbooks.com
E-mail : orders@atlanticbooks.com

Branch Office: Chennai
Phones : +91-44-48531784, 28291383
E-mail : chennai@atlanticbooks.com

Printed & bound in India by Atlantic Print Services

Acknowledgements

Writing a research paper or editing a book is a responsibility. Though it is my 22nd book still I feel the pressure of being accurate. None of this would have been possible without my wonderful husband. He never stopped me; he only encouraged me. That is true friendship. Thank you Sanjay. I'm eternally grateful to my awesome children Anuj, Shubhangi, and Shashwat for giving their constant support in my academic endeavours. I would be failing in my duty if I don't acknowledge the help that I received from my dear friend Dr. Dheeraj. He stood by me in every struggle and all my successes. I would also like to acknowledge the active support from all the contributors and my publisher Atlantic Publishers and Distributors Pvt. Ltd., New Delhi. Thank you Harjeet sir for making this journey so smooth for me.

Neeru Tandon

Preface

Whenever we refer to modernist approaches to literature, we usually refer to a radical break with the past and the convergent search for new forms of expression. We all know that modernism captures a period of experimentation in the arts from the late 19th to the mid-20th century, particularly in the years following World War I. Disillusionment and fragmentation were in abundance in Postwar Modernist Literature. Eliot's *The Waste Land* (1922) is considered as a seminal modernist work, which inspires rather forces the reader to take an active role in interpreting the text.

There is no agreement of considerable importance regarding the literal meaning of the terms—modernist and postmodernist. Modernist approach focuses on the writer and interiority, while postmodernist on the reader and exteriority. Modernist fiction is determined by alienation, unreliable narrator, rejection of realism and literary conventions, and free use of idiosyncratic language. On the other hand, postmodern literature is open and inter-textual, which uses simple language and does not hesitate to use parody of literary conventions. In this context, I strongly feel that it depends on the writer, subject, reader's approach, and the critical response.

How far is it justified to call a text modern or postmodern just because of the time period in which it has been produced? Probably, we should accept that in many cases a straight yes-or-no answer just won't be possible. There shall be shades of grey. Still, the matter of whether a work of fiction—its setting and characters, its interactions and preoccupations, etc.—feels authentic or realistic may have much to do with how it is being judged. But, before that we should determine what do we mean by authenticity? Since we can hardly ask for documentary accuracy from fiction, what is it exactly we're looking for? Authentic literature refers to narrative and expository texts that are written in the original, natural language of the authors. These texts are not written with a controlled vocabulary or rewritten to achieve a particular score according to a readability formula (Routman, 1991). Authentic literature is often referred to as 'real books' or 'trade books' (Rudman, 1989).

The modernist approach is directly concerned with describing reality correctly. I consider replacing 'modernist' and 'postmodernist' with 'interiority' and 'exteriority'. In my use of 'modernist' and 'postmodernist', I exercise the possibility to use terms in a modified way, more suited to communicate my line of thought.

There are some more questions which have been tried to be answered by the contributors, like how realistic does a work of literature has to be before it is a work of realism? Do the events that it relates have to be symbolic, representative, or emblematic of some wider social reality?

This anthology consists of analytical and critical essays on fiction. The articles in this anthology persuasively argue that recent literary fiction has moved away through formal innovation. It offers an academic treatise on authenticity related with modernist approaches to English fiction. The book covers the discourse in a range of postmodern novels, works that focus not on plot or character development but rather on meta reference to create a narrative assemblage for the reader. Among the contributors, some are established critics and have many published work to their credit, the others are voracious readers and budding scholars. All the contributors have taken great pains to ensure the quality of their articles.

I sincerely wish that this anthology may serve its purpose of creating a desire to know "how the fiction of the early twenty-first century is growing by the day". It is a must not only for scholars of contemporary literature, but also for anyone interested in the modernist approach or the idea of authenticity in contemporary fiction.

Neeru Tandon

Contents

Contributors

Anuradha Marwah, theatre scriptwriter and novelist of repute, has been teaching literature at Zakir Husain College, University of Delhi, for more than 25 years. She has written three novels and her first full-length script, *Sarkari Feminism*, was staged at the Shri Ram Centre for Performing Arts.

Mariam Karim Ahlawat, known for her novels and plays, is a pedagogue of French Language and Literature, freelance editor, and a writer of fiction for children and adults. Her first novel *My Little Boat* was published by Penguin in 2003. She was nominated for the IMPAC International Award, 2005, and the Hutch Crossword Award. Her second novel *The Bereavement of Agnes* was long listed for the Man Asian Prize, 2009.

Jayshree Singh, Head, Department of English, Bhupal Nobles Post-Graduate College, Mohanlal Sukhadia University, Udaipur, Rajasthan, India.

G.K. Das, eminent educationist and Professor of English Literature, is a former director of Delhi University's South Campus and Vice Chancellor of Utkal University, Odisha, India.

Ikuko Torimoto, B.A., M.A., Ph.D., is an Associate Professor of Modern Foreign Languages at St. Norbert College. She has published and edited several books, including *Okina Kyūin and the Politics of Early Japanese Immigration to the United States, 1868-1924*; *Globalization Redux: New Name, Same Game*; and *SAT II: Japanese with Listening*. Also, she has published numerous articles and book reviews in her field.

Eiko Ohira, feminist and a critic of repute, is a Professor of English at the Department of English, Tsuru University, Yamanashi, Japan. Her area of interest includes Indian English Fiction.

Hameeda Nayeem is a Professor at the Department of English, Kashmir University, Kashmir, India.

Binod Mishra is an Associate Professor of English at the Department of Humanities and Social Sciences, IIT Roorkee, Uttarakhand, India.

Motaleb Azari is an Associate Professor at the Department of Studies in English, Payame Noor University, Iran.

Noriko Kubota is a Professor at the Department of English, Otsuma Women's University, Tokyo, Japan.

Neeta Shukla is an Associate Professor at the Department of English, DGPG College, Kanpur, India.

Jaydeep Sarangi is a bilingual writer, editor, interviewer, translator, and creative writer. He currently serves as Chief Editor of international poetry journal *Teesta*, and also helped found the Intercultural Poetry and Performance Library (IPPL) in Kolkata, India.

Banibrata Mahanta is an Associate Professor at the Department of English, Banaras Hindu University, Varanasi, India.

Panchali Mukherjee is an Associate Professor at the Department of Humanities, Christ Academy Institute for Advanced Studies, Bangalore, India.

Swati Rai is a Research Scholar at the Department of English, Banaras Hindu University, Varanasi, India.

Neera Singh is an Assistant Professor at Department of English, IGNOU, New Delhi, India.

Kalikinkar Pattanayak is a former Assistant Professor at P.G. Department of English, Khallikote (Auto) College, Brahampur, India.

Ambika Bhalla is a Doctoral Scholar at the Department of Management and Humanities, Sant Longowal Institute of Engineering and Technology, Sangrur, Punjab, India.

Chitra Thrivikraman Nair is an Assistant Professor of English at Central Polytechnic College, Trivandrum, Kerala. She has also served on deputation as the Principal, Institute for Civil Services Examination Training Society, Scheduled Castes Development Department, Government of Kerala, India.

Gharge Sunita Sunil is an Associate Professor and Head at the Department of English, Rayat Shikshan Sanstha's Savitribai Phule Mahila Mahavidyalaya, Satara, India.

Meenakshi Sundaram is an Assistant Professor at the Department of English, Government P.G. College, Bundi, Rajasthan, India.

Nidhi Arora is the Director of Dr. Ambedkar Institute of Management Studies, Bangalore, India.

Kavita Tewari is an Associate Professor at Noida Institute of Engineering and Technology (NIET), Greater Noida, Uttar Pradesh, India.

Koyal Chakrabarty is an Assistant Professor at ITM University, Gurugram, India.

Reshu Shukla is an Assistant Professor at Axis Group, Kanpur, India.

1

The Second Coming of Indian Fiction in English: 1990s and After

Anuradha Marwah

Recently, I met the editor of the book's section of a national English magazine and in the course of conversation he said that he receives more than thirty books a week for review. This shows the quantum of only reviewable English books published in the country and obviously does not include textbooks or subject-specific/technical books that would be many more in number. Most of the books he receives would be fiction or other kinds of leisure reading.

All of us know that the number of Indian novels in English has seen a geometrical progression in the last decade or so and also that a lot of Indian writers are well known all over the world. However, we have yet to start an academic theorization of these changes or ask the question whether the transformation of the market is also accompanied by changes in the *kind* of literature that is being written these days. When my friend Neeru Tandon spoke to me about a special issue on fiction, I thought it would be a good opportunity to explore contemporary writing in English from the perspective of these recent changes.

Karthika V.K., chief editor, HarpenCollins, observed in the year 2007, "To a certain extent, names like Arundhati Roy, Kiran Desai and Jhumpa Lahiri, who have brought India on the international map, have gone a long way in making the initial buzz about Indian writing." Arguably in 1997 when *The God of Small Things* (*TGST*) landed like a comet on the international publishing firmament, a new chapter began for Indian fiction in English. Not only did more Indian writers—especially women—begin to get international recognition; the domestic publishing scene also became bigger and more vibrant. If Salman Rushdie is credited with the debut of the Indian novel on the world stage in 1981; Arundhati Roy may be acclaimed for leading its second coming in 1997. Roy's novel was welcomed as 'rooted' and more authentically Indian but the market phenomenon it became remains unprecedented. It highlighted the pre-eminence of market forces in the making of Indian literature in English and established the cult of author celebrities in India. It follows that fifteen years after the *TGST* or Roy phenomenon, readers and critics, along with their recognition of the increased national and international visibility of Indian fiction in English and celebration of its indigenization, have begun to voice their doubts regarding the accelerated commodification of books and authors.

In this short piece I will focus on some of the changes that have taken place in the international publishing scene and why Arundhati Roy's debut novel may be identified as their harbinger in India.

Modes of Production and the Issue of Commodification in the Present Time

There has always been a market for literature in the sense that books have always been bought and sold. Correspondingly, the relationship of literature with the market has been a legitimate area of study since at least the first half of the twentieth century since Q.D. Leavis wrote *Fiction and the Reading Public* in 1932. However, the last two decades have shown an intensification of global market activity like never before. Conglomeration and globalization of publishing companies rapidly increasing production figures; emergence of new and competing leisure industries and information technologies; and the switch of publishing power from editorial to sales and marketing have completely transformed the literary marketplace.

Takeovers, mergers and the rise of conglomerations in the last two decades have led to the concentration of the publishing industry in very few hands in the West. In the US, the largest market in the world, for instance, just five publishing houses—Random House, Penguin, HarperCollins, Simon Schuster, and Hachette account for 80-90 per cent of all books sold year after year. The large size and global nature of publishing houses may mean cut-throat competition and obsession with profits; conglomerations might also mean that the specificity of the book trade is likely to be sacrificed to general principle of business. Whatever debate there might be about competition and literary quality, all in the business agree that the old order has given way to a new one in which marketing departments play far important roles than they ever did before.

Problems Associated with Big Business

Sandra Ponzanesi delineates the shift in the focus/aims and objectives of publishers in the twenty-first century:

> As the earlier transition from industrialization (focus on production) to advanced capitalism and globalization (focus on worldwide spreading of consumption based on the outsourcing of development countries) the literary industry now—with a different intensity and of course with different modalities—has shifted its focus from supplying potential audiences to planning them. Rather than merely reading submitted manuscript and discovering new talent, they now proceed as if on a hunting campaign aiming to locate authors even before they have attempted to write, and commissioning subjects, topic, and area to reach one major goal: to create a demand for the product, a real thirst for consumption prior to production. (16)

Various problems may have arisen due to the expansion of the publishing industry and its re-definition a big business. As market becomes paramount, publishing that was conventionally regarded as a gentleman's endeavour (and sometimes a labour of love) is taken over by savvy whizz-kids who are attempting to run it like 'any other business'. The tussle to retain the distinction of books had started early in the world of publishing. In England, Allen Lane, the founder of Penguin regretted his decision to mass-produce literature and complained about the jazzing up of book covers as early as 1967: "So much dignity was going out of my books. Some of the frightful young marketing whizz-kids just wouldn't realise a book is *not* a can of beans" (Squires 45). Almost fifty years later, the fear that the uniqueness of books is under threat from the market has transmogrified into cynicism about best-selling non-books in certain quarters. In an article in *The New York Times* bewailing the death of publishing and the shift of power in the business to distributors Barnes and Nobles, Michael Wolff comments:

> I mean, books suck. Most books are dopier than television or movies or even advertising (many books tend to be just collateral promotions or the lesser offspring of dopey television, movies, and advertising). Even if there are precious exceptions, the overwhelming number of big-money, industry-sustaining books are incontrovertibly dum-dum things. More cynical, more pandering than any other entertainment product. Calling them *books* may be a substantial part of the problem with the book business it provides undeserved and unfair dignity (perhaps there should be a way to certify something as an *actual book*). Working at a magazine where every day random books come flying in by the bushel along with the calls from sluggish book publicists), you get a sense of the magnitude of the wasteland. Books may be the true lowest-common-denominator medium.

As books begin to resemble other commodities (cans of soup!), there is also a sea change in the author's social role—simultaneously more and less exclusive than before. Authors—especially of fiction—are now seen to be closer to entertainers than to intellectuals. Successful authors have become modern-day celebrities with images as saleable as their books. Tracing the beginning of the cult of celebrity authors to the nineteenth century, Joe Moran observes, "Celebrity images promote the body as product, the self as marketable commodity" (5). Emphasizing the importance of the visual media in creating 'personalities', he provides instances in which publishers ask for videos of first-time authors and suggests that their ultimate decision may be governed by the author's performance in certain cases (5).

The cult of celebrity in literature allegedly performs the function of status quo by hiding much more than it reveals about social processes. Moran explains, quoting from Bourdieu:

> Literary celebrity conforms to Marx's notions of the fetishized commodity—it works actively to suppress the intricate network of social relations that has produced it. As Bourdieu puts it, this process of individualization "directs attention to the apparent producer, the painter, writer, or composer, in short, the author, suppressing the question of what authorizes the author, what creates the authority with which authors authorise". (9)

Based as it is on myths and half-truths, the celebrity cult may be inimical to the higher purposes of literature. Literary theory has been foretelling the death of the author for a considerable period now. In an influential essay entitled "Death of the Author", published in 1967, for instance, Roland Barthes had argued against limiting the reading of the text to the intentions of the author and made a persuasive case for broadening out the focus of creativity to language and readers. By dislodging the 'Author-God', Barthes (1977) meant to challenge all authoritative 'meaning' ascribed to the text by 'Critics', who performed the priest-like function of mediating between the writer and the readers. He was reconceptualising writing as a truly secular and democratic activity embracing various cultures and points of view.

The reverse seems to be happening today as the market plays a pre-eminent role in projecting writers—by fair means or foul—as literary phenomena expressing a particular fetishized culture. In a certain sense, publishers with their arsenal of editors, designers, agents and publicists have become influential middle-persons (priests?) between the reading public and the text. They manufacture author idols misusing biographical information, nationality and sometimes stated intentions of the author. Due to close and often incestuous relationship between powerful publishers and the literary establishment, the mediation by reviewers, literary prizes, etc. only serves to consecrate and anoint the select few from the already constructed idols. George Garrett's condemnation of the industry in this regard is quotable: "The great corruption...of the last half of the century has been the attempt on the part of the publishers to create (by fiat as much as fact) its own gallery of stars and master artists" (15).

A salutary example from Indian fiction in English is Arundhati Roy's novel *TGST* that became a literary sensation even before it actually came out in print. It is said that it had been read by all of fifteen people when it was pronounced a bestseller. Commenting on the fairytale-like publishing history of *TGST* that began with agent Godwin getting on a plane to Delhi to negotiate with the author, Squires makes a dig about contemporary publishing mores:

> One of the earliest mentions of the novel in the national press was almost a year before UK publication, by Patrick French in the *Sunday Times* (French, as aforementioned, is another of Godwin's clients, and so his reference to Roy indicates how closely networked, even nepotistic, the publishing world can be). (138)

Several such incidents of the aggressive marketing of *TGST* have been cited by various critics.

Liberalization and Changes in the Indian Publishing Industry

Although *TGST* was published by a small independent publisher in India, it came out at a time when marketing had become very important in the country. The growth spurt had started in early nineteen nineties and by 1997 the industry was focused on the market like never before.

Tejeshwar Singh designates the period after 1991 as the 'Return of the Multinational' in his article on Indian Publishing in English (57). With the replacing of the FERA by the Foreign Exchange Management Act in 1999, the country has seen Picador, Random House, Routledge, Pearson Education, Buttersworth, HarperCollins, Scholastic and Cambridge University Press, Hachette come into India with wholly owned subsidiaries or with majority-owned partnership and with the intention of developing an Indian book publishing programme. Singh concludes his article by discussing new trends like the rapid growth of chain bookstores and indicating a large and growing readership for books in the country. He adds a caveat—"publishers have to find ways to reach their readers" (58).

The reported sale of 30,000 copies of Arundhati Roy's *TGST,* six months after its publication by India Ink set a remarkable record for the Indian trade. It established the power of international publicity campaigns and indicated a large market waiting to be tapped in India.

Literature and Commerce

To conclude, there seems to be general agreement among the critics that the publicity that attended the publication of *TGST* made it a market phenomenon in India and worldwide. *Midnights Children* may have got a similar ovation, but it was only after Salman Rushdie won the Booker. *TGST* became a phenomenon even before being published. However, when it comes to the tricky question of literary merit, there can be no easy answers. Some critics have celebrated *TGST* for its experimentation with language and its bilingual flavour; others have panned it for being over-written and badly edited. Similarly, some have seen it as truly subversive in its liberative gender and anti-colonial politics; others have pointed out in it surrender to marketability and exoticism demanded internationally from Indian writers.

In several ways, *TGST* stands at the crossroad of Literature and Commerce and provides in valuable material to the critic who would want to investigate their relationship. Exploring its theme, style, and marketing history might provide us with insights into how Literature and the Market are interrelated. Comparing and contrasting it with earlier novels—especially with Rushdie's oeuvre—might for one establish continuities of

Indian fiction in English and, for another, indicate a definitive change that connects also with the change in the economic status of the country. In the 1980s when Rushdie's *Midnights Children* came out India was still a protected space; in 1997 it was a liberalized, confident, and assertive India that Roy was projecting via her work. Such associations provide a rich seam to tap and this issue might only scratch the surface. However, if it plays the role of identifying an area that needs academic attention, it would have fulfilled its purpose.

WORKS CITED

Barthes, Roland. "The Death of the Author". Book Constant 1977. N.pag. Web 23 June 2008.

Garrett, George. "Once More Unto the Breach, Dear Friends, Once More: The Publishing Scene and American Literary Art". *Review of Contemporary Fiction* 8.3(1988): 15. Print.

Moran, Joe. *Star Authors: Literary Celebrity in America.* London: Pluto Press, 2007. Print.

Ponzanesi, Sandra. "Boutique Postcolonialism: Literary Awards, Cultural Value and the Canon." *Fiction and Literary Prizes in Great Britain.* Ed. H. Klein and W. Gortschacher. Vienna: Praesens Verlag, 2006: 107-34. Print.

Squires, Claire. *Marketing Literature: The Making of Contemporary Writing in Britain.* London: Palgrave Macmillan, 2009. Print.

Singh, Tejeshwar. "Publishing Scenario: English." Ed. D.N. Malhotra. *60 Years of Book Publishing in India: 1947-2007.* New Delhi: The Federation of Indian Publishers, 2007: 51-58. Print.

2

Problematics of Translation and Writing in a Second Language

Mariam Karim Ahlawat

This is basically a discussion on the meta-cognition of writing and translating processes in the minds of authors and translators, taking as an example *My Little Boat*. It takes a look at posteriori at what may have been the dynamics in play at the moment of production of the literary text.

Writing in English as a second language in parts is bound to be a translation of thoughts and structures that originate in other languages. To my mind, this constitutes not a weakness but richness.

As we have all experienced, we use language as a vehicle for thought and expression not only using words and sentences but its cadences, its tonalities, its rhythms, and of course, the idiom. This comes into play especially in poetry and other literary genres. Not only for a translator but for a producer of literary material describing a culture or using a setting where the language of the text is not the language of thought and expression of the characters in the text is perhaps the most challenging task. We may choose to ignore it as do many authors, but a text could be far more significant, more expressive, and more communicative if we can recreate something close to the original possibilities.

Comparative literature, translation and writing in a second language constantly pose the question of the possible rapports with another. Through the language it becomes incumbent upon the translator or the writer in a second language and also the editors and publishers—to transmit a certain understanding of the world. The question is what do we chose to transmit? What do we choose to translate and what do we choose to represent? And How? Meaning, to what do we attach value? In order to attach value, one must at some level make judgments. It is these judgments which will ultimately guide the choices we make in writing or translation or publishing.

The traditional approach to literary translation advocates the search for proper equivalents for lexical items and syntactic structures. But recently features like style, genre, figurative language, and connotation are considered more and more important. Writing in a second language often poses the same problem as diachronic translation.

The points under consideration for translation or production of literary texts in a second language may be: The semantico-cognitive, semiotic and poetic aspects, the structural aspect which in the case of diachronic work, can include etymology, phonetic, semantic, lexical, syntactic evolution, etc.; the stylistic aspect and the linguistic aspect, which can bring up the question of "equivalence in difference" (Jakobson 1963).[1]

The ideological and social aspect of such writing or translation is interesting because it examines the forbidden, the prohibited, taboos, political correctness. Here too, choices have to be made. For example, the recent deletion of the 'N' word from Huckleberry Finn is termed as a 'compassionate' decision, which I would consider extremely condescending and othering in nature. It expresses the need for the perpetrator of racist crimes to wipe out his past and not put balm on the wounds of the victims as it is projected to do.

The most relevant for us today is the intercultural aspect wherein we examine questions of cultural and linguistic interferences and resistances, of dominant and dominated cultures and languages, and the creation of a global cultural capital through translations and second language texts.

Prof. Hasan Anamur of the University of Ankara states "among the problems of translation the one the hardest to surmount is that of the transmission of equivalent socio-cultural values in a given context". He interprets the issue of dominant and dominated cultures and languages in terms of geographical spread. The exigencies for each exchange would be different depending on the target language/culture and the relations with/ratio to the source language/culture.

The hierarchy of languages follows the hierarchy of economies and levels of technology in societies which in turn affects cultures. This leads to the choices we make in translation and in producing texts with transliterations, interferences, and intertextuality. Also of import is the image of one culture that one seeks to project in another culture when the target language or culture is dominant and the text originally or the cultural context is that of a dominated culture or of a smaller distribution. This would be particularly relevant to the choices made by editors and publishers.

For example, when Sarat Chandra was asked which of his works he would like to have translated into English, he immediately said *Sreekanto* as it was his seminal work. But this did not happen and *Sreekanto* was translated into English a hundred long years after its publication in Bengali, and it became an instant best-seller.

Todorov, working between languages (he was of Bulgarian origin and wrote in French), not entirely accepting the dogmatic approach of a preliminary truth of universal human values upon which writing/translation can be based, adopts a more immanentist view of literature, and advocates accepting the fact that the truth of the other often escapes us and we need to go looking for it. A work such as *My Little Boat* in which the journal of the protagonist carries on a dialogic critique of the existing reality and may be understood through a Todorovian analysis, but is hindered by the editorial expectations from a work emerging from a dominated culture and written in the language of a dominant culture.

"Even when I was at school, words never made the same sense to me as they did to other people...the sense they were supposed to make. They were sounds, they were pictures, they were melodies, but they were not at my beck and call, for they had a life of all their own, and they smiled and winked at me from the book, creatures by themselves. My teachers said my grammar was faulty, but the words just put themselves in my sentences, because they were happy there, quite comfortable, even if grammatically incorrect. They got along well with their neighbours, when you said them aloud, and that seemed more important to me than the actual sense they made. To me, they did make sense, a sense of their own, a valuable sense.

I tried hard to be like other people, use words as slaves, be their mistress, but the stories within the words always sang in the background and the thousands, the billions of sentences in which they must have been used, the infinite combinations they must have made, all spoke from behind, and the words were not mine, never mine. Because when you use words, you cannot ignore their past, and if you do not ignore their past, you become someone else, they change you, for they are saying what they mean and not what you mean to say. And they slipped on my tongue and they slipped through my fingers when I tried to hold them, because I did not let them change me, they wanted revenge, and knew I would never have any sameness with all those people who owned and enslaved words, and used them to be what they thought they wanted to be.

And when words beckoned and called to me, and I said them as they wanted to be said, no one understood me and I was left ununderstood, un-translated, as Qamrun Bua.

And if I became what the words wanted me to become, how would I follow the path I was supposed to follow, the path of the soul?

I suppose I was always ajam, without words, and will always have to make do with saying what I really don't want to say, and always remain without sameness until I meet Zamurrad again."[2]

The above extract from the book could be understood in Bakhtinian theory, at one level and at a personal level it is a common human experience. The Hindi poet/writer Agyey, too, speaks of the *paroksh* and the *pratyaksh* and the insufficiency of language in expressing emotion, resorting to silences between words in his poetry.

In *My Little Boat* when Shamsher quotes the *Bhagavad Gita*, there is again the question of silence and the secret—

> I am the Silence among things that are secret.... And I really like that part.
>
> And....

Javed's realization of the paucity of words too expresses the same frustration of human beings.

"Words fall short, she once said, when the essential has to be expressed...image, colour, sound, metaphor, metonymy, synecdoche, paradox...the essential is inexpressible, just as the true image of God is unseeable with your two eyes...."[3]

The French author Nathalie Sarraute coined the word 'tropismes' for "things that are not said and the movements that cross our consciousness very rapidly;" they are the basis of most of our life and our relations with others—everything that happens within us which is not spoken by the interior monologue and which is transmitted by sensations.

Strikingly close to sociologist Andre Petitat's theory of the irrepressible movement of history and society being constituted of the swinging back and forth between the visible and the invisible, of the shadow of the secret protecting half the world, the book *My Little Boat* begins on the note:

> The power of the unrevealed moves this world...moves civilizations. Millions of men and women walk this earth carrying within them a million secrets each...powerful secrets, loves, hates, desires, dreams, images, unrevealed. Unuttered, unacknowledged, they knock about us, gathering momentum, until they cause us to engage in the unexpected, sometimes the unwanted....[4]

Language (Petitat) being the "tool par excellence which can express the perceptible as well as intangible thought...it welcomes imaginary distortions, and one can either respect or transgress the rules of usage".

A lucid example of polyglossia, heteroglossia, and dialogism in Bakhtinian terms, *My Little Boat* finds itself in troubled waters. A story of transition from the West to the East, it is an unexpected mélange of eastern symbolism and occidental theory. The eastern symbols of the little boat, the legend of Al-Khizr, the colour green and the revelatory role of the emerald, all point to the eco-feminist positioning of the novel.

The above complexities of the novel were entirely missed by its editors who wanted to declare plainly in the book that the protagonist was 'insane', and did so on the back cover for which they did not require the permission of the author. Although totally unexpected, this is extremely interesting as in the novel itself, the backward looking, patriarchal elements held the same opinions as the editors. I would like to touch upon Foucault's interpretations here: the text wells out of any gaps in discourse, driven by the inherent power and sexuality in all human beings—it creates itself in a free play of words, but is constrained by the limits put upon it by society which makes all the laws. The power of society permeates all discourse, at all levels, creating distinctions such as sane-insane, truth-error, natural-unnatural, sickness-health. Foucault claims that modes of discourse, not interchange between observation and hypothesis, position and maintain the above distinctions. The power of society also suppresses the truth and controls the truths that we can recognize. This is discussed in the novel taking the example of the folk tale of Babban Hajjam:

> Women must be immutable, to serve, and not be. To listen, and never tell, like Babban Hajjam. To vomit secret poisons into wells of loneliness that grow, like sinuous trees around them and ultimately strangulate them in their truths. To kill the truth is only to see it grow more dangerously in mutant forms. Then we will refuse to recognize it....[5]

Madness is a social construct changing with time and societies. The inability of the editors to interpret the intricacies of the novel made them desirous to declare the protagonist insane. How such ideas can affect our interpretations as well as our choices in translation and texts in a second language and what is "permissible" in such texts is now clear from the above. The interpretation of behavioural patterns, truth and error, sane and insane, might all also need to be acceptable in the dominant culture if issuing from a dominated culture. Publishing is prey to and deliberately sensitive to such issues when making choices. What becomes dangerous is when authors themselves, instead of wanting to be part of the "irrepressible movement of history and society", pander to power structures (as Todorov remarked in his lifetime) and linguistic and cultural hierarchies.

Sociologists and even economists such as Amartya Sen today recognize communities of discourse overlapping loose assemblages with no sharp boundaries, having common beliefs, interests, and styles of expression. It is not necessary that language and culture can create a community of discourse by themselves. Why translations or reading of translated works and multicultural works are important because we need to understand other communities of discourse, but first choosing to accept that universal human values can be modified within contexts and also that we need to go looking for the truths of "the Other". Translation and writing in a second language should help to diminish the distances between communities of discourse. And not taking too extreme an approach, one can also to some extent adopt an immanentist attitude towards literary texts, to save literature from serving political goals. We can, through translation and writing in a second language, highlight the importance and value of "the Other" in its very "otherness" rather than look for similarities and equivalences and therefore looking to reproduce ourselves, seeking to recreate our own truths in our production and translation of literary texts. And if we go back to the swinging back and forth between the visible and the invisible, the enigma of the "otherness;" of texts such as these, would appeal to the very nature and dynamics of human existence.

I think that writing in a second language permits one to transgress many rules, for example, the transliteration of idiom and the creation of sentences where the verb and the subject are not in their normal places as in the target language, in the language in which the text is read or produced—writers should use these linguistic and cultural interferences, not reject them when they appear in their conscious or unconscious minds in the form of sentences, and in rhythms because they can enrich the text enormously.

In the translation (*My Little Boat*), from English to French for a reading of extracts my translator, Mme Marie-Claudette Kirpalani (my literature teacher in JNU and who now teaches at the Sorbonne in Paris) used to ask me to speak the sentences out aloud, so that the meaning may become clearer and similar cadences could be retained in the translation.

It is these rhythms of the play of language which match the rhythms of social interactions, the dialogue between thought and action, between meta-cognition, linguistic deformations which reveal and which dissimulate, the transgression of rules, creating puzzles to be solved...the very appeal of such texts would lie in their similarity to the rhythms of society and of history of which writers and translators, and even editors and publishers, would want to be a vital part.

NOTES

1. R. Jakobson, *On Linguistic Aspects of Translation, Essay*, 1959.
2. Karim Mariam, *My Little Boat*. India: Penguin Books, 2003.
3. *Ibid.*
4. *Ibid.*
5. *Ibid.*

3

Translation: A Social Fact and Practice

(Hindi Short Stories by Ravi Nandan Sinha)

Jayshree Singh

Introduction

In the words of Simeoni Daniel (2009), "Translations are 'textual artefacts' whose functions are inscribed in the particular social culture that hosts them." Peter Newmark made a detailed differentiation between semantic translation and communicative translation. He defined semantic translation as "an attempt to render as closely as the semantic and syntactic structures of the target language allow the exact contextual meaning of the original" (63). According to him, the words as signs or as images presents literal information of the contemporary understanding of the things prevailing in the surroundings. The signifier, i.e. meaning of the words conveyed in language construction is per se the mental, social, and personal outlook of the speaker or the writer in an independent creative work. The signs and signifiers in the source language relate to self-raising and self-propelled idea of the signification and communication in which semiotic device depends on the structure and meaning of the language more specifically. In source language, the semantics, i.e. signs refer faithfully the indication of cultural phenomenon and dimensions in the exact sense; while in target language, i.e. (in case of the rendering versions) the signs, words, symbols get free from the indigenous framework and they are reframed or adapted to their 'semiotic niche'. For instance, the translator

Ravi Nandan Sinha in English rendering of the stories—titled *Atonement*, assuringly retains the original title in print *Prayaschit*. This is because in Indian cultural phenomenon and social dimension the word *prayaschit* denotes larger sense than mere apology for doing something wrong. The translator aims to describe the meaning of the original word as it is actually used in a particular "geographical origin and social class membership of speakers" (56). His perspective as regards the representation of a sign is to refer to the traditional connotation of a specific geographical origin. Indeed it contradicts the Ferdinand de Saussure's conception of linguistic semantics, in which Saussure prescribes the meaning of the word in structure of a language as it should be, while Ravi Nandan Sinha unfollows the prescriptive expression of meaning and applies his descriptive comfort zone for communicative meaning.

The Social Facts and the Social Practice

The translation of a source text into a target language is a human activity. Paradoxically, a faithful rendering of the original text reinforces one's insight, knowledge and linguistic ability and translatability. In the article "Translation and Social Praxis in Ancient and Medieval India", Debendra K. Dash and Dipti R. Pattnaik write that:

> Translation has been perceived as an ideological enterprise and studied as a potential site for raising issues related to practices of power and knowledge within a community or culture.

In Indian context, translational and linguistic transactions are commonly practised due to multilingual society. On account of this, there are challenges as regards meaning and felicity of expression during translation activity. Yet, the exchange between the two languages is an aesthetic experience, because translation involves the 'peripheral aspect of exegesis' (133). In translation, it integrates knowledge and power. The translator is a time-binder who challenges the metaphysical notion of authorship by situating text materially. His interpretation of the source text goes across the space-binding because he recreates the linkage of language to knowledge in the target language.

For instance, the translator Ravi Nandan Sinha legitimises the multilingual nature of Indian society and ontological status of different languages of India by transcreating the Hindi short stories in order to let them reach to a wider range of readers. His rendering not only caters to the intellectual taste but also to the social needs. The activity of retelling and subverting the text of short stories not only takes into account the narrative dynamics but also internal and external forces of intercultural and exchange relationship while the process of translational transactions. The translation of Hindi short stories in English language assimilates freely the linguistic and lexical materials. The heterogeneity of local language is healthily intermixed and consolidates the co-existence of source language with the target language.

Ravi Nandan Sinha in translating the original story *Puruskar* titled as *The Reward* written by Jaishankar Prasad, retains the original author's source text conventional symbolic signs, because he could not find equivalents in the target-oriented literature or language. The words such as *Adra Nakshatra, Bhadre, Bhadra, Devi, Chanwar, Kalash, Kumkum, Prahar, Shrawan* (Sinha 34) signify ethno-philosophies, ethical-cultural subject of an indigenous ethical system at the primary level. Secondly, the element of transcoding such ethical words indeed violates the essence or the conscience of the nature-culture frame. Therefore, the translator attempts to recognise the terrain of culture in aboriginal mother-tongue. The translator metaphorically does representation of aboriginal concepts in the performing art of literary translation as word and image. He presents these symbols in "generalizable semiotics" (Spivak 242). Similarly, the translator Sinha emphatically prints the original title: *Goonge*, besides translating it as *Dumb People*. The author intends to focus on the acoustic, receptive, and auditory perspective of the word in the native Indian tone as well as the perception towards such people of disabilities in Indian social settings and realities. Besides he wants to reach inside "the corresponding conceptual structure of the discourse" and to search "the problem of the transposition of the subject" in the target language by avoiding semiotic deviations (Gill 31-36).

The translator while narration faithfully adheres to the linguistic pattern of sentence structure expressed as in source language. Indeed there is grammar-translation and vocabulary-translation, yet he constitutes his rendering on the model of "natural-method" (en. wikipedia) alike Maxmilian Berlitz who preferred to avoid target language as an expression for communicating the tone/voice of the original object, rather he lets ongoing interaction between the word and the sentence per se source language. In the story *Prayaschit*, the translator not only sticks close to religious sensitivities of the speakers of native language, but he maintains a relationship between the rendered version and social perspective of the vocabulary for indigenous readers. He translates the maid's reaction while preserving the standard in the normative structure of source language "Are Ram, the cat is dead. Ma ji your daughter-in-law has killed the cat. It's indeed a very serious matter". Further the translator attempts to create normative linguistic entity while translating the standard behaviour of native speaker in the lines spoken by Pandit Paramsukh on the event. He said in a grave voice, "Hare Krishna! Hare Krishna! It is a terrible sin. Killing a cat early in the morning! The scriptures prescribe the Kumbhipak hell for such a killer. Ramu's mother, this is really a serious matter" (Sinha 91).

The translator tries to constitute separate and autonomous entities. To keep religious adherence in order to perform linguistic stability between source language and target language, a critic writes that "languages remain insulated from one another" (Lewis 21). The author does not want to stabilize the normal selection of a social, regional speech pattern at a certain point, while he progressively includes "standard forms of the lexical, morphological, phonological and syntactic mixtures of the target language" (22). This manifests the translator's efforts to achieve normalization and standardization for determining translatability and traditional linguistics in "cultural, social and situational possibilities in communicative acts" (23). The translator R.N. Sinha while communicating meaning in the rendered version establishes relationship between signs which are to be interpreted by readers and the readers have to disseminate the information if they belong to the source language group, and if they are from target language group then they have to decipher the mixed or hybrid/non-standard cultural and linguistic context. For example, the story originally written by Rangeya *Goonge* titled conveys metaphorically the difference between the sense-oriented and sign-oriented function, that are two kinds of typical strategies to interpret communication. Communication is a monolingual activity but when the translator or interpreter works on the semantic content and mental representation of the transposition process, the activity turns bilingual. The translator chooses deftly words as concepts to indicate signification and communication. It is apt to go through a passage from the story "Dumb People" to understand the difference in sense-orientation and sign-orientation. He writes the English rendering version in this way—'Gesturing with her fingers', Chameli asked to the dumb boy, "then what happened?"

The dumb boy covering his face with his hands to indicate a veil replied in a sign-language: She ran. Who ran away? It was sometime before people could understand what he was trying to say. He was saying: "When he was young, his mother who wore a veil left him. That happened because 'father' represented by a gesture of handlebar moustaches, died. And he has been brought up by—by whom? The boy's reply to this question was not clear to anyone, but everyone understood that those who brought him up thrashed him frequently" (Sinha 80).

The gestures, signs, expressions indeed explain the image or object that the speaker aims to draw, but when it comes to kinaesthetic, the mental representation has to be decoded and for that translator has to have consciousness raising insight, even if it appears to be an anomaly symbiotically. While doing translation from the psycholinguistics point of view, the meaning has to be drawn from the sense of the concepts, but not from the factual idea of the word/sign. In this context, it is apt to quote a literary translation theorist to understand Ravi Nandan Sinha as the professional translator/interpreter who focuses on the "sense for sense process which consists of the deconstruction of sign into sense and reconstruction of sense into sign. His bilingualism is mediated by the possession of a single store of logical and encyclopaedic entries for concepts but distinct language-specific stores of lexical entries for the languages involved. For such translator the sign in the target language is called up by the concept, by the sign in the source language" (Bhargava 55).

The Social Nature of Translation

Literary translation tends to increase knowledge and dissipates ignorance. It enlightens and instructs interpreter or reader or audience with information and instruction regarding socio-cultural realities and socio-political context of the society, man and norms. It designs mental faculty with intellectual vigour to explore the primitiveness prevailing in socio-cultural phenomenon of the original text. It manifests in its utterance the characteristics of conventions and intentions of the historical, ideological, "social and political functioning" (Culler 36) of a culture or community.

Literary translation is a skilful device to transmit the reflections of culture and to discuss the relevance of past nature-culture frame in the present times and context. The social nature of rendered version carries ideas, attitudes, and values of the contemporary times of the original text, but at the same it significantly indicates resistance and inquiry in the meaning of the complex at three levels of rendering—"linguistic, ethnographic and pragmatic" (Herman 78). For example, the translator Ravi Nandan Sinha in the rendered English version of the book *Great Hindi Short Stories* picks up the Hindi short stories that falls within the span of last hundred years. His observations and experimental approach bring out his mediation, consideration, direction, depiction, and dimension capacities as regards the societal conditions of India; he surfaces the matter-of-facts that shows conformity of the socio-cultural aspects. He changes "these from one language into the other language to retain the sense" (Smithy 1958) with the realisation that in contemporary times such issues need change and thoughtfulness as well as "hermeneutic approach in translation to apprehend performance rather than existence of diverse identities of human species" (Harvey 295-320). The translated English version story entitled *She had Asked Me* (originally titled as *Usne Kaha Tha* written by Chandradhar Sharma Guleri) gauges gender-consciousness and gender-language issue in literary translation. The interpreter Sinha sets before us the conventional assumptions of identification and self-identification that are perceived and treated differentially, in relation to women's status and the notion of gender imposed by society. He writes that in Amritsar the big coachmen unlike bamboo cart-drivers while picking their way through the narrow, winding lanes of Amritsar say with patience their brethren "*Save yourself Khalsaji*", "*Wait a minute brother*", "*Let me pass Lalji*". Their tongue cutting, their way like a sweet knife, when drive past some old women (who) despite being asked middle of the road, they say to her, "*Hut ja jeene jogiye, hat ja karma walie, hut ja putten puriye, bach ja lambi umara waliye!*"

Ravi Nandan Sinha translates and it means "You deserve to live, you are fortunate, you are loved by your sons and you have a long life ahead of you; what do you want to die under the wheels of my cart? Please let me pass!" (Sinha 2).

Conclusion

The translator here acts as a revisionist to such gender symbolic and he integrates from the source text the gender sensitive language into the target text. The translator rejects the traditional images of the source text; while translating he distils "the traditional usage of the modern language, and do not translate word by word, rather communicates with his creative genius the sensitivity, individuality as well as the target texts' conception of the source text in particular and of textuality in general" (Zellermayer 75). There is "shifts of expression in the social nature of translation" (Toury, ed. 75). The translator focuses more on "the contextually conditioned culture-specific structures of meaning, rather on the lexical differences of the language peculiarities or on the reproduction of the linguistic expression in its exact completeness. The translator internalises connotative context of the text" (Talgeri 86). Thus, the native cultural reference either the translator has retained the sense in its originary or he has decontextualised the verbal culture of SL into TL contextual situation for the sake of consciousness-raising regarding heterogeneous cultural sensibility.

WORKS CITED

Anderman, Gunilla (2011). "Linguistics and Translation". *A Companion to Translation Studies.* Eds. Piotr Kuhiwczak and Kiran Littau. New Delhi: Orient Blackswan.

Bhargave, Rajul (1999). "The Psychological Perspective in Translation Studies". *Literary Translation.* Ed. R.S. Gupta.

Culler, J. (1997). *Literary Theory: A Very Short Introduction.* Oxford: OUP.

Daniel, Simeoni (2009). "Translation and Society: The Emergence of a Conceptual Relationship". In *Translation—Reflections, Refractions and Transformations.* Eds. Paul St. Pierre and Prafulla C. Kar. New Delhi: Pencraft International.

Gill, H.S. (1999). *Translation: A Semiotic Perspective Literary Translation.* Ed. R.S. Gupta. New Delhi: Creative Books.

Harvey, K. (1998). "Translating Camp Talk: Gay Identities and Cultural Transfer". *The Translator.* Vol. 4, Issue 2.

Herman, Theo (2011). "Literary Translation". *A Companion to Translation Studies.* New Delhi: Orient Blackswan.

Lewis, Anthony R. (2009). "Language and Translation: Contesting Conventions". In *Translation—Reflections, Refractions and Transformations.* Eds. Paul St. Pierre and P.C. Kar. New Delhi: Pencraft.

Newmark, Peter (1981). *Approaches to Translation.* Oxford: Pergamon. En.wikipedia.org/wiki/semiotics

Niranjana, T. (1972). "Setting Translation". *History, Post Structuralism and The Colonial Context.* Los Angeles: University of California Press.

Spivak, Gayatri Chakravorty (2000). "Translation as Culture". *Parallax.* Vol. 6, Issue 1. Taylors and Francis Online.

Talgeri, Pramod (1999). "Intercultural Hermeneutics and Literary Translation". *Literary Translation.* Ed. R.S. Gupta.

Verma, Bhagwaticharan (2013). "Prayaschit"—Atonement. *Great Hindi Short Stories*. Trans. R.N. Sinha. New Delhi: Anubhuti Foundation Mission.

Zellermayer, Michal (1987). "On Comments Made by Shifts in Translation". *Translation Across Cultures*. Ed. Gideon Toury. New Delhi: Bahri Publication.

4

Slow Winds of Change: The Woman's Question in Contemporary Fiction in India

G.K. Das

A 'feminist' theoretical perspective is not quite an appropriate or adequate base to approach the woman's question or representation of women in contemporary fiction in India. In the ideological context, 'feminist' literary theory in India is an import, like several other imported ideas/commodities.

The feminist movement in general has a 'bad time' in the West: "It is down at the moment and we are trying to find the reasons..." declares Gisele Halimi, a Tunisian-born lawyer who, along with Simone de Beauvoir, led the feminist movement in France. "Perhaps we got everything women wanted too fast-contraception, abortion, and divorce. And the problems that face women to-day are not strong enough to give the movement new force and strength" (1987).

We have no quarrel with Western feminism(s). There should be no particular problem in using theoretical formulations from Western feminism either, so long as their priorities are also our priorities. In an age of increasing cultural globalization, application/adoption of a theory European feminism, Russian formalism—for instance, by another country, can indeed be a common phenomenon. But Western feminist ideology, Simone Beauvoir's female-physiology/anatomy-based-one, for instance, may only partially serve as a relevant reference point in gender discourse in India in the absence of a more culture-specific formulation that can perhaps be devised. For purposes of a fuller exploration into any aspect of the woman's question in a composite culture like India's made of diverse social and ethnic identities, it will remain insufficient. However, the constituents of womanhood in India in existential terms vary significantly from those of womanhood in Europe or in the Anglo-American world, although biologically they may be similar. Their divergence should be more conspicuous in ideological terms, however. Ideology is usually formed by tradition coming in collusion with empiricity, so differences in both the constituent factors would be natural on account for the heterogeneity of ideology of the two cultures. A particular cultural ideology may, of course, influence, or even supplant another, within an imperial political structure, for instance. This is what apparently has, by and large, happened with 'feminist' perceptions/representations of the woman's question in India.

Not many writers, or scholars/critics on the subject seem to question whether the aims and agenda of the feminist movement, at various stages, in the post-industrial Western world, are wholly relevant to the woman's question in India, or whether those considerations, as such, are culturally as profitable parameters to evaluate the changing position of women in India. It seems to me that to *understand* the woman's question in India, we need to evolve a more humane philosophy than the humanism of enlightenment; and to *interpret* the woman's situation in our country we similarly need to build more insightful, more pragmatic, and more value centred parameters than the ones provided by the politico-economical feminism of the West, if one may so put it.

Several of our country's mythologies, older literary classics, and oral histories give an elevated position to womanhood. But in actual history, women in India who did hold exalted positions in the past have been few and far between, like the Rani of Jhansi, or more recently Indira Gandhi, who stand out as iconic figures. In contemporary literary representation, the discourse has been more varied and polemical, however. Ruth Prawer Jhabvala in her belles-lettrish novel *Heat and Dust* (1975) depicts the familiar sight of un-worrying deprivation of women in India in her portrayal of Inder Lal's mother, the fat and jolly, "earthy looking peasant woman" Maji (83), who is supposed to represent the quintessential Indian womanhood, if there ever can be one. Rajinder Singh Bedi's acclaimed Sahitya Akademi Award winning novel *Ordained by Fate* (originally titled *Ek Chadar Maili Si* in the Urdu version) on the other hand, is a far more authentic and compelling narrative in many ways, representing, as it does, the sad and hopelessly beleaguered situation of the rural woman in a tradition-warped rural community, where she has no choice of her own.

Politically, the woman in India is a free citizen with a vote of her own, but that means little to her; economically she is hardly independent. Woman-empowerment programs in our country still have a long way to go. Gender sensitization is slow. Property laws are not unambiguous, and often disfavor the woman. The long hands of a diehard patriarchal society more often than not strangle a woman's life; alternatively, without hope she kills herself. Voices of protest have been raised against this dispensation by women novelists of the subcontinent, e.g. Kamala Markandaya, Mumtaz Shahnawaz, Basanta Kumari Patnaik, Mahasweta Devi, Krishna Sobti, Indira Goswami, Pratibha Ray, Shashi Deshpande, Manju Kapur and others. Though less conspicuous, there have been powerful male voices of protest also, such as that of the late Upendra Kishore Das of Odisha, in his avant-garde narrative *Mala Janha* (1923; titled *The Dying Moon* in the English version, 2006).

The question of representation almost always is tied up to a focal idea, or an ideology. Take for example the varied representations of Sita in the *Ramayana* or of Draupadi in the *Mahabharata*. In a delightfully eclectic and intriguing recent book titled *In Search of Sita: Revisiting Mythology* (2009), Malashri Lal argues in favour of a 'gendered approach' to Sita. "The diversity of India encourages the depiction of many Sitas.... She speaks not just for women but also for the marginal people, the ones who are compelled to receive the dictates of power. We wish to foreground Sita's voice and her subversive authority. Daughter of the Earth, touched by the anguish of mortality, she is both a conformist and a rebel, mystic yet real" (87-88). In yet another rather controversial book *The Hindus: An Alternative History* (2009) by University of Chicago's famed Professor of Divinity, Wendy Doniger, Sita is portrayed as a 'highly sexual woman,' and Doniger argues that Sita's sexuality "may explain not only why Ravana desires her but he is able to carry her off". Well, one can, like the Creator, construct/re-construct a Sita in one's own image. Post-modernism certainly makes handsome allowance, today, for all and sundry representations of popular culture.

In literary representation, as distinguished from the historical Balarama Das's *Jagamohan Ramayana* (16 c. AD), traditionally a household text in the Odiya home, represent Sita by and large as the original *Valmiki Ramayana* does in the image of a glorious victim. She starts out as a martyr in the cause of Indian womanhood's image of purity, nobility, and wifely chastity. In another curious text, the *Vilanka Ramayana,* which is more or less contemporaneous with Balarama Das's *Jagmohan Ramayana,* there is a strikingly different representation of Sita however, in that it is she not Rama who eventually comes out as the true hero of the *Ramayana.* Sita is a vivacious woman with an impetuous libido in the *Vilanka Ramayan;* with an over-domineering femininity she succeeds in subduing the patently unconquerable demon-king of Vilanka; and only then—at a weak moment on the part of the demon-king—Sita prompts the despondent Rama to shoot him and become victorious and save numerous gods and sages living in an oppressive regime in Vilanka.

There are two different background ideas behind the two different representations of Sita in the Odiya narrative tradition that I refer to above. The representation by the Vaisnavite sage and poet Balarama Das was inspired by an ascetic and saintly idea of womanhood which was supposedly the *'ideal'* womanhood; while the representation by the other (anonymous-disputed rather) author in the *Vilanka Ramayana* accentuates Sita's sexuality, taking an anthropological/androgynous stance, as it were, that anticipates the avant-garde feminist notion of womanhood of our time.

Representations of Draupadi similarly vary. The one in the *Mahabharata* (1981) by William Buck, a profoundly lyrical prose rendering of the epic, is that of an impassioned admirer of Bhima whose impressive body movements, virile strength and spectacular bravery she adores. A very remarkable passage describing Draupadi's feeling for Bhima is suffused with sexual symbolism, and reads thus:

> One day Draupadi was sitting in the morning air when the northwestern wind blew into her lap a white lotus with a thousand petals. She had never known a flower so fragrant and beautiful, and she carried it to Bhima and said, "Look what a wonderful flower! Oh Bhima, even when Arjuna is here, I tum to you for help.... If only I had several of these flowers, I could make our home of branches and boughs so beautiful."
>
> "Where did you get it?" asked Bhima.
>
> "It blew down from the mountain."
>
> Bhima picked up his bows and arrows. "I'll go and look," he told her, "and if I find anymore I'll bring them back for you".

Then Bhima left their home near the giant tree and began to climb the forests and meadows above in search of the home of the thousand-petaled lotus. Peacocks danced on the branches to the dancing bells of *Apsaras* that they alone could hear; they danced as if it was about to rain and spread their tail like crown for the trees. Black bees stuffed with honey were resting on flowers everywhere. As he went higher and higher in the forests and glens of Kailas, deer gazed at Bhima with grass ill their mouths, and, all unseen, the wives of Yakshas followed him with their eyes....

When Bhima returned with Draupadi's flowers, the rain began to fall and all Earth was peaceful.... (156, 167)

The representation of Draupadi in Pratibha Ray's gripping narrative *Yajnaseni: The Story of Draupadi* (1995) is no less vivid and evocative; but it is also markedly different. Ray's Draupadi is a down to earth woman of the tradition-bound Hindu home of the past (should I say) who is given in marriage to five husbands in accordance with 'Dharma', though we are to understand. With a bowed head Yajnaseni is shown at the outset brooding: "...a woman going to bed at the same time with more than one husband—how shameful and painful..." (65). Mother Kunti tries to comfort her: "The situation you are in today is necessary for the preservation of Dharma on earth" (66).

Draupadi (also called Krishnaa) dutifully brings herself to reconcile to Dharma. "I became the subtle thread for keeping the five flowers bound together, whom no one would see; whose pain and anguish no one would know; word of whose torment would reach none" (68). A respecter of Dharma, Pratibha Ray's Draupadi accepts self-denial as her religion and *raison d'être* of her existence. Ray de-romanticizes the 'mythic' to make Yajnaseni come through in real flesh and blood and to make her largely representational of countless submerged women of our country today. Yajnaseni's suffering is Ray's saga of the unending martyrdom of a woman in India.

In an "Afterword" to the 1995 edition (sixth impression) of the novel that won the prestigious Moortidevi Award (1993), Pratibha Ray writes that "Draupadi is a challenge of womanhood, the embodied form of action, knowledge, devotion and power" (400). Also, Ray goes on to add that the narrative depicts "a relationship of spiritual love". There, one can see is Ray's credo—an avowedly non-political, existential, but tending to be mystical one—that has guided her representation.

Representations of woman in contemporary fiction in India, by and large, thus show multiple variation colored by shifting ideological belief or predilection of the author. In contrast to which trend, representations in woman-centred fiction in the Anglo-American world, or in Europe, patently tend to be stereotypical. Doris Lessing's Anna Wulf (1962) is not very different really from D.H. Lawrence's Gudrun Brangwen (1920). Both are iconic representations of the new 'free woman'—"drifting lives that have no roots" (*WL* 424).

Although Sita, Draupadi, and Sri Radha syndromes appear to dominate representation of the Indian woman in contemporary fiction, one can notice remarkable innovations also, as one proceeds from one writer/text to another. In Pratibha Ray's later fiction, for instance, where the woman's question goes beyond the consideration of gender and gets intertwined with broader social, psychological, and moral questions. Her anthology of short fiction titled *Ullanghan* (1998) links the social concerns, especially those related to the woman's question, to the broader domains of ethics, village politics, criminality, justice, Gandhian thought, etc., as it happens in well-known classics on the human condition like Dostoevsky's *Crime and Punishment,* or Phaniswar Nath Renu's *Maila Aanchal.*

A crucial question for Pratibha Ray's representation of social and moral issues is that of 'violation' ('*ullanghan*'), which forms the title of her 1998 book of short fiction. When and in what situation is 'violation' of a code of personal social, moral or religious ethic justifiable moral act? A woman attending upon an ailing, elderly father-in-law, for instance, comes to suspect illicit motive on his part; would she or would she not, be justified in distancing herself even if that amounted to neglect of her husband's ageing father? The choice she eventually makes is misunderstood by her husband, who thinks she is unkind and brutal. Who is right, who isn't—remains a mute point in the title story "Ullanghan".

In yet another story, Ray sketches a situation where a young village girl cycling back home from college is stopped on the way, gang-raped and murdered by a bunch of vagabonds. And ironically police harass the father of the deceased—a Gandhian of sorts—who is accused of negligence of his daughter. Who violates the law of the land, or of home, in this case: the rapists, the father of the girl, the girl herself, or the police—a question not too easy to decide!

Ray's focus on the issue of '*ullanghan*' thus points to an existential dilemma that goes beyond the considerations of gender. That dilemma haunts the life of two young couples in Basanta Kumari Patnaik's classic *Amada Bata* (*The Untrodden Path*, 1957) where two gifted young women and their remarkably sensitive husbands find themselves pitted between the two horns of a dilemma. The problematic of marriage entails the crucial questions: Is marriage 'freedom in togetherness', to use D.H. Lawrence's words, or is it a double bind? Is it a means of self-fulfilment, or is it indeed violation ('*ullanghan*') of one's own inviolate self? Is sexuality a violation ('*ullanghan*') of the other?

'*Ullanghan*' may come to be socially criminal and morally reprehensible. But is it not indeed true that in '*ullanghan*,' not in conformism, there is life's abundance, the elixir of a world beyond. Humankind would not be there, on this earth, if the first parents had not transgressed. Isn't 'transgression', then, nature's law? Did not Jesus transgress the hard frame Judaism to establish a more humane religion? Did Gautama Buddha not do so? Did he not transgress the Hindu *dharma* of '*Grhasthashram*' (sacred law of the family) and go on to preach *Nirvana*? Did Gandhi not violate the law of the land to lead the country to *Swaraj*? Is '*ullanghan*', then, not a fifth *Purusartha*, really?

Let me discuss the point a little further by referring briefly to the outstanding novel I refer to earlier: *Ordained by Fate* (2007) by Rajinder Singh Bedi. Originally written in Urdu and titled *Ek Chadar Maili Si*, the book received the Sahitya Akademi Award in 1965. It is a story of a woman living in a farming community set in north India. Traditionally, in India and abroad the farming community has been a rather stable social organization. The farmer's home has been a 'naturally' regulate institution, dedicated to the ethic of labour and productivity in which women, men, and children have defined roles to play co-operating in an ongoing, year-round family occupation. Of late, there has been a marked change, however leading to disruption in the older ethos.

The organic nature of family/communal life and occupation has become a rarer feature now. New mode of labour degrading the farmer to almost a tool, exploitative use of capital 'genetically modified' foreign seeds, and increasingly competitive ways of international/domestic marketing—all these factors combine to complicate farming as an occupation and way of life and take away the peace and contentment of the farmer's home. They might have contributed to the growth of isolated pockets of monetary prosperity here and there, they indeed have considerably added to stresses and strains of the emotional and private life of the farmer in general. We are familiar today with instances of suicide by farmers in several parts of the country. The burden of loans, the pressures of competitive mass production and the increasing loosening of family bonds—are all new factors in their situation to cope with; negotiation with those might bring occasional dividends, but it does involve grave liabilities and hazards.

The changing social ethos willy-nilly leads to the fast deteriorating position of the woman of the farming household that we see in India today. The farmer's spouse, daughter, daughter-in-law, or sister-in-law is no more a self-responsible, confident participant in a shared home. She has little sense of belonging or even sense of purpose. That is the sad scenario to Rajinder Singh's narrative, which is an illustration of the slow winds of change that blow today in rural India.

A multi-caste and multi-community village is the scene of action in *Ordained by Fate*. Largely, the inhabitants are farmers growing food crops and cotton. They are the last generation of low-income landowning farmers before economic liberalization and globalization were to make inroads in India. Profit-making, food adulteration, sale of condensed milk were becoming familiar features and premonition of the hard days to come. Some of the inhabitants, like the Choudhry brothers, are wealthy, lustful, and corrupt. There are also the 'menial' classes who live as outcastes by the gutters and garbage heaps.

Rano, the protagonist of the novel, is a young widow of the deceased down at the heels all life *ekka* driver Tiloka who lived in a farming family. After Tiloka's murder Rano has no right to live in the joint household, and must quit but for her four children needing looking after. Her best confidante and sister Channo tells her she could stay on only if she got married to her deceased husband's younger brother Mangal. Rano cannot swallow the idea as she had looked after Mangal, who is ten years younger than she is and has been like a son to her. Whereupon Channo, once bursts out in a fit: "We are trying to do our best for you, you bitch! And there you are going absolutely berserk.... Do you or don't you want to live in this village? Do you want to appease the hunger in the hell of a belly of yours or not? Do you want to cover your shame or not? Who do you think with all these moralistic pretensions of yours...?"

"Just think how many women get a chance to marry not once but twice? Once a woman is married to a man she is married to him for good. In between, you have a couple of affairs, but do you think it is a good thing? You are scared to death all the time.... Oh yes! In the case of a man things are different.... This is a man's world...."

Rano cannot rebel; she has no alternative but to acquiesce to a second marriage against her own will and desire. She's married to the dissolute and unresourceful Mangal who at the time of marriage is in a drunken and badly bruised state, having been lynched by an angry crowd for allegedly dishonouring a woman belonging to their own religious community. Ranu and Mangal's marriage is ambiguously consummated, if at all, and it consigns Rano to perpetual slavery to be relieved only occasionally, as when her daughter Waddi's wedding is held and there is a frenzied celebration at the shrine of Devi Ma.

Rajinder Singh Bedi's representation of woman is not a fable. It is not imaginary. It is representational of numerous women in India today who live in the blind slavery of the household and cannot violate the unjust, unequal, and inhuman 'law of the threshold'. If one or two do violate, they may, if fortune smiles on them, know freedom; but for how long one cannot say! We wish them luck, however.

WORKS CITED

Bedi, Rajinder Singh. *Ordained by Fate.* Trans. from the Urdu by Avtar Singh Judge, New Delhi: Sahitya Akademi, 2007.

Buck, William. *Mahabharata.* Delhi: Motilal Banarsidass, 2000.

Das, Balarama. *Jagamohan Ramayana* Vols. 1 and 2. Bhubaneswar: Dr. K.C. Sahoo, 1995.

Das, Chakradhar. *Vilanka Ramayana.* Cuttack: Dharma Granth Store, nd.

Das, Upendra Kishore. *The Dying Moon.* Trans. from the Odiya by Supriya Kar. Bhubaneswar: Rupantar, 2006.

Doniger, Wendy. *The Hindus: An Alternative History.* New York: The Penguin Press, 2009.

de Beauvoir, Simone. *The Second Sex,* London: Vintage Books, 1997.

Jhabvala, Ruth Prawer. *Heat and Dust.* London and Sydney: Futura, Publications, 1984.

Lal, Malashri and Namita Gokhale (eds.). *In Search of Sita: Revisiting Mythology.* New Delhi: Penguin Books, 2009.

Lawrence, D.H. *Women in Love.* London: Penguin Classics, 1996.

Lessing, Doris. *The Golden Notebook.* New York: Bantam, 1973.

Pattanayak, Basanta Kumari. *Amada Bata* (Odiya). New Delhi: NBT, 1957.

Ray, Pratibha. *Yajnaseni: The Story of Draupadi.* Trans. from the Odiya by Pradip Bhattacharya. New Delhi: Rupa & Co., 1995.

——. *Ullanghan* (Odiya) Cuttack: Adya Prakashani, 2001. "Transgression", Trans. from the Odiya by Bikram K. Das. *Indian Literature* 210, July-August 2002: 35-50.

5

Nagai Kafū and Okina Kyūin and the Literary Portrayal of Japanese Immigrant Women in the U.S.

Ikuko Torimoto

Japan was still in a period of national isolation (1639-1854) during the Tokugawa Shogunate, whereas California, which became a state in 1850, already was attracting immigrants from all over the world. The California Gold Rush (1848-55) marked the beginning of the history of Asian immigration to the U.S.: Chinese coolies—many of them against their will—arrived in North America, the so-called "land of opportunity".

On June 8, 1869, the first contingent of six Japanese immigrants arrived in Gold Hill near Coloma, California, under the leadership of John Henry Schnell, a German soldier of fortune and an ardent follower of Matsudaira Katamori, the last feudal Lord of the Aizu Domain. The Pollack Pines Press Congressional Record mentions that the Schnell party arrived at San Francisco aboard the side-wheeler China of the Pacific Mail Steamship Company on May 27, 1869. These Japanese pioneers proceeded to Sacramento by riverboat and then by horse and wagon to Gold Hill, where John Henry Schnell bought 160 acres of land for $5,000.00 from Charles M. Graner. In the fall of 1869, sixteen more Japanese followed (including Itē Okei, nursemaid to the Schnell household, which consisted of Matsu and Kuni). The colonists brought with them silk cocoons,

50,000 three-year old Kuway Trees (of the Mulberry family) for silk farming, tea plants and seeds, grape seedlings, five-foot long bamboo roots, and sapling wax trees. The colonists hoped to transform the arid California soil in order to grow tea and silk cultures, treasured in their native Japan. Okei was brought to the Wakamatsu Colony by Sakurai Matsunosuke, a middle-aged former samurai from Aizu-Wakamatsu, who arranged for her passage from Japan to serve as a nursemaid in the household of the Schnells several months after their daughter Mary's birth. In 1870, after the Wakamatsu Colony failed, its members disbanded. Some stayed in the U.S., but we do not know what happened to most of them. Okei stayed at Gold Hill even after most of the colonists had left, hoping that one day in a not too distant future, someone would come to get her; sadly, the following year, in 1871, she died from malaria and never saw her home country again.

The Meiji Government was the first to authorize emigrants, known as *Kanyaku Imin* literally, "government contracted Japanese immigrants," to travel to Hawaii, a practice that began in 1885 and ended in 1894. As a consequence of terminating the *Kanyaku Imin* program, the Japanese Government lost control over the Japanese immigration population; government-licensed private agencies soon took over the recruiting of Japanese immigrants, and a large number of self-contracted immigrants started arriving in Hawaii. After 1895, one can see a rapid increase of the number of Japanese emigrants to Hawaii, and before long they began arriving on the American West Coast. For the next thirty years, the Japanese population in the United States steadily grew, reaching a peak in the early 1920s. But, by 1924, it began to decline rapidly. Looking at the evolution of the number of Japanese immigrants in Hawaii and on the Pacific Coast during the periods 1885-1907 and 1908-24 reveals the evolution of Japanese immigration and its relationship with such factors as the 1908 Gentlemen's Agreement, various land laws, as well as immigration acts and laws periodically enforced during this period until the Japanese Exclusion Act was enacted in 1924.

Japanese emigrated to the U.S. to find work and to make a better life for themselves and their children. Japanese were willing to engage in manual labor at near-subsistence wages. Japanese men were employed as bellboys in hotels, as housekeepers, and as manual laborers on the railroads, for example. Many Japanese men brought their families with them; unlike Chinese women immigrants, many Japanese women could enter the U.S. with their husbands, as family members. However, most single Japanese men worked as laborers in the United States and did not have enough money to go back to Japan to find a wife, so they got married to a so-called picture bride. Exchanging pictures with their bride-to-be in Japan through a proxy, who also arranged to have their marriage registered in Japan, permitted the husband to bring his new wife to the United States. In those years—twice a month—women from the Orient (specifically Japan) would disembark, often times provoking unfavorable reactions among Americans.

Anti-Japanese protests had escalated every year since 1900 and many new anti-Japanese movements were organized. The first Gentlemen's Agreement in 1908 prohibited the immigration of males as laborers; however, the parents, wives, and children of laborers already in the United States could remain, as could laborers who were already working in the United States. However, the 1913 Alien Land Law Act prevented ownership of land by "aliens ineligible to citizenship". Japanese (and other Asian) immigrants were prohibited from becoming naturalized citizens, but there was still hope for their children born in the United States to become citizens. Therefore, since the 1908 Gentlemen's Agreement, the number of single Japanese males looking for a wife from Japan, using the traditional Japanese practice of meeting and marrying through pictures, "*Shashin Kekkon*," escalated. New brides arriving in the United States soon became known as picture brides. Since Americans believed in dating and marriage based on love, celebrated in a church ceremony, most viewed the Japanese practice as immoral. However, Japanese men in the United States had virtually no chance of meeting eligible women, and the Japanese Government argued that arranged marriages created harmonious households in Japan and that Americans should respect cultural differences. The practice continued with thousands of picture brides arriving, whom white Californians increasingly viewed as a threat to their control over a growing Japanese immigrant population.

On October 26-30 and November 1, 1915, on the first page of the Nichi Bei, Yamazaki Hokusui published an essay in six parts titled *Shashin Kekkon Mondai* (*Problems with Picture Brides*). His October 29 article included statistics on the number of picture brides who had arrived in San Francisco: in 1912 (879), 1913 (625), and 1914 (768). Here, consider that the total number of Japanese males in the United States in 1914 was 37,221: in California 31,676; in Utah, 1,445; in Arizona, 473; in Nevada 569; and in Colorado 3,058. The total number of Japanese children in 1914 was 5,549 boys and 5,279 girls: in California (boys 5,362, girls 5,087), in Utah (boys 64, girls 48), in Arizona (boys 10, girls 11), in Nevada (boys 6, girls 6), Colorado (boys 107, girls 127); and the total number of births in those states were 1,145 boys and 1,122 girls [Yamazaki Hokusui, Nichi Bei (*The Japanese American News*) Oct. 29, 1915: 1].

Many Japanese women joined their husbands, living in one of the early West Coast settlements, a formative stage in the process of cultural transformation or cultural adjustment to America, which all immigrants went through. However, the evolution of Japanese women immigrants to the U.S. West Coast begins with the history of the Wakamatsu Colony at Gold Hill, where the grave of a young Japanese girl named Okei stands today as a solitary reminder of the past. Gradually, of course, increased immigration from the four corners of the world led to the formation of a hybrid culture very evident today in places, such as Seattle, San Francisco, and Los Angeles. However, until recently, scholars studying the lives of immigrants were primarily interested in the life of male immigrants, whose numbers were far greater. The experience of women, to the extent that it was described at all, typically, was told from a male point of view, as evident in two novelists I will consider next.

During my research on Japanese immigrants on the American West Coast, I discovered the extraordinary life story of Okina Kyūin (1888-1973), which present not only his own life story but also the life of Japanese immigrants on the West Coast. While Okina shared many common experiences with his peers who crossed the Pacific to look for a better future in the United States, his life took a different direction. For ambitious young Japanese like Okina, Japanese-American newspapers became the most valuable vehicle of communication available in which to express personal opinions on important social issues and, of course, to describe everyday life in their community, thereby making newspaper articles an invaluable source of information for scholars. Okina became incredibly productive in this regard, publishing numerous articles, critical essays, and novellas under the pen name of Okina Rokkei (occasionally Okina Rokkei-Sennin). His works also appeared almost daily in such major West Coast newspapers as the *Nichi Bei* (*The Japanese American News*), the *Shin Sekai* (*The New World*), and the *Taihoku Nippç* (*The Taihoku Daily News*).

Specifically, I will look at his portrayal of women in the Japanese immigrant community in the early twentieth century. However, Okina was not the only writer to give a literary account of women's life, which was every bit as tough as men's, if not more so. But, in his many descriptions of women, Okina, just like his contemporaries, for example, the novelist Nagai Kafū (1879-1959), who, in his novel, *Amerika Monogatari* (*American Stories*), nevertheless adopts a sympathetic point of view, tends to subject women to mostly negative stereotypes (waitress, prostitute, picture bride, run-away wife). Here, I would like to examine how Nagai Kafū and Okina Kyūin's stories and memoirs portray Japanese immigrant women and show how they consistently portray a certain type of woman in a negative light.

Nagai Kafū and Okina Kyūin both traveled to the U.S. and describe America in their literary works. Nagai Kafū, who went on to become one of the most important modern Japanese writers, lived in Tacoma and Seattle but also in the Midwest, in Chicago and Kalamazoo, Michigan. He became a student at Kalamazoo College, then traveled east, living in Pennsylvania and New York between 1903 and 1907. His well-known memoir titled *Amerika Monogatari* is a detailed and gripping account of his American odyssey. Nagai spent a total of four years in the U.S. His journey began at the age of twenty-three and lasted for four years; needless to say, he was not a teenager but was older and maybe more mature than the average Japanese immigrant, who traveled to the U.S. on a student visa. He left New York and continued to France, which apparently had been his primary destination all along.

As I stated above, there is not much literature dealing with the lives of Japanese Americans, particularly Issei women or Japanese-born women in the immigrant community during the early immigration period. In addition, although many Japanese women traveled to the U.S., few of them wrote about life in America, whether in Japanese or in English.

I am interested in how male writers portrayed women in immigrant society, and I will focus on Japanese women on the North American continent at the turn of the century. By looking at Nagai Kafū's journey to the U.S. and using his *Amerika Monogatari*, as well as several literary works by Okina Kyūin, who happened to be in the U.S. around the same time and who lived in the very same cities, I hope to promote a better understanding of the life of immigrant women. Both Nagai and Okina wrote novels about immigrant society and the life of Japanese people in the U.S., but their experiences, though apparently similar, were really quite different.

Nagai Kafū's father, Nagai Kyūichirū, was a scholar, bureaucrat, and successful businessman, who visited Europe on government business and later worked for the shipping company Nippon Yūsen. Nagai was his eldest son, and he was expected to follow in his father's footsteps and become a bureaucrat.

In 1898, Nagai Kafū began writing short stories under the guidance of a popular novelist, Hirotsu Ryūrū (1861-1928). In 1899, he helped write and stage a *Rakugo* (a comic story). At around the same time, he dropped out of the Tokyo Foreign Language School. In 1899, he began publishing short stories. In 1901, he worked briefly as a newspaper reporter and then began to study French. He was interested in the culture of the

Edo period and, as Iriye Mitsuko writes, "immersed himself in the lifestyle of a typical late Edo dilettante" (Iriye ix); he took *shakuhachi* (bamboo flute) lessons, visited the Yanagibashi geisha quarter (the red-light district in Tokyo), and frequented Kabuki theaters. As Edward Seidensticker mentions in his book titled *Kafū the Scribbler*, "he was sent to the United States [because] his father had given up hope of making a bureaucrat of him, and had decided that a degree from an American university might start him on a commercial career" (Seidensticker 18).

Around the same time, Nagai Kafū also became interested in French literature and devoured many of the French naturalist Émile Zola's novels (which he read in translation). His novel titled *Yume no Onna* (*The Woman of the Dream*) was published in 1903 and told the story of a prostitute; the work is very "Zolaesque" and reminiscent of Zola's masterpiece, *Nana*. As Edward Seidensticker writes, when Kafū first appeared on the literary scene, he was called an anti-Naturalist because he never could bring himself to admit that flat, seemingly passionless and objective reports ought to be the ultimate goal of writers of fiction (Seidensticker 14-15). But then the categories used in Japanese literary history are sometimes quite curious, since essentially European schools of thought were imported piecemeal and never consistently applied. Kafū's most famous statement about literary naturalism can be found in the epilogue to his second story: "There can be no doubt that a part of man is beast.... He has built up religious and moral concepts from customary practices and from the circumstances in which he has found himself, and now at the end of long discipline, he has come to give the darker side of his nature, namely sin" (Seidensticker 14). Such a statement suggests that Nagai Kafū did have some sympathy for literary naturalism, which holds that man is a prisoner of social forces beyond his control; however, as anyone who has read his collected works knows, Nagai Kafū's literary characters are not all as powerless as the people who make up the world of Zola's multi-volume frescos of life in late nineteenth-century France, the cycle of novels titled *Les Rougon-Maquart*. Nor does the narrator explore the life story of his characters in the same depth as Zola.

By comparison, Nagai Kafū's point of view is superficial and almost dilettantish. Zola's stated goal was to improve society by exposing its faults; nowhere does Nagai Kafū express a similar didactic position.

In September 1903, Nagai Kafū departed for the U.S.; he was one of the fortunate young Japanese who came from a privileged family background, and he had both wealthy patrons in the U.S. and financial support from his parents. Nagai Kafū arrived in Seattle and settled in nearby Tacoma. He quickly wrote his first story, in November. In 1904, he sent it to Japan, where it was published in a magazine the following January. In October of the same year, the Furuya-shēten Trading Company, Tacoma branch office, hired him. Next, in November, he moved to Kalamazoo, Michigan, and enrolled at Kalamazoo College, a well-known and distinguished liberal arts institution. He wrote another story, titled *Okano Ue* (Atop the Hill), in December. He left Kalamazoo in 1905, staying in Pennsylvania before heading to New York City. He needed to save money to go to France and found a small job at the Japanese Consulate; later he also worked for the Yokohama Specie Bank. During his years in the U.S., his fourteen short stories were published in various magazines in Japan. He left for France in July 1907 and went first to Lyon. Upon returning to Japan in 1908, he published a collection of short stories under the title *Amerika Monogatari* (*American Stories*). He also published *Furansu Monogatari* (*French Stories*) in 1909. The translator of *Amerika Monogatari*, Iriye Mitsuko, states that "no such work had ever been published in Japan" (Iriye xvii) and that this work presented a novel view of life in America, which retains its charm even today.

This collection of short stories opens with *Funabç Yobanashi* (*Night Talk in a Cabin*), recounting how the narrator boarded a ship bound for America in Yokohama harbor. The story is cast in typical autobiographical form but uses various framing techniques to bring in other, sometimes quite colorful characters who tell the actual story. The narrator simply sets the stage for them to tell their stories and writes in a modern style typical of the second half of the nineteenth century, which seeks to create the illusion that characters are perfectly natural and unaffected.

The story just mentioned is a good example of this technique. The narrator makes friends on board. One stormy night, he invites them to his cabin for drinks. As they get to know each other, one of these new friends, Yanagida, tells the story of his life. After graduating from university, he was hired by a company and transferred to Australia. When he returned to Japan, he never doubted that he was highly valued and could obtain a desirable position based on his experience abroad; however, he was assigned a translation job at the head office and paid a very small salary. He was very disappointed by this treatment and therefore decided that it was time to take a wife. He thought that surely it would be easy for a man like himself to attract a lady. Eventually, he did meet a lady, the daughter of an aristocrat; however, she turned out to be married, and her husband was a graduate of the university that Yanagida despised the most. Yanagida was devastated but recovered by deciding to embark upon another foreign expedition. He found a position with a raw-silk company, which wanted him to investigate the silk market in the United States. Then, the story suddenly ends.

At this point, while the evening is still young, another new friend, Kishimoto, tells his story. He is married and has a child. At one point he started working for a company, but he did not have any prospects for career advancement because he did not have a college degree. When his wife inherited some money, he begged her to let him use it to study in the U.S. He promised her that he would return to Japan upon receiving a university degree. His wife did not want her husband to strain himself to succeed, as she did not want to be separated from her husband and believed that he ought to accept his limitations and live peacefully. "Yet, faced with her husband's resolute entreaties, in the end she yielded and tearfully saw Kishimoto go off to a faraway land" (Iriye 7).

The reader immediately notices that Nagai was no ordinary traveler: here was a first-class passenger with his own cabin, which included a comfortable sofa, and the right to order drinks through room service. Nagai was a bourgeois through and through, unlike most Japanese on their way to Seattle at the turn of the century. Moreover, Nagai's female characters are usually presented through a male narrator. For example, Kishimoto describes his wife, who sacrificed her own feelings and helped her husband advance his career even if it meant that he would leave her to travel to a faraway country. Kishimoto's wife is described as a devoted and loving partner of her husband, the ideal traditional Japanese wife.

The story titled *Makiba no Michi* ("A Return Through the Meadow") takes place in the late fall. The narrator has decided to buy a bicycle and spends time cycling around the prairie with a friend from Tacoma. His descriptions of the late autumn prairie are most vivid and colorful. Nagai uses the same narrative technique as in the first story, letting his companion tell a story as they approach the Washington State mental hospital. His friend begins his story by explaining that there are a few Japanese confined in the asylum, adding mysteriously that they are "laborers" from Japan. Here Kafū gets agitated; when he hears the words "laborers from Japan," his ears ache, since he remembers how he crossed the Pacific with a group of laborers. In this story, Nagai adopts a new tone, expressing his genuine feelings for people who were treated as something less than human, as cargo packed tight in the bottom of a ship full of immigrants. During good weather, they would come up on deck to watch the ocean and smoke. He describes those laborers this way: "unlike the rest of us, oversensitive souls, they do not seem particularly struck by any feeling" (Iriye 11). Nagai expresses deep sympathy with those farmers who left farmland that had been passed on to them from their ancestors, believing that three years of hard work "abroad [will] sow the seeds of ten years' wealth and happiness after they go back home...[they] remain patient all through humiliations such as immigration regulations and health examinations" (Iriye 11).

Now his cyclist friend tells the story of a laborer who lost his sanity. The man arrived in Seattle, together with his wife, to earn a living. At that time, much of immigrant society was characterized by lawlessness; many people who came to work in the U.S. ended up falling into traps set by crooked employment brokerage firms, innkeepers, or smugglers of prostitutes. When immigrants stepped ashore, they might be approached by some con artist or other. One such man guided the narrator and his wife to an inn. They paid a commission, and the husband was taken to the woods and given a job as a woodcutter while his wife stayed in town and worked in a laundry shop. One day his fellow workers cautioned him that it was as dangerous to leave his wife alone in Seattle as it was let a small child play alone at the edge of a river; a woman, they said, was a treasure worth as much as a thousand dollars. Pimps were always on the lookout for new prostitutes. When the poor man heard these scary stories, he could not bear the thought that something might happen to his wife, yet he could not do much in his present situation. His friends then suggested that he bring his wife to live with him in the woods; he followed their advice. One day after work, his fellow workers started drinking and singing and then asked matter-of-factly if they might borrow his wife for the night. The poor man turned dead pale, and began to tremble, but he could not do anything with his wife crying at his feet. He fainted, and when he regained consciousness he had lost his mind and had to be committed to a mental hospital. In this story, Nagai Kafū gives a vivid portrayal of life in immigrant society, with its often primitive mores. Women are described as male sex objects that satisfy carnal desire and as precious objects, since women were scarce in an immigrant society dominated by males. In this sense, one might argue that Nagai is a Naturalist, simply because he described what he saw and the laws that seemed to govern human behavior.

Nagai's story titled *Akuyū* ("Bad Company") focuses on a particular Japanese woman who works as a barmaid in a whorehouse in Seattle. The story begins one evening as Nagai is engaged in conversation with his friends. One of his friends asks: "Is it true that there are a lot of Japanese prostitutes over there?" (Iriye 81). He recalls a certain waitress, a very suave and good-looking woman, who worked at Daruma, a tea-stall restaurant in Seattle. He found out that her husband was a well-known thug in Seattle but also a college graduate with fluent English. As a newcomer to America, he is impressed by the contrast between good and bad. Evidently, society has many disgusting characters that make a living by "seducing, kidnapping or smuggling women...so called pimps" (Iriye 82). One of his friends, Shimazaki, knows the woman, who is around twenty-six or twenty-seven years old, tall and with a slender face. He recognizes her husband as a close friend of his deceased older brother. Shimazaki begins his story at the request of his friends. He arrived in Seattle three years ago. He was glad that he had landed safely, but he was at a loss for what to do next. Then he met a man who said he was the desk clerk in a Japanese inn and took him to the area of town known as Japan town, where he checked into a dingy wooden inn. He describes the surroundings from the inn's window at night:

> There was also the sound of samisen everywhere...followed by women singing and men clapping their hands.... Just imagine. Against the surrounding American view, you have on one hand the noise of "the West" presented by the whistling of ships, the bells of trains, and band music played by gramophones, and on the other, long-trailing, howling, moaning, and sleepy country songs from the Kyushu region, accompanied by the brief, intermittent sound of the strings. No music is sadder, giving rise to such a discordant, unpleasant, and complex, even if monotonous, sensation (Iriye 85).

One evening he was unable to sleep as the sound of the *samisen* was ringing in his ears, so he took a walk in the entertainment quarter, following a crowd of laborers. There were "huge crowds of Japanese everywhere, from the archery grounds and billiard parlors to various restaurants, and...from the windows of wood-frame houses, women's faces could be seen on and off..." (Iriye 86). He continues to describe those women as "women from the western part of Japan, with flat noses, narrow eyes, and flat faces. Their hair was swept back in a bun at the back with bangs at the front, and they wore what appeared like Western-style gowns. But for me, just a glance at them was enough to make me feel satisfied—or rather, queasy—anyway, I could not bear to get closer to them" (Iriye 86).

Suddenly, he saw several distinguished-looking gentlemen coming out of a dark doorway. One looked vaguely familiar; as it happened, he was none other than the close friend of Shimazaki's late older brother, a man who used to come to see him quite frequently. This gentleman, named Yamaza, took Shimazaki to a Japanese restaurant in the same alley; there, Yamaza spoke with a waitress who sat down close to him and who happened to be his wife (Iriye 90). Small world!

In *Nezame* (Rude Awakening), Nagai describes the fate of yet another Japanese immigrant. The protagonist of this story, Sawazaki Sabur?, is appointed manager of his company's branch office in New York; "he left alone for the United States in high spirits, leaving behind a wife and children at his home in Tokyo" (Iriye 105). After several months, he feels "desolate," living all by himself in a foreign land. He explains "he is more and more given to feeling the inconvenience of daily life as well as the loneliness of his lot" (Iriye 106). He misses a morning bath in a Japanese tub and enjoying grilled eel with a shot of warm sake; back home in Japan he had a wife who willingly did everything he asked; and there was also a time when he secretly kept a mistress. He feels foolish for leaving the "comfort" of the life he enjoyed in Japan (Iriye 106).

The reader of this story may be inclined to feel sympathetic toward single company men transferred abroad; this particular protagonist works hard and essentially promotes himself to manager of the New York branch of his company. However, Nagai seems to be primarily interested in letting Sawazaki talk about his marriage, showing how this man married his wife as a convenience, as though he was hiring a maid, according to custom, and as though his home was just for the sake of appearances, for the sake of decency: "just a gateway for show, his children, ones to bring up primarily because they had been born.... That was all there was to it, and it felt quite unmanly and cowardly to worry about wife or home" (Iriye 106).

I came to Nagai Kafū after reading Okina Kyūin, and so asked myself the question: "How does Okina Kyūin measure up and compare to Nagai Kafū?" This question admits of no easy answer but does reveal both some distressing similarities and some obvious and far-reaching differences. Let me now focus on the life of Okina Kyūin and one of his major literary works, *Akuno Hikage* (Shadow of Evil) published in the *Nichi Bei* (*The Japanese American News*) in 1915.

Okina Kyūin traveled to the U.S. around the same time as Nagai Kafū and he, too, lived for a time in the Seattle area. Both men were exposed to immigrant society and wrote extensively about immigrant life. However, whereas Nagai Kafū remained a spectator constantly on the move, Okina assimilated into immigrant society and tried hard to establish himself in the U.S.; even his Japanese wife Kiyoko joined him in the U.S. Okina had met Kiyoko Ishiguro when he made a short visit to Japan. Kiyoko's younger sister, Fusako, was married to a Japanese man who had emigrated to America and now ran an orchard in Florin, near Sacramento. Kiyoko approached him—rather passionately, it seems!, expressing her desire to return to America with him as his wife (*Zenshū*, Volume II, 361). He was married to Kiyoko Ishiguro in 1913. Kiyoko took care of Okina's father briefly and, then, on March 10, 1915, was reunited with Okina in San Francisco before they went to live in Stockton.

In February 1914, Okina left his new wife with his father in Japan and returned to the U.S. In November 1914, he left Seattle to go to San Francisco by boat. After arriving in San Francisco, he moved to Stockton and started working for the Benri-sha. In 1915, Okina's wife, Kiyoko, joined him in Stockton. When he went to meet her, he saw that the ship carried several hundred Japanese women—no less than 210—and not many men.

Looking at these picture brides, Okina tried to fully comprehend what he was witnessing. Their faces showed no emotion and appeared quite expressionless; they had just crossed the Pacific Ocean and were about to take their first steps into a new unknown world. "What were they thinking?" he wondered. They looked anxious and scared but, at the same time, appeared to be both relieved and excited about finally arriving in San Francisco, as if they had suddenly emerged from backstage and found themselves on center stage, in the spotlight. Most of the women were wearing kimonos; not many wore Western clothes, and the simple and plain way they were wearing their kimonos suggested that they most likely were from some forlorn province in rural Japan and not from a big city. Some were holding *furoshikibukuro* (a Japanese cloth for wrapping); but those women looked more urbane, waving and talking to someone waiting for them on the pier; one could easily tell that they were returnees back from a visit to Japan. Looking at the group of women, one man on the pier asked another, "Which one is yours?" He answered, "Maybe that one? I think so, yes, she is thc one."

Of course, Okina was also searching for Kiyoko among those women while he was thinking about the "picture brides" phenomenon, which he knew to be a controversial issue in anti-Japanese propaganda.

Okina was anxiously looking for Kiyoko among the picture brides marching off the ship. Saeki, who had driven the whole way from Stockton, had been waiting for her to disembark for thirty minutes. He approached Okina and asked, "Is she wearing a Western dress?" Okina replied, "I am not sure but... Oh, look at that woman wearing the kimono." When Kiyoko saw him waving his hat, she smiled back. Okina introduced her to Saeki. He tried to shake her hand, but she hesitated for a moment. She was not used to the American way of greeting someone. It was also the first time for Kiyoko to ride in a car. They drove through downtown San Francisco, passed through Chinatown, then went up a very steep hill and stopped in front of the Imperial Hotel, where they stayed the night.

Okina's years in Stockton (1914-17) inspired his literary works on immigrants. Living in Stockton, he interacted with Japanese immigrants and had the chance to meet many influential people in the area, including leaders of the local Nihonjin-kai (Japanese Association). Okina described his life and his involvement with immigrants as he became active in the community, an experience that had a profound influence on his writings. On June 5, 1914, Okina started writing articles in the *èfu Nippç* (*The Sacramento Daily News*) under the pen name Okina Rokkei. His articles and essays appeared almost daily on the front page of the newspaper. Some articles recounted his impressions of Sacramento and, more generally, of California. Okina began writing criticism for the New Year's special editions of the nine Japanese-American newspapers on the West Coast, urging the establishment of a pure immigrant literature. Okina emphasized the importance of a realistic literature based on the everyday life of immigrants; he felt that if the immigrant experience were seen through rose-tinted glasses, it would seem meaningless.

By 1915, Okina's literary works spanned virtually every genre. In addition to publishing articles and essays, Okina continued to write fiction and later comedy. As an advocate of literature about immigrants' experience, and with the support of Yamanaka Magae of the *Nichi Bei*, he wrote a lengthy novel titled *Aku no Hikage* (Shadow of Evil), which appeared in the Nichi Bei in 1915, in 99 installments (*Aku no Hikage*, *Nichi Bei*, 99 installments between June 3, 1915, and September 16, 1915). At twenty-seven years of age, Okina was building a career as an editor at the publishing company and the *èfu Nippç*, and serving as secretary of the Stockton Nihonjin-kai (Japanese Association). He also enjoyed life with his wife Kiyoko, who had joined him in the U.S.

Aku no Hikage is about the lives of several young people: Ofumi, Okuni, Kumagaya, Kçno, Tajima, Tayama, and Tomura. He modeled two of the female characters (Ofumi and Okuni) on the waitresses he had befriended in the Maneki restaurant, four of the male characters (Kumagaya, Kçno, Tajima, Tayama) on his personal friends, and Tomura on himself. All four are young Japanese immigrants who happened to be schoolmates in the same junior high school in Japan and arrived in Seattle in the same year and struggled to make it in their new country. Tajima and Tomura became students, and Tayama went to Alaska to work. The story begins when Tajima and Tomura visit the cemetery where Tayama is buried; he was killed four years before the story starts, after getting in trouble with a woman. Okina has very good powers of observation; he bases his story on some episodes that happened in the community and on some of his own experiences with women, as well as on actual drinking establishments, waitresses working at several Japanese restaurants, houses of prostitution, hotels, and streets, including their physical layout, which is why some characters and episodes in the novel are so realistic, as if they were part of a documentary. One example is a love triangle set in a drinking house, the *Maneki*, or the *Yachiyo* in the Japanese quarter (*Zenshū*, Volume III, 26-34). As the story progresses, it often becomes difficult for those people who know Okina well to distinguish between his own life and the fictional actions of the character Tomura, especially when Tomura describes his feelings for various women. Those readers familiar with his *Zenshū* (Volumes II and III) are aware of the topics described in his diary and can easily relate them to Tomura's experiences with a white girl, who happened to be Okina's schoolmate in Union High School in Bremerton (Selma Pittack, who later became a silent film star). These readers also recognize his experiences with waitresses at the Maneki restaurant, the *Zabuton* (Japanese cushion) incident, the prostitutes in King Street, his visits to Tacoma with his friend and meetings with a lady who openly expresses her feelings toward Tomura. The story ends rather unexpectedly when Tomura suddenly loses his passion for her because he is disappointed by her rather rude behavior while she was drinking. She leaves town and disappears. Okina's story was well received by critics and many readers, who considered it the most vivid and realistic description of immigrants that they had ever read. He received many comments from his readers, most of whom were pleased with his story.

Finally, let me attempt to define the significance of Nagai's and Okina's life and work and how women are portrayed in their stories. Both writers were exposed to all sides of immigrant society and wrote about the life of immigrants. Although they had similar experiences in America and described many of the same experiences in their work, Nagai Kafū remained aloof, knowing full well that he had other options, chief among them a visit to France (which he had been preparing all along). His journey to the U.S. recalls the French Symbolist Charles Baudelaire's famous poem titled "Le Voyage," which Nagai quotes at some length:

> Mais les vrais voyageurs sont ceux-là seuls qui partent
> Pour partir; cœurs légers, semblables aux ballons,
> De leur fatalité jamais ils ne s'écartent,
> Et, sans savoir pourquoi, disent toujours: Allons!
> "Le Voyage" (Baudelaire, *Les Fleurs du mal*)
> But the true voyagers are only those who leave
> Just to be leaving; hearts light, like balloons,
> They never turn aside from their fatality
> And without knowing why they always say: "Let's go!"

In Nagai Kafū's stories, the Japanese female figures include the wife of a man who comes to the U.S. to get a college degree, a laborer's wife who is gang raped, a waitress whose husband is a pimp, an assortment of prostitutes, a young female student attending college, and the wife of a businessman who left her behind in Japan. These women are all quite helpless; more importantly, they are usually victims, objects of male desire, particularly the prostitutes, but also the laborer's wife who is raped, the wife who was abandoned in Japan and whose marriage was a marriage of (male) convenience, and even the student pursuing a degree from an American college. All are portrayed as objects lacking emotions and passion.

Okina, on the other hand, actually did become an American in the sense that he lived and worked in America for many years. Okina's work is important for historical reasons, because he helps us understand the lives of ordinary people in Japanese immigrant society. This is the personal journey of a young Japanese man who wanted to come to America, the land of his dreams, in order to experience success. In so doing, he became an advocate for immigrant literature, a new genre of writing by, for, and about immigrants. Okina often used events that happened to him and to people in the Japanese community as material for his novels and stories. He believed that their experiences made up the essence of immigrant literature. In Okina Kyūin's stories, the Japanese female characters are rather few and limited to waitresses or daughters of Japanese immigrants. Often, his stories involve a young man's struggle to make a living as an immigrant, tormented by love and lust, caught between his romantic feelings and his carnal desire. For example, when Okina Kyūin tries to describe a young man's passion for women, he often describes married women or waitresses. Needless to say, these women all arc portrayed as quite helpless and as victims of immigrant society. Okina knew the realities of immigrant life first-hand. Women did not have much choice, and it was difficult for them to escape from the conditions in which they lived (of course, the same could be said about many male immigrants at the time). Some women arrived in the U.S. without much knowledge about the country. For instance, they came as picture brides to strange men; sometimes one of these brides suffered so much that she ran away with another man. Other women accompanied their husbands but could not endure the harsh reality of immigrant life and left. In some cases, women were lured by sweet talk of easy money and tricked into coming to the U.S., where they sometimes ended up as prostitutes. If they were lucky, they found work as waitresses, for example, but most women immigrants did not have many options.

The women who appear in Okina Kyūin's stories are often women with whom the author himself was romantically involved, which means that their literary personae express the author's emotions and passions rather than those of the characters he intends to portray. Okinaūs romantic interludes ended rather quickly, though, and unfortunately were limited to women of a certain type, who did not reflect a cross section of immigrant society. Actually, Okina's experience with women was rather limited period. Moreover, he was not always able to make smooth transitions between scenes, characters, and themes, which frequently creates an awkward impression on the part of many readers. I believe that one reason for this "rushed" quality of his writing was that he was usually in a great hurry to meet a newspaper deadline. Many of his novels were serialized and appeared in 20, or 30, or more installments. Unfortunately, he did not have the genius of a Balzac or a Dickens—the unacknowledged masters of the genre—to whet the reader's appetite and to keep it in suspense, as it were, until the next installment appeared.

Okina Kyūin's world is dominated by the harsh realities of immigrant society. However, this is not enough to make of him a Naturalist, at least not in the accepted sense of the term; nor was Nagai Kafū a Naturalist in the French, Zolaesque sense of the term. Both writers met women in immigrant society, whom they later described in their literary works; however, although women were omnipresent in immigrant society, their stories almost always were told by male authors, not from a woman's point of view, but from a male's, so one might say that an immigrant woman's voice was seldom heard, if ever. Here again, I think of Okei, who was brought to the Wakamatsu colony and left all alone; she wished to return to her homeland but instead died in faraway America. Her grave stands as a solitary reminder of one Japanese woman immigrant's sad destiny and echoes the challenges that awaited other women immigrants from Japan.

In the final analysis, despite all their shortcomings and their narrow and even self-indulgent focus, both writers are eminently interesting to scholars studying Japanese emigration to the American West Coast because their works transcend literature proper insofar as they offer a wealth of information about Japanese immigrant society.

WORKS CITED

Baudelaire, Charles. *Les Fleurs du mal*. Paris: Garnier Frères, 1961.

Iriye, Mitsuko. *American Stories: Nagai Kafū*. New York: Columbia University Press, 2000.

Nagai, Kafū. *Amerika Monogatari*. Shinshēsha, Tokyo, Japan, 1951.

Okina, Kyūin. "Aku no Hikage." *Nichi Bei* (*The Japanese American News*) 3 Jun. 1915: 1-16; Sept. 1915: 1 (99 installments between Jun. 3, 1915, and Sept. 16, 1915). Print.

Okina, Kyūin et al. *Umino Kanatani*, Okina Kyūin Zenshv. Volume II. Toyama, Japan: Toyama Sugaki Company, February 1972.

——. *Konjiki no Sono*, Okina Kyūin Zenshū. Volume III. Toyama, Japan: Toyama Sugaki Company, May 1972.

——. *Sōsaku Aku no Hikage*, Okina, Kyūin Zenshū. Volume V. Toyama, Japan: Toyama Sugaki Company, May 1972.

Pollack Pines Press Congressional Record. Vol. 113, Washington. Wednesday 7 May 1969.

Seidensticker, Edward. *Kafū the Scribbler: The Life and Writings of Nagai Kafū, 1879-1959*. Ann Arbor: Center for Japanese Studies The University of Michigan, 1965.

Takeuchi, Kējirē. *Beikoku Hokuseibu Nihon Iminshi*. Seattle: Tairiku Nipposha, 1929.

Yamazaki, Hokusui. "*Shashinkekkon Mondai.*" *The Nichi Bei (The Japanese American News)* [San Francisco, CA] 29 Oct. 1915: 1. Print.

6

Midnight's Children as a Bildungsroman: A Narrative of Failure

Eiko Ohira

As M.K. Naik states Salman Rushdie's *Midnight's Children* (1981) is a "many-faceted novel...an autobiographical bildungsroman, a picaresque narrative, a political allegory,...a surrealist fantasy..." (*Studies in Indian English Literature* 46). Most critics have tended to focus on the modernity of its complex structure and its experimental style, and recent criticism tends to focus on the relationship between individual and political identity. However, the ways in which this bildungsroman is unique as a partition novel have not been focused on yet. As a partition novel it is unique in the way the grand narrative, which foregrounds the creation of a unified nation-state, is deconstructed through its depiction of the failure of the protagonist's psychological subject formation, a process which is chained to the formation and fragmentation of India.

Midnight's Children, which delineates the protagonist' self-alienation and fragmentation, is largely a narrative of failure. I would like to focus in this paper on how Saleem narrates the story of his life which ends with him as "specks of voiceless dust" (463) in a crowd, his autobiography a record of his defeat and dismemberment, and, by extension, of the defeat and dismemberment of India.

II

Saleem starts his autobiographical narrative with his birth, August 15, 1947, which, of course coincides with the date of the independence of India, and he ends his story with a prophecy of his death on August 15, 1978. Since he "had been mysteriously hand-cuffed to history", and his "destinies indissolubly chained" to those of his country, his autobiography is necessarily a history of India for those three decades. The new India, "a mythical land" only exists, he says, in "the dream we all shared" (118), but it reflects the "collective failure of imagination" of its parents. The partitioned India generated from this failure, as well as the origin of Saleem's birth and his family saga goes back to Kashmir in 1915. So we need to consider what sort of event caused Aziz Saleem's grandfather, to fall into a life of fragmentation in Kashmir in 1915.

How and where do we come from? This is a universal question for all children. Saleem finds his answer in his grandfather's "holy, mutilated square of linen" (10). This is his "talisman" and "open-sesame" which enable him to "commence the business of remaking" his life from "the point at which it really began" (10). Saleem also says that he is "a swallower of all lives," and that things around him could be "guided only by the memory of a large white bedsheet with a roughly circular hole some seven inches in diameter cut into the center" (9-10), stained with "three drops of blood," from which the Creator formed Man according to the Quran.

The hole in Aziz was made when he "hit his nose against a frost hardened tussock of earth while attempting to pray" one Kashmir morning in 1915, after which he "resolved never again to kiss earth for any god or man" (10). The vacancy in him made by this decision left him "vulnerable to women and history" (10). But this is not really an explanation of anything since it mostly begs questions. What does this vulnerability to women and history mean? By this traumatic experience, what exactly did Aziz lose and what sort of situation did he fall into or what sort of desire was aroused? Why is his grandfather's experience in the early spring of 1915 fatal to Saleem? Why is "a hole" referred so obsessively in this text?

To begin to answer these questions, we need to consider the psychology of infancy. Traumatic separations are retrospectively and repeatedly rehearsed in many autobiographical stories. An infant suffers from the absence of a mother, which causes a psychological trauma. *Midnight's Children* is full of images which suggest such a traumatic experience. Is Saleem, as garrulous narrator, playing a game of "fort da" (peekaboo) in a symbolic replay of the traumatic separation in order to appease anxiety? Since his story includes a saga of his family and of modern India, is this whole narrative a gigantic game of peekaboo?

III

To explore these questions, I would like to examine first what sort of character Saleem is. He has various nicknames such as "Snotnose, Stain-face, Baldy, Sniffer, Buddha and even Piece-of-the-Moon" (9), which suggest his bewildering multifariousness. As T.N. Dhar asks, is he "no 'character' at all" but "an embodiment of history", "no more than a voice", "a world in himself—history encapsulated into a human frame", "a receptacle of what has happened and is happening around him?" (*History-Fiction Interface* 106). Is he a hole to absorb all the lives and things around him? Saleem says, "...there are so many stories to tell, too many...I have been a swallower of lives; and to know me, just the one of me, you'll have to swallow the lot as well. Consumed multitudes are jostling and shoving inside me" (9). He asks, "Who am I?" and answers, "I am the sum total of everything that went before me, of all I have been seen done, of everything done-to-me. I am everyone everything whose being-in-the-world affected was affected by mine" (383).

He is "a swallower" of the world, but, on the other hand, he is doomed to inherit the legacy of his grandfather's magical sheet, reflecting the hole inside Aziz, meaning he cannot hold what he swallows. So, he is both omnipotent and impotent; his life is doomed to fragmentation. This also reflects infant psychology. A baby before the fatal separation from the mother is helpless but nevertheless fantasizes s/he is omnipotent. Saleem is self-aggrandizing (174); he sees himself as a "protagonist" (237) and claims "a place at the center of things" (238). As he swallows the world, he identifies with it, and later he projects his ideal unified ego towards Jamila, his sister or Mother India, but this projective identification causes his self-sacrifice, castration, and self-loss. Saleem and Mother India are represented as if they were following a standard subject-formation process: parasitic fusion between a baby and the mother, loss of the object, and identification with the lost object.

Is he an Object petit (a Lacanian concept), an image of the objects which are loved, identified with and separated from by the subject, and thus finally an image of self-love? A baby embraces any old objects but those loved objects are abandoned in the process of subject formation. Thus, the speaking subject (the narrator Saleem) separates them (the loved objects) from his/her body. Does Saleem symbolize this separation, a hole in consciousness which sets a signifying system in motion? Saleem's narrative, which is guided only by the memory of his grandfather's perforated sheet, suggests a metonymic movement to cover the hole in himself which signifies a lack of love.

At the same time, Saleem foretells his own death, and a death drive definitely lurks throughout this text. This drive is generated by a nostalgic desire for a symbiotic relationship in the imaginary with the maternal body. Saleem tells us obsessively about how he is chained to India, and in the repetitive narratives of the fatal connection between the two, we are given variations of representation, which make the bond far from simplistic. Saleem says, "I had been mysteriously hand-cuffed to history, my destinies indissolubly chained to those of my country. For the next three decades, there was to be no escape" (9). Saleem and India are not only chained to each other a "twin-in-birth," but they are also "joined at the hip, so that what happened to either of us, happened to us both. If I, snot-nosed stain-faced etcetera, had had a hard time of it, then so had she, my subcontinental twin sister" (385). Later, he tells us they are in fact Siamese twins joined at the hip, then adds, "...my truly incestuous feelings were for my true birth-sister, India herself" (385). He then significantly asks, "Had I simply transferred on to her shoulders the adoration which I now perceived to be a vaulting, all-encompassing love of country? When was it that I realized that my truly-incestuous feelings were for my true birth-sister, India herself?" (385). However, Saleem also represents this sister as Bharat Mata, Mother India. "Women had made me; and also unmade...is not Mother India, Bharat Mata, commonly thought of as female? And, as you know, there's no escape from her."

Even though already joined too closely, Saleem desires fusion with this composite figure. What does this incestuous desire for India as a maternal body suggest? Mother India creates and destroys him, which suggests she is the devouring mother whom an infant imagines at a certain growing stage. He becomes impotent because of his incestuous feelings for Jamila, his real sister, to whom his true desire for Mother India is transferred. His castration, then, suggests punishment for his forbidden love for the maternal body. When he kisses Parvati, he sees "her face changing, becoming the face of a forbidden love; the ghostly features of Jamila Singer replaced those of the witch-girl" (396). Not only that, but Jamila "had begun to rot, the dreadful pustules and cankers of forbidden love were spreading across her face; now the rancid flower of incest blossomed on my sister's phantasmal features, and I couldn't do it, couldn't kiss touch look upon that intolerable spectral face" (396).

In fact, Saleem's whole narrative is proleptic: "I will soon be thirty-one-years old. Perhaps. If my crumbling, over-used body permits. But I have no hope of saving my life, nor can I count on having even a thousand nights and a night" (9). His castration and elimination are constants. He wonders how he should end the story, and chooses an ending in which he will be trampled underfoot by crowds, many-headed monsters, and reduced to "specks of voiceless dust," one of the thousand midnight children who are both "masters and victims of their times" (463). As such, he says, "I shall never reach Kashmir, like Jehangir Mughal Emperor. I shall die with Kashmir on my lips" (462).

What does Kashmir signify for him and his grandfather? Is it a lost homeland for his grandfather, a lost Eden for Saleem? Saleem's conclusion suggests, at least, that he shall never attain the object of his desire, the origin of his being. He dreams repeatedly of Kashmir (329, 338, 404, 406, 462), but this dream is never realized.

But in what sense does Kashmir signify a lost homeland for his grandfather? When he came to the temple to sacrifice himself, he was trying to recall "his childhood springs in Paradise, the way it was before travel and tussocks and army tanks messed everything up" (11). However, after he was hit on the nose by a tussock and took an oath not to pray to any god or man, he could not re-unite himself with "an earlier self" (11). This experience encapsulates his alienation and identity crisis. Aziz did not know whether he was Kashmiri or Indian (107). He was "caught in a strange middle ground," trapped between belief and disbelief which reminds us of Mrs. Moore's double vision in *A Passage to India* (1924). His alienation is represented as the "middle place" and "permanent alteration: a hole" (12). "In the succeeding months and years, he fell under what I can only describe as the sorcerer's spell of that enormous—and as yet unstained-perforated cloth" (24).

Doctor Aziz, who became vulnerable to history and women, fell in love when he was requested to examine a woman through a perforated sheet. He gradually came to have a picture of Naseem in his mind, "a badly-fitting collage of her severally-inspected parts. This phantasm of a partitioned woman began to haunt him, and not only in his dreams.... Glued together by his imagination, be accompanied him...he could smell her scent of lavender and chameli; he could hear her voice and her helpless laughter of a little girl; but she was headless, because he had never seen her face" (25). He had come to think of the perforated sheet as "something sacred and magical," because through it "he had seen the things which had filled up the hole inside him which had been created when he had been hit on the nose by a tussock" (27).

How could this emptiness and fullness, this alienation and love, be related to each other? The key word in this text is "a hole". The one in Aziz is caused by his vulnerability to women and history, since that hole in his inner chamber is a vacancy which sets desire in motion. It also means Aziz is caught in time. Being born again to time means you are exiled from Eden, a timeless space. A hole is also a "middle place" and "permanent alteration". This means that a hole signifies the lack in the other which starts a system of signifiers, where you are doomed to be confined to endless alterations of self-reference, as well as a metonymic movement to cover the vacancy of desire with magical words, images or things. Aziz identifies himself as neither Kashmiri nor Indian. He neither believes nor disbelieve in God. Saleem inherit this legacy and is thus caught in endless self-reference and in the succession of this infinite multiplication of signifying processes. He will be castrated and eliminated because it is the other who label and stigmatizes him.

His grandfather was spellbound by a woman whose partitioned body he was forced to see as a doctor through an unstained perforated sheet, and he "came to think of the perforated sheet as something sacred and magical, because through it he had seen the things which filled up the hole inside him" (27). But he had lost a perspective from which to see the world as a whole, and had fallen into the world of time where he had to collect and glue fragments together always with something missing, which suggests a lost Eden. Saleem, his grandson, represent all these fragments and fail to unite them, and is thus doomed to crack and be reduced to "voiceless dust".

IV

This is a bildungsroman in which a protagonist grows to be a grotesque, deformed and drained man with cracks all over his body and reduced to "specks of voiceless dust". Saleem's deformity, impotence and bodily disintegration are mentioned again and again, along with the loss of his telepathy, memories, and stories. Saleem is not only an ugly goose but also a changeling. Yet, he remains self-delusive: "...I was the sacrificial lamb with which they anointed their love" (297),

"...my parents loved me...my parents ruined me for love" (301). Clearly, he is afraid of losing his parents' love because of his deformity. "Had I not inflicted upon myself one more deformity to add to bandy legs cucumber nose horn-temples staincheeks? ...Was it not possible that my mutilated finger had been..., for my long-suffering parents, the last straw? That I was no longer a good business risk, no longer worth the investment of their love and protection?" (240).

His historical role, in part, is to mirror the fate of India's prime ministers (86). So Rushdie has Jawaharlal Nehru write, "Dear Baby Saleem, ...it [your life] will be, ...the mirror of our own" (122). Saleem thus has to "bear the burden of history" (382), and his version of India is supposed to reflect "all the more-than-hundred-million" versions of India. Though cracks are spreading all over him in 1956, Saleem tells that he is expected to be "the mirror of our own" (167), and in 1976, during an emergency, Saleem tells Padma again that the role of mirror-of-the-nation was bestowed upon him by Nehru, Indira Gandhi's father, so he of course resists the slogan, "Indira is India and India is Indira" (427).

The historical role of Nehru, the father of the new-born nation-state, in relation to Saleem becomes clearer after an explosion in a mosque. Because of this explosion, his "mother's silver spittoon" hits the back of Saleem's head, which sets Saleem free from all memories and purifies him. Saleem is empty because "all the Saleems go pouring out of me, from the baby...to the eighteen-year-old with his filthy dirty love, pouring out goes shame and guilt and wanting-to-please and needing-to-be-loved and determined-to-find-a-historical-role" (343). When his memories are later restored something new is born in him. His wrath becomes targeted at "everything which I had, until then, blindly accepted: my parents' desire that I should repay their investment in me by becoming great; ...should I have to bear the burden of history?" (382). Apparently, the expectations that marked the beginning of the Indian nation-state under Nehru were unrealistic, and therefore doomed.

In psychological terms, the subject (a product of the symbolic) under the subjugation of a system of signifiers is imprisoned in an endless metonymic movement of desire for self-reference, and is doomed to suffer from a sense of helplessness, loss, and fragmentation, and this pain arouses the memory of dismemberment before the mirror stage. To form an ideal ego, he has to identify with the other, which causes his imprisonment in the other as well as fragmentation and loss of self, because it is the other who labels and stigmatizes him. He has been a receptacle of the other's desire. Saleem blindly accepted his parents' desire that he should become great, because he wanted to be loved by them, and wanted to please them, which is the way to repay their investment in him. He is burdened with a heavy debt, to repay his parents' love.

His ideal wholeness is imprisoned in the other, so he has to seek for an other who can reflect his unified self. Saleem is expected to reflect the unity of India. He is both privileged and burdened with the unity of the other, the new-born nation-state. India is also expected to accept his love for her. Primary narcissism in the imaginary is suggested. Two mirrors are set facing each other at the hip of Siamese twins, Saleem and India. And Saleem, as a narrator, is the one who should effect a separation. At one point he voices confidence about this, saying, "...while Aadam Aziz remained the sheet's victim, I have become its master..." (121). Clearly, again, this is self-delusive.

V

Saleem's desire for unattainable wholeness is represented as incestuous. This is referred to incessantly: "unspeakable sister-love" (315), "unnatural love" (316), "the unspeakable secret of my love for Jamila Singer" (320), "his own love to his open-mouthed sister" (325), "my true birth-sister, India herself" (385), "forbidden love" (396), "under the Monkey's spell" (402). His desire for Mother India and his sister reflects his desire for wholeness, and he is seeking for the object of his projective identification, the ideal object with whom he can trust his unified self-image, though both India and Jamila betray him. He is the victim of his forbidden love, and is punished by Indira, his rival, who tries to banish midnight's children, since she yearns for a place in the centre of Indian history. Indira is represented as a devouring mother figure, and Saleem is doomed to sacrifice himself for her. He says, "there's no escape from her" (404).

In fact, this text is full of unavoidable women who make and "unmake" (404) him: the "unavoidable Widow" (346) "Amina (his mother), Jamila (his sister), Mary (his nurse), Nashim (his grandmother), and Pia (his aunt)". "Women and women and women" (405) from whom there is no escape. Saleem asks, "How are we to understand my too-many women? As the multiple faces of Bharat-Mata? Or as even more...as the dynamic aspect of maya, as cosmic energy...? Too-many women: are they all aspects of Devi, the goddess?" (406). Though Mary Perreira (a mother figure for Saleem) sang "Anything you want to be, you kin be," he says, "I no longer want to be anything except who I am" (383), but he also says, "I am the sum total of everything" (382). He is expected to reflect all the dreams the others (women) have had, and is a victim of the others' desires, from which his anger is born, but finally he says, "the Widow drained anger out of me along with everything else" (382). He thus learns "the lesson of No Escape".

VI

Since it is Mother India, an unavoidable woman, who chains Saleem with an umbilical cord, it seems impossible for Saleem, the signified, to cut it. Yet as an autobiographer, it is Saleem's role to complete his story. Thus, Saleem, as a player of "fort da," must take the role of an absent mother, and repeat the drama of traumatic separation. He then discards a doll (the signified Saleem). Castration anxiety (= separation anxiety, anxiety over loss of the object) is all too evident in this text, and Saleem's storytelling helps reinforce this anxiety by repeating the traumatic drama of separation. So Saleem, a victim protagonist needs to be annihilated in the end.

Images of Saleem's fragmented body are repeated again and again (no less than 20 times) in this text. When Saleem begins his "autobiographical enterprise" (121) and his family saga, he says that his body is already "over-used" and "crumbling" (9), and suggests that he shall die before his thirty-first birthday. Thus, he refers to the cracks on his body or his mutilated or disintegrating body incessantly: "...I have begun to crack all over like an old jug—that my poor body, singular, unlovely, buffeted by too much history, subjected to drainage above and drainage below, mutilated by doors, brained by spittoons, has started coming apart at the seams. In short, I am literally disintegrating" (37). "As history pours out of my fissured body, my lotus is quietly dripping in" (38). "...as cracks widen within—I can hear and feel the rip tear crunch" (383). "Rip crunch crack, ...I, too, am being hurried towards, disintegration" (384). "...the ghostly essence of that perforated sheet, which doomed my mother to learn to love a man in segments, and which condemned me to see my own life—its meanings, its structures—in fragments also" (107). "... the cracks spreading all over me, radiating like a spider's web from my navel" (166). "...When I've lost my struggle against cracks" (211). This litany continues till the end, and Saleem concludes his story with his cracked body reduced to "specks of voiceless dust" (463).

This obsession with his fragmented body suggests the traumatic separation which arises at the mirror stage of child development. "The baby sees its own image as a whole, and the synthesis of this image produces a sense of contrast with the uncoordination of the body, which is experienced as a Fragmented Body" (Dictionary 'mirror stage' 115). The "gap between man and nature" which causes the subject's division is "evident in the mirror stage" (Dictionary 71). The baby's mirror image as a whole retrospectively makes its previous experience of the fragmented body clear. "The mirror stage shows that the ego is the product of misunderstanding and the site where the subject becomes alienated from himself" (Dictionary 116), because "the ego is formed by identification with the specular image in the Mirror Stage" (Dictionary 51). The ego is based on vacant illusion, and the moment of jubilation when "the baby sees its own image as whole" is replaced by depression caused by his helplessness compared to the omnipotence of the mother. This is the moment of the fall into the world of history, the moment of lost Eden (Gallop). Adam and Eve may have been made to look like God, but they knew they are naked and incomplete.

If the ego is the product of paranoiac misunderstanding, the subject is alienated from himself and eternally imprisoned in an illusive self-image, like Dorian Gray, who is killed by his portrait, that receptacle of his negative self. Saleem always suffers from the cracks in his body and finally is reduced to voiceless dust, but at the same time he sees himself as an omnipotent writer of history and a receptacle of all lives and things around him, an all-embracing figure who looks like Brahma, within whose dream we are existing. He says, "I am the sum total of everything that went before me, of all I have seen done, of everything done-to-me...to understand me, you'll have to swallow a world" (383). "...I was somehow creating a world; that the thoughts I jumped inside were mine, ...I triumphed, 'There isn't a thing I cannot know!'" (174). "...the spirit of self-aggrandizement which seized me then was a reflex, born of an instinct for self-preservation. If I had not believed myself in control of the flooding multitudes, their massed identities would have annihilated mine" (175). He repeatedly tells us that he himself is a world; however, he is suffering from his dismemberment, and envies the wholeness Jamila, his sister, acquires, as well as the omnipotence of Mother India and of other women who have both made him and unmade him. His "unnatural love," forbidden "unspeakable sister-love" (315), his incestuous desire for his sister, he says, can be traced to her wholeness. He adores in her "the fulfillment of my most private dreams" (316). We can thus see Saleem as a paradoxical Narcissus figure who misunderstands himself and is alienated from himself.

Saleem, like "the Buddha" who is finally "emptied of history" (350), learns to be submissive and becomes a citizen of Pakistan. This marks a failure to recreate history, which would constitute resistance, an act of rebellion. Thus, this narcissistic narrative becomes a history of modern India, and the history of the nation-state becomes a story of selfhood deformation. This narrative shows how self-reference is impossible for both for Saleem and India. Saleem's desire for the maternal body and his anxiety about disintegration and dismemberment run parallel with the disintegration of the newly born nation-state, the partitioned India. The fates of both reflect the twisted psychology of narcissism.

WORKS CITED

Appignanesi, L. and S. Maitland. *The Rushdie File*. London: Fourth Estate, 1989.

Baral, K.C. "Imaging India: Nation and Narration". *Rethinking Indian English Literature*. Eds. Nanavati, U.M. and Kar, Prafulla C. Delhi: Pencraft International, 2000.

Beniwal, Anup. *Representing Partition: History, Violence and Narration*. Delhi: Shakti Book House, 2005.

Bharucha, Nifufer E. and Vilas Sarang. *Indian English Fiction 1980-90: Assessment*. Delhi: B.R. Publishing Corporation, 1994.

Bhatnagar, M.K. *Political Consciousness in Indo-Anglian Fiction*. Delhi: Allied Publishers, 1990.

Brennan, Timothy. *Salman Rushdie and the Third World: Myths of the Nation*. London, Macmillan, 1990.

Chakraborti, Basudeb. *Indian Partition Fiction in English and in English Translation: A Text on Hindu-Muslim Relationship*. Calcutta: Papyrus, 2007.

Chakravarty, Joya Ed. *Indian Writing in English*. Delhi: Atlantic, 2003.

Cleary, Joe. *Literature, Partition and the Nation State: Culture and Conflict in Ireland, Israel and Plestine*. Cambridge: Cambridge University Press, 2002.

Crane, Ralph J. *Inventing India: A History of India in English Language Fiction*. Houndsmill, Basingstoke: Macmillan, 1992.

Cundy, C. *Salman Rushdie*. Manchester: Manchester University Press, 1996.

Dhar, T.N. "Micro-Macro Symbiosis: The Form of Salman Rushdie's Midnight Children." *Journal of Indian Writing in English* (Jan. 1985).

——. *History Fiction Interface in Indian English Novel*. New Delhi: Prestige, 1999.

Evans, Dylan. *An Introductory Dictionary of Lacanian Psychoanalysis*. London: Routledge, 1996.

Fletcher, M.D. Ed. *Reading Rushdie: Perspectives on the Fiction of Salman Rushdie*. Amsterdam and Atlanta, Rodopi, 1994.

Goonetilleke, D.C.R.A. *Salman Rushdie*. London: Macmillan, 1998.

Harrison, James. *Salman Rushdie*. NY: Twayne Publications, 1992.

Hasan, Murhirul. *India's Partition: Process, Strategy and Mobilization*. Delhi: OUP, 1996.

——. *Legacy of a Divided Nation; India's Muslims Since Independence*. Delhi: OUP, 1997.

——. "Memoirs of a Fragmented Nation: Rewriting the Histories of Partition." *Economic and Political Weekly* 33, No. 41 (10 October 1998), 26-44.

——. *Pangs of Partition: The Human Dimension*. Eds. S. Setter and Indira Baptista Gupta. New Delhi: Manohar, 2002.

——. *Inventing Boundaries: Gender, Politics and the Partition of India*. Oxford University Press, 2000.

Jain, Jasbir. Ed. *Reading Partition/Living Partition*. Rawat Publications, 2007.

Jassal, Smita Tewari and Eyal Ben-Ari. *The Partition Motif in Contemporary Conflicts*. New Delhi: Sage Publications, 2007.

Kirpal, Viney. *Postmodern Indian English Novel: Interrogating the 1980s and 1990s*. Delhi: Allied Publishers, 1996.

——. Ed. *The New Indian Novel in English: A Study of the 1980s*. New Delhi: Allied Publishers, 1990.

Kudchedkar, Shirin L. "The Second Coming: Novels of the Partition" *Indian English Fiction 1980-90: An Assessment*. Eds. Bharucha, Nilufer E. and Vilas Sarang. Delhi: B.R. Publishing Co., 1994.

Kumar, Sukrita Paul. "On Narrativizing Partition". *Pangs of Partition: The Human Dimension*. Eds. S. Setter and Indira Baptista Gupta. New Delhi: Manohar, 2002.

——. *Narrating Partition: Texts, Interpretations*, Ideas. New Delhi: Indialog Publications, 2004.

McHale, Brian. *Postmodernist Fiction*. NY: Methuen, 1987.

Mee, Jan. "After Midnight: The Indian Novel in English of the 80s and 90s." *Rethinking Indian English Literature*. Eds. Nanavati, U.M. and Kar, Prafulla C. Delhi: Pencraft International, 2000.

Mehrotra, S.R. *Towards India's Freedom and Partition*. New Delhi: Rupa Co., 2005.

Mukherjee, Meenakshi, Ed. *Rushdie's Midnight Children: A Book of Readings*. New Delhi: Pencraft, 1999.

Mukhopadhayay, Anindita. "Partition Relived in Literature." *Pangs of Partition: The Human Dimension*. Eds. S. Setter and Indira Baptista Gupta. New Delhi: Manohar, 2002.

Naik, M.K. *Studies in Indian English Literature*. New Delhi: Sterling, 1987.

Naik, M.K. and Shyamal A. Narayan, Eds. *Indian English Literature 1980-2000: A Critical Survey*. Delhi: Pencraft International, 2004.

Nanavati, U.M. and Kar, Prafulla C., Eds. *Rethinking Indian English Literature*. Delhi: Pencraft International, 2000.

Pathak, R.S. "History and the Individual in the Novel of Rushdie". *The Commonwealth Review*, 1/2 (1999), 118-34.

Paranjape, Makarand. "Inside and Outside the Whale: Politics and the New Indian Novel." *The New Indian Novel in English: A Study of the 1980s*. Ed. Viney Kirpal. New Delhi: Allied Publishers, 1990.

——. *Towards a Poetics of the Indian English Novel*. Shimla: Indian Institute of Advanced Study, 2000.

Ramachandran, C.N. "The Empire Lingers On: A Note on the Rushdie Phenomenon." *Makers of Indian English Literature*. Ed. C.D. Narasimhaiah. Delhi: Pencraft International, 2003.

Rao, Madhusudan. *Salman Rushdie's Fiction: A Study*. New Delhi: Sterling Publishers, 1992.

Rao, V. Pala Prasad, K. Niruparani and Digumarti Bhaskara Rao. *India Pakistan: Partition Perspectives in Indo-English Novels*. New Delhi: Discovery Publishing House, 2004.

Rushdie, Salman. *Midnight's Children*. 1981. London: Vintage, 1995. Setter, S. and Indira Baptista Gupta. Eds. *Pangs of Partition: The Human Dimension*. New Delhi: Manohar, 2002.

Shanna, K.K. and B.K. Johri. *The Partition in Indian English Novels*. Ghaziabad: Vimal Prakashan, 1982.

Shastri, Susha. "Tamas and Midnight's Children: From the Historical to the Postmodernist." *Rethinking Indian English Literature*. Ed. U.M. Nanavati. Delhi: Pencraft International, 2000.

Ten Kortenaar, Neil. "Midnight Children and the Allegory of History." *ARIEL: A Review of International English Literature*, 26.2 (1995): 41-62.

Tharu, Susie. "Rendering Accounts of the Nation: Partition Narratives and Other Genres of the Passive Revolution." *Oxford-Literary Review* (OLR). 1994; 16(1-2): 69-91.

Walder, Dennis. *Post-Colonial Literature: History, Language, Theory*. March 1998, Wiley Blackwell.

7

The Reluctant Fundamentalist: Proposing an Alternative Postcolonial Epistemology

Hameeda Nayeem

Today postcolonial theory and literature especially the novel has come a long way of since the defining moment of postcolonial theory in 1966 in the journal *Tricontinental* but continues to derive its inspiration from the anti-colonial struggles of the colonial era (Young 16). Ashcroft et al. also use the term in a comprehensive sense, "to cover all the culture (literature) affected by the imperial process from the moment of colonization to the present day" (*Empire Writes Back* 3).

Though there are others who contend that postcolonial studies is more concerned "with the lived condition of unequal power sharing globally and the self-authorization of cultural, economic and militaristic hegemony than with a particular historical phenomenon such as colonialism" (*Beginnings* 3).

Postcolonial theory gets adapted to almost all changing paradigms in critical and philosophical thought like Marxism, postmodernism, historicism, existentialism, psychoanalysis, theory of Hermeneutics, which have attempted to situation the notion of truth, power and knowledge in historical, economic and political contexts and contested and interrogated the monologic, hegemonistic and power-inflected epistemologies.

Literature, the novel form, in particular, has responded to the shifting, ever-widening perspectives of postcolonial thought by both reflecting and contributing to this shift to openness. It has expanded its boundaries by incorporating all forms of dominations and neo-colonial projects within and outside the former colonies in which the novelists interrogate various forms of domination and constructed world views circulated for global consumption.

The main motifs of postcolonial novel can be identified as: "the relationship between the self and the other which encompasses a whole lot of areas; the nature of the encounter, the way a self is constructed, the role of tradition, of religion, the economic power and social relationship. It also takes into account cultural formations and how civilizations are viewed by themselves and others" (Jain 21). If colonialism employs a strategy of subordination and appropriation as a mean of controlling native identity, postcolonialism works through search for alternatives—alternative history, education and epistemology. It looks for equality and the articulation of "difference". It seeks to retrieve self-respect and lost, forgotten and hidden history of the colonized or of the East. It undertakes to problematise, decentre and invalidate eurocentrism, imperialisms and hegemonistic epistemologies. It seeks to validate alternative epistemologies by reversing and interrogating the existing hierarchies and sovereignties.

The Reluctant Fundamentalist (2007) by Mohsin Hamid, the young Pakistani novelist, is an enchanting piece of work by a sophisticated mind. It got instant international critical acclaim and was published in 23 languages simultaneously to lavish reviews by major newspapers, journals and magazines in Europe, America and the subcontinent. This understated writing abounds in italics which signal tremors and are suggestive of the cadences of Hamid's analytical mind at work. It captures through an extended monologue the shifting relationship between the self and the other from exuberant hope and trust to distrust and debilitating suspicion. The present paper focuses on how the novel explores this shining perspective and tries to provide an alternative postcolonial perspective on the American neo-colonial project in the name of war on terror after 9/11.

The protagonist's initial acceptance and later rejection by America is allegorized by his relationship with a beautiful high society American girl Erica (America) who increasingly recedes into nostalgia for her dead childhood boyfriend Chris (Christianity) symbolizing American regime's regression into forgotten Christian puritan identity backed up by the construct of the clash of civilizations theory to dominate and colonise Islamic countries in particular. Architectonically, Changez tells his story of personal and public pain in twelve chapters which could broadly be divided into three waves or phases.

The first one-third deceptively familiar—a superb tale of the American dream comes true now so often told and retold that it lulls one into lazy complacency.

The second wave relying on the strength of that bond between the reader and the narrator, the narrative ventures into more and more emotionally disturbing territory where the narrator feels oppressed and attacked by what Foucault would call "epistemic violence". Changez decides to return to Lahore as his shining and lucrative career has been overtaken by resentment of the United States for its changed attitude to the people from the East, bombing of Afghanistan and all that it stands for. At the outset of the novel, there is a divide between the outside voice and the inner tale of Changez. But as the novel progresses, the two voices merge with each other. The open confession of an immigrant is soon laced with bitterness—a hovering disappointment with the American dream. His crucial decision to leave America as he loses the fire to work for the financial company is precipitated by his Chilean host (in Chile, where he had gone on a business evaluation trip), who tells him about Janissaries—the young Christian boys who were taken by Ottomans in childhood and who fought for them wholeheartedly as they had no memories of their native land. Since Changez has memories, he cannot resist the pull of filiations and decides to return to Lahore. In the first phase, his filiation which embodies given ties of family, home, class and country seem to have been swamped by his affiliation with Erica and New York—an acquired allegiance part voluntary and part historically determined, of critical consciousness to a system of values (not a clear sentence). His story is an exquisite blend of autobiography, family history, geographical spaces and human destiny. In the third phase where the novel actually begins, Changez is back in Lahore, working as the lecturer in the Punjab University and being followed by the police and possibly by American agents for leading protests which he explains are actually for greater independence of Pakistan in deciding domestic and foreign policy but are viewed by the US, backed government as anti-American.

The novel, in the form of an extended dramatic monologue weaves, a narrative within a narrative in which Changez, a Pakistani, is in conversation with a mysterious unnamed American who could even be a CIA agent to get him, in a café of Anarkali Bazaar in Lahore. The American never speaks but his responses, reactions and queries to whatever Changez says or to whatever is going on in the vicinity of the café, is articulated by the monologuer himself. That is what makes it a dramatic rather than the sickening interior monologue of the modernist novel, which concentrates on the outpourings of a single individual consciousness, representing the cult of individualism. This device breaks monoglossia to make room for heteroglossia to which I will return later. The form of the novel with the narrator and his audience acting as characters on equal footing, allows the author to mirror the mutual suspicion with which America and Pakistan or the Muslim world look at one another, particularly after 9/11. The Pakistani narrator wonders: "is this just a normal guy or is he a killer out to get me". The American man who is his audience wonders the same. The ever-persistent notion of the American listener's life being threatened by Changez and the reader is given hints that the former may not have benign intentions either, superbly captures the mutual suspicion after 9/11 of "East and West". The form of the novel is like an invitation which, if the reader accepts, will in turn implicate him because the reader will be called upon to judge and shape its ending.

Just as in/while watching a film, we enter another world in a dark room, the same way we have an intermediary here who allows the readers to move from their world into the world of the narrator and to discuss that movement. The fact that the reader moves from his world into another is how the boundaries of self and the other are broken. This has the effect of positioning the reader's mind differently and making him a joint player in the game, rather than putting him in the oppositional mode.

The hybrid utterance to Bakhtin is a passage that employs only a single speaker—the author, for example. The juxtaposition of the two different speeches brings with it a contradiction and conflict in belief systems. Bakhtin's view of heteroglossia has often been employed in the context of a postmodern critique of the perceived teleological and authoritarian character of the modernist art and culture or its monoglossia. It is precisely the monoglossia of the American vision and its invisible assumptions by which it operates after 9/11 which Changez sets out to contest in the narration of his life story to the American. But the book is not merely about the 9/11. It is about the meaning of such events and their effects on the individuals who live through them. The novel is at its heart, a probing meditation on the construct of East-West divide which besides laying bare the American neo-colonial foreign policy points to "dizzying multiplicity of positionalities" as Ella Shohat derogatively calls it, because the narrator himself is a divided self. His filiation and affiliation is in a constant state of tension.

Hamid does not give ideology as something formed and hardened like Updike in *The Terrorist.* He reflects upon a process going on all over the world after 9/11. By addressing the American, symbolizing the American audience, he provides them the opportunity to experience their own changing and confused reactions as part of the fluid moment. Are they the imperialists? As the narrator indicates? Are they a beacon of opportunity for the talented or ruthless emissaries of global business as the narrator had experienced? Must immigrants shed their allegiances and perspectives as America invades their countries? This set of questions would gradually penetrate the membrane of fixed mindsets and ideologies. Hamid keeps the readers hurtling toward the edge of new and discomforting perspectives, generates an "unsettling dialogue within the readers, raids theirs complicity, forcing them to actively talk back, unable to retreat to their national borders with complacent certainties" (Mariana Budhos, 2007).

In order to trace the source of the present mutual suspicion and mistrust, the narrator dives into the sea of his past memory of Princeton and New York and scoops up the relevant details for his narrative. He begins his recapitulatory narrative from his days in Princeton. A first class Princeton graduate, Changez has been the rising star of an elite New York finance company, Underwood Samson, which in a way symbolized American dream, its worship of efficiency rather than creativity. Infatuated by Manhattan and in love with an American beautiful and wealthy girl Erica, he lived the American dream for a while but the romance is soon soured by fear and mistress after 9/11 and by the time we meet Changez back in Lahore, the air of the menace of suspicion is very thick. What Lukacs says in *The Historical Novel* (1960) is very relevant here: that a historical novel can come to life only in a specific social and ideological setting because history itself is seen as a kind of mass experience which offers concrete possibilities for men to comprehend their own existence as something historically conditioned, for them to see in history something which deeply affects their daily lives and immediately concerns them; this experience has links with social transformations and people's awareness of their relationship with national and world history" (24). Changez tells the American "I am telling you a history...it is the thrust of one's narrative that counts, not the accuracy of one's details. Still I can assure you that everything I have told you thus far happened...more or less as I have described" (*TRF*, 118).

Accordingly, the thrust of the narrative shifts to the aftermath of 9/11, the turning point in the story when on a business evaluation assignment to Manila, he watches the World Trade Center come down on TV. He tells the American, "I smiled, yes, despicable as it may sound, my initial reaction was to be remarkably pleased. I was caught up in the symbolism of it all, the fact that someone had so visibly brought America to her knees" (*TRF*, 72-73). On his return to New York, he finds palpable change in attitudes towards him starting right at immigration. His name and his face render him suspect. He is subjected to intensified scrutiny at the airport and later he receives physical threats from commoners in the American society and his co-workers become markedly less effable (*TRF* 75), though his boss remains unchanged in his behaviour toward him.

To add to his woes, the ongoing trouble between India and Pakistan over Kashmir intensified by the attack on Indian Parliament on December 13, 2001 urge Changez to visit his home in Lahore. Despite his parents' advice to the contrary, the pull of filiation is too strong to be averted.

Back home in Lahore he realizes that he has changed in a way that shames him "I was struck at first how shabby our house appeared...I was saddened to find it in such a state. This was where I came from and it smacked of lowliness" (*TRF* 124-25). But soon he is awakened from corrupting affiliation, exorcises "the shameful feelings" and once again appreciates the "unmistakable and idiosyncratic charm" of his home "Far from impoverished, it was rich with history" (*TRF* 125). On his return to New York, he asserts his identity by letting his beard grow to the chagrin of his co-workers and average Americans, though his managing director Jim cares only for efficiency. Both 9/11 and the American reaction to it awaken Changez's hitherto latent Islamist, nationalist sympathies. He comes to the resentful realization that life in America has made him a traitor to his identity and made him a mercenary for American interests. "Finance was the primary means by which the American Empire exercised its power. It was right for me to refuse to participate any longer in facilitating this" (*TRF* 167). He returns to Lahore to use the imperialist's tools to dismantle the house that American imperialism has built.

He takes this decision after his postprandial conversation with his Chilian host Juan Bautista who tells him the story of Christian boys captured by the Ottomans and trained to be soldiers in a Muslim army, at that time the greatest in the world. "They were ferocious and utterly loyal and fought to erase their own civilization. Having no memories, they had nothing else to turn to" (*TRF* 150-51). Having memory of his country, this story intensifies deep resentment in Changez and he sees himself as a modern-day Janissary working for American Empire which is destroying Afghanistan and colluding with India in putting down his own country, Pakistan. His resentment coupled with his adopted country's "growing and self-righteous rage, slackens his working pace and he is fired in debilitating disenchantment. The clash between his filiation and affiliation tear him apart and his decision to leave is precipitated by Erica's failure to help him as she regresses more and more into nostalgia for her dead boy-friend Chris and is committed to a mental institute. After a brief relationship with Changez, Erica loses balance as she becomes obsessed with past memories triggered by 9/11 events, "the attacks churned up new thoughts in my head, I keep thinking about Chris. I don't know why" (*TRF* 105). Erica's downward mental spiral symbolizes America's regression into nostalgia of a mythic past as she refuses to accept the present warm embrace of the "other" and instead embraces disappearance from the scene or perhaps death. Changez tells the American that "It seemed to me that American, too was increasingly giving over to a dangerous nostalgia at that time. There was something undeniably retro about the flags and uniforms about generals addressing cameras in war rooms and newspaper headlines featuring such words as *duty and honour.* I had thought of America as a nation that looked forward. For the first time I was struck by its determination to look back. What your countrymen longed for was unclear to me, a time of unquestioned domination? of safety? or moral certainty? I do not know" (*TRF* 114-15). The novelist actually ridicules this nostalgia both in Erica for her dead boyfriend because Americans are supposed not to believe in sentimental non-sense and the country's nostalgia for a mythical past as he believes it to be forward looking.

As American "epistemic violence" grows stronger, for, everyone with a beard and Muslim name is persecuted and attacked, so does her "monolithic epistemic sovereignty" grow dangerous and destructive.

But in reaction Changez also regresses into nostalgia for his homeland and his sympathy for Muslim world like Afghanistan that comes under American attack immediately after 9/11 is awakened. His filiation overcomes his affiliation and his desire for self-aggrandizement. Spivak's theorizing is very relevant here as she extends Foucault's argument and situates it within a larger global context, suggesting that the narrative of political and economic development in Europe and by extension in America is part of a broader narrative that included imperialism and the definition of Europe/America in relation to the colonial "other". Whereas to Spivak "certain knowledges" in both Europe and colonized countries were subjugated or "disqualified as inadequate" (*CPCR* 267), America aggrandized her own epistemology by redefining its relationship with the East as one of clash of civilizations where its civilization is presented as superior and stronger and the "other" decadent, barbarian, obscurantist and what not. Mohsin Hamid tells his story in such a way as to be critical of American Imperialist Policy and the show of civilizational superiority but at the same time displays deep attachment to that country for having spent much of his time there "where he learnt English before he learnt Urdu". The narrator has to wade his way in the monologue through myths and doses of demonology which are paraded as gospel truths about the "other". He tells alternative stories about his own country in particular, and about the Islamic world, in general at various points of his narrative. Religion, he tries to point out is a "demarcator of difference" to use Ayesha Jalal's expression rather than a marker of superiority of one over the other. Neither religious difference nor ideological disagreement between East and West are the source of trouble but America's unjust and imperial policies in the East, "inviting" attacks on World Trade Center as a symbol of American imperialism. Changez tells the American: "It seems to me...that America was engaged only in posturing. As a society you were unwilling to reflect upon the shared pain that united you with those who attacked you. You retreated into myths of your own difference, assumptions of your own superiority. And you acted out these beliefs on the stage of the world so that the entire planet was rocked by the repercussions of your tantrums, not least my family, now facing war thousands of miles away. Such an America had to be stopped in the interests not only of the rest of humanity, but also in your own" (*TRF* 167-68). His initial reaction of pleasure over the destruction of World Trade Center gives way to a constant murmur of reproach as he introspects while walking by floral motifs in the shrines to the dead and the missing that had sprung up in his absence in New York. These reminded him of his inhuman response when he was actually caught up "in the symbolism of it all".

Yet, he immediately contrasts it with other reproaches that were far louder "Your country's flag invaded New York after the attacks, it was everywhere, on toothpicks in the shrines, on windshields and windows, large flags fluttered from buildings. They all seemed to proclaim: *We are America, not New York which is the mightiest civilization the world has ever known. You have slighted us, beware our wrath*" (*TRF* 79). Here Hamid again gives us an alternative perspective on his country to contrast it with the American claim of her superiority and perception about herself. He starts with self-mockery to cast the reader trap and then imperceptibly moves to describe the past glory of his country when America was almost non-existent. Perhaps because we currently lack wealth, power or even sporting glory—the occasional brilliance of our cricket team notwithstanding, we Pakistanis tend to take an inordinate pride in our food. Here in old Anarkali that pride is visible in the purity of the fare on offer. "They are *predatory delicacies* imbued with a hint of luxury, of wanton abandon. Not for us the vegetarian recipes one finds across the border to the East, nor the sanitized, sterilized processed meats so common in your homeland. Here we are not squeamish when it comes to facing the consequences of our desire...."

"For we were not always burdened by debt, dependent on foreign aid and handouts, in the stories we tell of ourselves, we were not the crazed and destitute radicals you see on your TV channels but rather saints and poets—yes—conquering kings. We built the Royal Mosque, the Shalimar Gardens in this city and we built the Lahore Fort with its mighty walls and wide ramp for our battle elephants. And we did these things *when your country was still a collection of 13 small colonies gnawing away at the edge of the continent*" (*TRF* 101-02). That is how he deflates the claims of American superiority.

Such comparisons are everywhere in the novel. But his aim is not to assert the superiority of his own culture and civilization over the "other" but to humble the other by re-articulating the past glory of his nation, the difference of his culture, to assert its distinct identity. This is not to reject the other but to provide an alternative perspective on things, to make room for epistemological pluralism by placing it side by side with the singular epistemology the America privileges over others; to problematise the assumptions of her superiority and not to inferiorize her. After having spent many years in the US, the narrator is at core a divided person, he is not sure where actually he belongs to as he confesses to the American. "I lacked a stable core. I was not certain where I belonged, in New York, Lahore, in both, in neither and for this reason when Erica reached out to me for help, I had nothing of substance to give her. Probably this was why I had been willing to take on the persona of Chris because my own identity was so fragile" (*TRF* 178).

Towards the end of his inconclusive open-ended story he admits: "I had returned to Pakistan but my inhabitation of your country had not entirely ceased. I remained emotionally entwined with Erica and New York and I brought something of her with me to Lahore or I lost something of myself to her that I was unable to relocate in the city of my birth.... Such journeys have convinced me that it is not always possible to restore one's boundaries after they have been blurred and made permeable by a relationship, try as we might, we cannot reconstitute ourselves as the autonomous beings we previously imagined ourselves to be. Something of us is now outside and something of the outside is now within us. Perhaps you have had no such comparable experience, for you are gazing at me as though at a raving madman" (*TRF* 172-74). Those who are mobile know, according to Changez, that we inhabit various territories simultaneously. Hence, there is no articulation of the terms of struggle—of a clash that is neither the one nor the other but something else which contests the terms and territories of both.

Homi Bhabha's theorizing on the untenability of absolute political positions is very sound, though not the ground on which he bases his argument in view of what the narrator experiences in the novel. Bhabha using Stuart Hall's insights maintains that political positions cannot be charted out in advance as true or false, progressive or reactionary and I must add morally valid or vapid, ideologically fixed or fluid prior to the specific conditions in which they emerge. In this sense, they are marked by "hybridity and the ambivalence of the process of emergence itself" (*Location of Culture* 22). This is a way of acknowledging the force of writing, its metaphoricity and its rhetorical discourse, as a productive matrix which defines the "Social and makes it available as an objective of and for action" (*LC* 23). Bhabha here uses writing in a Denidean sense signifying the intrinsically metaphoric nature of language and discourse, their inability to make statements which are absolutely clear and unequivocal since they are constituted by a vast network of signifiers in which any given position is structured by what is outside of it, this externality infecting with its diversity and ambivalence, any presumed internal coherence of the position itself.

In this connection, Bhabha cites J.S. Mill's essay *On Liberty* which describes knowledge and a given political stance as arising only through continual self-questioning and confronting at each stage of its articulation other stances that are opposed to it. As Bhabha interprets it, "Mill sees the political as a form of debate and dialogue". The political is dialogic not by abstractly acknowledging other perspectives and then circumventing them, but by recognizing its own limitations in their light, is at every point riven by ambivalence. It is this discursive ambivalence in the subject of enunciation itself that marks the truly public and political (*LC* 24). This type of political "negotiation", says Bhabha, goes beyond the unsettling of the essentialism or logocentrism of a received political tradition, in the name of an abstract free play of the signifiers (*LC* 25).

Mohsin Hamid believes with Bhabha that the language of political critique is effective not because it maintains rigid oppositions between binaries like master and slave, East and West but because it overcomes the given grounds of "opposition and opens up a space of translation, a place of hybridity" (*LC* 25) which engages in the construction of an alternative epistemology. Such a language will be dialectical as it is in this novel without recourse to a "teleological or transcendent history". The event of theory or writing becomes the negotiation of contradictory and antagonistic instances that open up hybrid sites and objectives of struggle and destroy those negative polarities between knowledge and its objectives and I should add between the East and the West, between theory and practical political reason. Bhabha notes that there could be "no simplistic, essentialist opposition between ideological miscognition and revolutionary truth". Between these is a "historical and discursive difference" (*LC* 25). Hence, our political priorities and referents—such as the people, class, struggle, gender difference "are not there in some primordial naturalistic sense. Nor do they reflect a unitary or homogenous political object" (*LC* 26). All of this makes us recognise, claims Bhabha, that the question of commitment is "complex and difficult".

Bhabha's argument sows the seeds of its own contradictory position and untenability for being uncritically founded on Derridean notion of difference which is itself abstract, his third space is unrepresentable and the notion of hybridity bears within itself the seeds of polarities it was intended to transcend.

But divested of Derridean sources of the notion of difference at the level of language and the unrepresentable third space argument, one can see its truth value in relation to transnational intellectuals and novelists by re-orienting and grounding it in the psychological truth of the lived and living experiences of those who inhabit the in-between space.

Mohsin Hamid's ambivalence and oscillation between two cultures can be seen in this background. He says in an interview that "a novel can be a divided man's conversation with himself because in the internally that other party, the American side was speaking very much and I was thinking of his responses".

That is why the monologue is full of conflicting perspectives but the novelist's aim is not to create or add to confusion but to enlarge the mental landscape, to dethrone monologic epistemic sovereignties, to call the bluff of the clash of civilizations, by highlighting other stories, other epistemologies, other narratives to remove the blinkers from Euro American eyes, to demystify constructed myths of imperialistic regimes; to turn the kaleidoscope and show different colour patterns as forming the complex web of humanity which transcends borders both physical and mental. Changez is wedded to both the civilizations but subjects both to a penetrating critique though one more than the other.

WORKS CITED

Bakhtin, M.M. (1930s, 1981). *The Dialogic Imagination: Four Essays.* Ed. Michael Holquist. Trans. Caryle Emerson and Michael Holquist. Anstin and London: University of Texas Press.

Bakhtin, M.M. (1986). *Speech Genres and Other Late Essays.* Trans. by Vern W. McGee. Austin, Tx: University of Texas Press.

Bhabha, Homi K. (1994). *The Location of Culture.* New York and London; Routledge.

Bill, Ashcroft et al. (1989). *The Empire Writes Back: Theory & Practice in Post-colonial Literatures.* New York and London: Routledge.

——. eds. (1995). *The Postcolonial Studies Reader.* New York and London: Routledge.

Habib, M.A.R. (2005). *A History of Literary Criticism: From Plato to the Present.* Malden MA, Oxford: Blackwell.

Jain, Jasbir (2006). *Beyond Postcolonialism, Dreams and Realities of a Nation.* Delhi, Mumbai: Rawat Publications.

Rao, P. Mallikarjuna, Mittapalli, Rajeshwar and Rao, K. Damodar eds. (2003). *Postcolonial Theory and Literature,* Delhi: Atlantic.

Said, Edward (1985). *Beginnings: Intention and Method.* New York: Columbia University.

——. (1978). *Orientalism.* New York: Vintage.

Shohat, Ella (1992). Notes on the "Post-colonial", Social Text 31/32, 99-113. Quoted in *Young.*

Shukla, Sheobhushan and Shukla, Anu (2004). *Postcolonialism and Fiction in English.* Delhi: Sarup & Sons.

Spivak, Gayatri Chakravorty (1999). *A Critique of Postcolonial Reason.* Cambridge, MA and London: Harvard University Press.

Young, Robert J.C. (2001). *Postcolonialism: A Historical Introduction.* Oxford: Blackwell.

——. *Postcolonical Critic.* Arena 69; 47 to 63. Quoted in Habib.

8

Jhumpa Lahiri's *The Lowland*: A Narrative Pattern of a Broken Family

Binod Mishra

Jhumpa Lahiri, who rose to fame with her *Interpreter of Maladies* (1999), continues with her favourite theme of diaspora, alienation, acceptance and adjustment in her other works too. There is no denying the truth that the issue of cultural confrontation is developing in a complex and progressive way in a multi-cultural global world. Her latest work, *The Lowland* (2013), which had been long listed for the Man Booker Prize 2013, echoes with the complexities of immigration and exile in a Third World. The novel with its context, inter-text, pretext and subtext covers the complex reality of some initial Mao-movement, immigration of a family to the United States and gradually its cultural assimilation therein. According to James Clifford, "Everywhere individuals and groups improvise local performances from (re)collected pasts, drawing on foreign media, symbols and languages."[1] Such attempts of immigrants mostly lead to despair and dissatisfaction.

The present paper endeavours to explore not only the movement of an individual to United States for his education and his gradual entanglement into the culture of the country with Bela and Gauri but it also examines the narrative of a broken family bent on finding some tissues with which the family may be reorganized. The novel also deals with the phenomena of hybridity and cultural dislocation. Further, the paper dives deep into the psychological realities of Gauri's existence, seeking reasons for her disinterestedness in social relationship. An attempt will also be made to discover the phenomenological reason of Bela's complete assimilation in American culture.

The Lowland very subtly discusses the plight of an Indian family that witnesses the trials and tribulations of all sorts. While the two brothers Subhash and Udayan had a very secluded childhood at Tollygunj, their education separates them forever. The elder brother leaves for United States while the younger Udayan, highly influenced by Naxal movements decides to submit himself to the cause of his native land. He refuses his brother's proposal of going to USA and being 'indifferent to building up a career', he tells Subhash: "How can you walk away from what's happening? There, of all places?"[2] (30). As time moves, Udayan gets closer to Gauri, the sister of his friend and later marries her. It was Gauri's love for indigenous things and traditional practices that Udayan gets attracted to. Unaffected by the waves of changes that most girls of her age often nourish an infatuation, Gauri is mostly afraid to go out with her fiancé and even avoids going to the movies with him. The novelist draws Gauri's simplicity and cultural hiccups in the following lines: "It was one thing to fall into conversations with him on the portico, or at the Coffee House or to walk over to the College Square to watch the swimmers in the pool. They had not yet stayed from that immediate neighbourhood, where they were simply fellow students, where it was always unreasonable for them to be" (*TL* 60).

The novel shows the first break-up in the form of two brothers separating because of their different goals. Subhash's academic pursuits prompt him to apply for Ph.D. programs in the U.S. while Udayan confines himself to the happenings in his country. Despite Udayan's realization of his being 'nothing' without Subhash, the latter's action appears selfish to Udayan. Initially, Subhash feels isolated and seems to gather strength through recollections of his native land—its pulls steeped in his brother's letters which also smack of revolutionary approaches. The concluding line of his brother's letters unsettles Subhash who foresees the immanent fears that would distance them in the times to come. Lahiri records: "He felt their loyalty to one another, their affection stretched half-way across the world. Stretched to the breaking point by all that now stood between them, but at the same time refusing to break" (43). Subhash feels ill at ease at Rhode Island in the beginning but he learns to leave without the familiar voices of his family members. Eager to know about the happenings in Calcutta, he relies on letters yet feels helpless, unable to fulfil his parents' wishes of not disregarding them as Udayan did. He consoles them by offering reassurances but becomes a part of the impending web of globalization where cutting off from inmates and ignoring them become an integrated affair.

Gauri, a student of philosophy, gets won over by the innovative and original ideas of Udayan who preferred simplicity and idealism over everything. Buoyed by the thought of Marx and Rousseau whose books Udayan had given her to read, Gauri eloped with him and married. But their marriage could not last longer because of Udayan's rebellious escapades and explosive views. As ill luck would have it, this marriage proved only a medium to nurture Udayan's Naxal views which finally devastated Gauri and her in-laws. Udayan got killed in the broad daylight at the hands of the police for his complicity in a murderous act of a policeman. Gauri became a widow in the prime of her life. She became a bad omen for the family members who held her responsible for the tragedy. Her notion of independence abruptly got stalled and she became an object of neglect and indifference. Gauri's existence in her in-laws' house didn't matter to anyone till Subhash, Udayan's younger brother visited Kolkata. At an early age of 23, Gauri had to fall in line with other widows who were meant to dissociate themselves from all sacred ceremonies. Lahiri outlines Gauri's brokenness in the following: "The vermilion was washed clean from her hair. The iron bangle removed from her wrist. The absence of these ornaments marked her as a widow. She was twenty-three years old.... She was given white saris to wear in place of coloured ones so that she resembled the other widows in the family. Women three times her age" (*TL* 108-09).

Udayan's death shatters the entire family. Subhash, who used to receive gifts sent from India every Durga puja gets a telegram during Puja in 1971 and is broken to read the lines: Udayan killed. Come back if you can. Driven by the despair, Subhash returns to India and endeavours to know about the circumstances that resulted in his brother's death. The discovery that his brother was a Naxalite adds to his shock yet his parents' blind love towards Udayan surprises him at times.

On his return to India, Subhash is haunted by the memory of his brother. His last meeting with him had created mixed feelings. While it was quite usual not to find his parents at the airport, what shocked him more was their indifference even to him. The disorientation of the house and the depression of his parents fell heavy upon him:

> His parents asked no questions about America. Inches away, they avoided looking Subhash in the eye. He wondered whether his parents would ask him to remain in Calcutta, to abandon his life in Rhode Island. But there was no mention of this. Nor was there any mention of the possibility of their arranging a marriage for him. They were in no position to plan their wedding, to think about his future. An hour often passed without their speaking. The shared quiet fell over them binding them more tightly than any conversation could. (*TL* 96)

Subhash is shocked to see Gauri widowed at such a tender age. Gauri is devoid of all delicacies at 23. As his acquaintance grows with her, he feels sympathetic and starts nursing the idea to take her to U.S. to provide her with the basic requirements. He faces opposition from all quarters yet decides to give Gauri what his brother failed to provide when he was alive. He was of the view that the American world of larger culture would help Gauri assimilate with the worldly challenges where the helplessness behind the rigours of Indian culture go in oblivion and help her begin life afresh. The reality that Gauri had Udayan's child in her womb doesn't deter Subhash's determination to marry her though in a small gathering, at the cost of several whispers making round. While Subhash married her on humanitarian grounds, Gauri had her own beliefs since in her isolated moments, she felt thankful for "his independence and at the same time she was bewildered" (126). Lahiri writes: "She had married Subhash as a means of staying connected to Udayan. But even as she was going through with it she knew that it was useless, just as it was useless to save a single earring when the other half of the pair was lost" (127-28). Gauri foresees the ghosts of uncertainty in America where she would be left both without Udayan and Manas, making her life an exile in true sense. Her miseries remind us of the predicament that most immigrants suffer from in a new country as well as in a new culture. Edward Said's observations about exile appear quite apt in this regard:

> It is the unhealable rift forced between a human being and a native place, between the self and its true home: its essential sadness can never be surmounted. And while it is true that literature and history contain heroic romantic, glorious, even triumphant episodes in an exile's life, these are no more than efforts meant to overcome the achievements of exile permanently undermined by the loss of something left behind forever.[3]

Subhash tries utmost to make Gauri comfortable and therefore tries to make her familiarize with the surroundings. But he is terrified to see Gauri's volte face after her return from such a gathering. She feels herself quite low and finds her status inferior. Finding nothing in common with the group, she also refrains from the idea of inviting them to their house. In addition, she destroys her Indian clothes and puts on a new look. She seems to get weary of her past and hence tries to rinse it. The phantoms of past and the meadows of future play hide and seek in her life. Her age as well as her bodily demands seems to shake her from within. Though an expecting mother, she visualizes her position as a forsaken woman whose existence depended only upon the child in her womb. The gap between the external and the internal world lacerates her entire being. Her personal life and her desire seemed to have an uproar which was unheard by the man who posed to live with her as husband. They posed as couple yet lived apart under the same roof. The walls of tradition and custom which she wanted to break appeared to chase her as ghosts. She realizes that while Udayan appreciated her independent moves and thoughts, Subhash distanced himself from all these though he lived in a far advanced country like America. Because of his predilection and reverence for his dead brother and his remains, Subhash feels ill at ease. The novelist throws light on his conflict and realization in the following: "He had inherited his brother's wife: in summer he would inherit his child. But the need for her physicality-waking up from the dream, in the apartment in which they were living both together and separately, he could no longer deny that he'd inherited that also" (*TL* 141).

Gauri gives birth to Bela in U.S. People in the surroundings treat Subhash and Gauri as couple yet the latter reassures herself that Bela belonged to Udayan. It is from here that Gauri's existential journey begins. Philosophy as her subject of study works as a solace to her. Interrogation about time, people and surroundings drive her to a new world where she tries to assimilate the brokenness of her life into a new form she could call 'a form of sustenance' (151). The new couple's relationship being as ordinary as anything enables Gauri to ward off the onslaughts of time in her own way. She most often attended philosophy classes in Rhode Island and developed a sort of nonchalance towards the physical realities of time and space. The novelist graphically describes the waves of Gauri's mind in the following ways: "She saw time; she sought to understand it. She filled note-books with her questions, observations. Did it exist independently, in the physical world, or in the mind's apprehensions? Was it perceived only by humans? What caused certain moments to swell up like hours, certain years to dwindle to a number of days?" (*TL* 151).

Gauri's childhood habit of 'waking up a staircase in darkness' and then her yearning for philosophy started its imprint on her real life the way things started shaping in her life. The Greek's concept of future as 'indeterminable' and Aristotle's teaching that "a man could never say for certain if there would be a sea battle tomorrow" (152) comforted Gauri. The continuum of space and time galvanized her existence more than anything else.

If philosophy acted as a soothing balm to the bruises of Gauri's existence, idealism and practicality perpetuated Subhash. While Subhash's external reality differed from his internal outbreaks, he seemed to derive satisfaction in posing himself as Bela's father. Bela's childhood joys were Subhash's perpetual concerns. In a world divided by space and time, Bela's growing childhood sutured the gaps in marriage solemnized between Subhash and Gauri. Lahiri records: "The point of their marriage was Bela, and in spite of the damage Gauri had wrought, in spite of her new schedule, her coming and going, the fact of Bela remained" (*TL* 176).

The wheels of time and fortune kept Gauri and Subhash at bay through Bela—'a filament' connected them. The growing child often got unnerved by Gauri's confinement in a room surrounded by papers and books. She understood later that her mother's Study also served as her bedroom. She also realized lately that in her shaping, the parents were never together. The child that connected her parents though in a make-believe bond, had her own suffering which was becoming not a part but a whole rather. The novelist records painfully the growing child's isolation and independence in the following lines: "There was no one to observe whether she had toast or cereal, whether or not she finished, though she always did, spooning up the last of the sweetened milk, putting the dirty bowl into the sink, running a little water in it so that it would be easier to rinse clean" (*TL* 204).

Bela's curiosity deepens on her visit to her grandparents' house in India. Her grandmother makes her wonder by pointing to a portrait as that of her father—a smiling teenager. The child in Bela fails to understand the implication of burning incense in front of the picture. Subhash later placates the puzzle by calling the smiling teenager as his late brother who died of illness caused by an infection "the doctors were unable to cure" (204). He also lies to Bela that he and Gauri couldn't marry because of the lack of time. Both Subhash and Bela, on their return from India are dismayed at the sudden disappearance of Gauri, who had moved to California for a teaching assignment.

The father calms the daughter by feigning ignorance about the reason of her mother's catastrophic decision yet the growing child is not at ease with the circumstances. Subhash tries his best to control the situation but in a way fails to fill the void left by Gauri. Both Subhash and Bela are affected badly. Bela's performance at studies suffers and later improves after several sessions of counselling by Dr. Grant. As time passes, Bela graduates to become an agricultural apprentice working on farms. She also becomes a victim of someone's physical contact and gets conceived.

Though Gauri had no contact with Subhash, Bela continued to pay visits to the former, who always longed for her company. He grew fond of Bela and her ideologies which smacked of Udayan at times. A bond which Subhash had himself forged both with Gauri and Bela, at times, intimidated him. While the bond appeared real to the outside world, its frivolous nature frightened him. Lahiri sketches Subhash's fears in the following lines: "And yet sometimes he felt threatened, convinced that it was Udayan's inspirations: that Udayan's influence was greater. Gauri had left them, and by now Subhash trusted to stay away. But there were times Subhash believed that Udayan would come back, claiming Bela from the grave as his own" (*TL* 225).

Gauri's decision of leaving Rhode Island for California is propelled by her existential anguish resulting from the forces of American dream where everyone can vie for a space of one's own. Broken from within, she had not been able to assimilate herself with Subhash who played a quasi-husband and with Bela who was unaware of her mother's split identity. Seen from Gauri's perspective, she was moving towards diasporic identity of people who were "constantly producing and reproducing themselves anew through transformation and difference".[4] Her sudden move to California may appal many of us but her further action of not keeping any ties either with Bela or Subhash provides her more time to build her own identity. It is quite significant to note that Gauri makes up her mind to see Subhash, instead of replying to his letter seeking a divorce. Finally, she decided to free Subhash to whom she had proved "an imposition, an intrusion" (*TL* 304). Unfortunately, she met Bela and her child, as Subhash was not at home. Gauri ruefully receives Bela's admonitions and admits of her fault but it's too late. The meeting between the mother and the daughter is bereft of any cordiality and becomes very tumultuous where Bela's daughter, Meghna works as a comic relief.

Bela inherits the brokenness left by her mother. A protected childhood in the beginning followed by a disturbed growth later take a heavy toll on her life. A second-generation immigrant, Bela decides to give birth to an illicit child, thinking it to be her single source of identity. Subhash's revelation about Udayan being her father had made Bela empathetic and empowered. She was following Subhash's model of bringing up a fatherless child, "an element of life that for different reasons they would share" (*TL* 271). She grew more intimate with Subhash and revered him more than her mother. Subhash had provided her stability while Gauri had abandoned her when she needed parental care more.

Thus, a close analysis of *The Lowland* attests to the fact that brokenness becomes the fate of all the characters. The novel acts a narrative of a broken family. Starting with the rebellion of Udayan, the novel takes in its web the intricate relation between Subhash and Gauri who stand united through a thin line of relational scale where the one always overweighs the other. Brokenness becomes a part of Subhash's parents who continued to remain isolated from their sons—one way or the other. It is only Gauri, who, despite several ups and downs, finally emerges from the breakdown and establishes her own identity though at a heavy cost. She loses Udayan, of course, because of cruel fate but chooses to severe her ties with Subhash and Bela only to allow them to assimilate with the demands of a diasporic and global world. Subhash proves himself to be a sheet anchor ready to shield those who need him—whether his parents, Udayan, Holly, Gauri, Bela, Meghna and Elise. He plays an instrumental role in uniting the separated ones and yet remains separated and solitary throughout. The myriad ups and downs of his life had taught him that happiness was but "the occasional episode in the general drama of pain".[5] And hence, several decades of his American life also couldn't propel him to compromise with his Indian faith and values of a family life, despite having any blood ties either with Gauri or Bela or even Meghna. On the other hand, Gauri, dislocated from her roots, learns to grow and to transform herself to a life of autonomy and freedom. Though reticent in her Rhode Island's house, she proves through her action that subalterns (women) too can speak. Gauri's indomitable spirit always runs parallel with Subhash's indefatigable act where both remain a loser to each other. The novel, thus, has woven intricately the narrative pattern of a broken family.

NOTES

1. Clifford, James. *The Predicament of Culture*. Harvard University Press, 1988: 14.
2. Lahiri, Jhumpa. *The Lowland*. U.K.: Random House India, 2013: 30 (All subsequent references have been quoted from the same edition of the book and their page numbers mentioned in brackets).
3. Said, W.E. *Reflections on Exile and Other Essays*. Cambridge Mass: Harvard University Press, 2001: 137.
4. Hall, Stuart. "Cultural Identity and Diaspora", in *Community, Culture and Difference*. Ed. Jonathan Rutherford. London: Lawrence and Wishart Ltd., 1990: 235.
5. Hardy, Thomas. *The Mayor of Casterbridge*. Chapter 45.

9

Separation as the Emergence of a New and Independent Self: A Psychological Study of Jhumpa Lahiri's *A Temporary Matter*

Motaleb Azari

Jhumpa Lahiri's writing is characterized by her 'plain' language and her characters—often Indian immigrants to America—navigate between the cultural values of their homeland and the host society (Wikipedia, *Lahiri's Works and Style*). Her art in characterization reminds us of John Ralston Saul's fiction in which the protagonists—normally from British and Canadian origins—travel to Asian countries and create fabulous stories in their search for identities in diaspora. Lahiri's fiction is, to some extent, autobiographical and frequently draws upon her own experiences as well as those of her family and friends in the Bengali communities with which she is familiar. In her fiction, she examines her characters' struggles, anxieties, and biases to chronicle the nuances and details of immigrant psychology and behaviour. Until *Unaccustomed Earth*, she focused mostly on first-generation Indian-American immigrants and their struggle to raise a family in a country very different from theirs. Lahiri's stories describe their efforts to keep their children acquainted with Indian culture and traditions and to keep them close even after they have grown up in order to hang on to the Indian tradition of a joint family, in which the parents, their children and the children's families live under the same roof (Smith 2011). Based on Nicole Smith's analysis, this article tries to explore the psychological effects of living in diaspora on the marital relation between Shoba and Shukumar in Jhumpa Lahiri's *A Temporary Matter* in her collection *of Interpreter of Maladies*. Told from the third-person perspective of the husband, the story deals with the disintegrating relationship of an Indian couple—Shoba and Shukumar. Their stillborn child has created distance between the two of them, and Shukumar observes as Shoba transforms from the attentive wife into someone more aloof and self-absorbed (Lahiri, *Interpreter of Maladies*). In his analysis of the story, Nicole Smith believes the fact that this short story is called "A Temporary Matter" is interesting on two levels. First of all, although the main action of the short story revolves around very important life events such as the death of a child or the end of a once happy marriage, the narrative is mostly centred on the little things in life. The change in the couple's relationship can be seen through the routines in life such as; dinner planner and dentist appointments, but what seems small or like a "temporary matter" is actually something important and complex. The title, Smith believes, is also interesting because it is almost a summary of "A Temporary Matter" by Jhumpa Lahiri because it seems as though the power outage might bring the couple closer together yet it is only a temporary matter, or a temporary respite to the pain the couple is feeling and is a brief moment in which they can reflect on what has changed between them. On the other hand, this is an ironical situation in which the only ray of light shine on the desperate lives of Shoba and Shukumar. For the writer, the most important is 'the little things in life' and this story seems to sum up that sentiment perfectly. Although the couple in "A Temporary Matter" by Jhumpa Lahiri has experienced great pain and this is made evident in the first several paragraphs of the story, there is little talk between them. Instead of addressing the pain directly, the narrator, Shukumar, discusses the changes he feels by talking about the 'little things in life' such as his wife's habits and his feelings about his work. For instance, even though it is clear that the couple is not feeling the same way they used to and are feeling as though things have changed, this is only truly visible through the little observations Shukumar makes. In one of the important quotes; "he ran his tongue over the tops of his teeth; he'd forgotten to brush them that morning. It wasn't the first time. He hadn't left the house at all that day, or the day before." While this may seem like an average and everyday observation, it masks a much deeper feeling. He is growing depressed and does not care about himself the way he used to. He can sit indoors and not want to go outside and is letting himself go, yet this is not as simple as it may at first seem (Smith 2011).

The fact is, at this point in the short story, he is finally realizing that there is something terrible and sad that is happening between him and the love of his life, yet he is at a loss when it comes to knowing what to do about it. The fact that his teeth are not clean masks his lack of concern about things that used to affect him deeply—things he used to care about. The reader knows he is a conscientious man, especially when one of his greatest admissions to his wife is that he cheated on an exam in college. As the story moves, the reader perceives how, both he and his wife, were and how far they have grown apart and moved away from things that used to be important to them. Although the title is "A Temporary Matter" none of these things seem temporary for people who are as steady in their lives as these two.

As mentioned earlier, throughout "A Temporary Matter" the little things seem to mask even the most important events in Shoba and Shukumar's lives. Interestingly, even when Shukumar talks about the day his wife went into labour, a very important event for any couple, his memory focuses only on images and "little" things. For instance, when he thinks of the day he left Shoba alone before she had the child, he doesn't remember that she was beautiful or happy, but only small things. He says, "Each time he thought of that moment, the last moment he saw Shoba pregnant, it was the cab he remembered most, a station wagon, painted red with blue lettering. It was cavernous compared to their own car. Although Shukumar was six feet tall, with hands too big ever to rest comfortably in the pockets of his jeans, he felt dwarfed in the back seat." In some ways, even though this might seem callous, this is usually how we realistically remember events from our lives. Important events do not happen in our memories as sequential narratives, but in a series of random feelings, senses, and observations. In this way, the story is narrated realistically, and the story tells us that it is the little things, the small, seemingly inconsequential memories that form our realities and memories. What we might call as 'homesickness' is the opportunity to recall the trivial memories we had with our families at home. The situation gets harder when the ability to remember these memories fades away by the routine life in the host society. At this moment, a completely different 'self' emerges, and the situation gets harder if it cannot sustain the characteristics of the 'real self'. At this point, the important realities in life seem trivial and the trivial things may bother the new self. This happens again in the story when Shoba speaks her confession and says: "You went to answer the telephone in her room. It was your mother, and I figured it would be a long call. I wanted to know if you'd promoted me from the margins of your newspaper." Instead of looking for clues about her future husband or finding something of Shukumar's life. Again, it is clear that the little things mask the greater realities while living in diaspora.

As mentioned earlier, the power outage is a 'temporary matter' and something that is not a great life event, and thus it cannot trump all of the little things that have been signalling a problem with the couple's marriage. In an article entitled "Psychological and Emotional Aspects of Divorce", O'Connell Corcoran recounts the psychological reasons and motivations of women for initiating divorce. Based on the statistics in the United States, she states that women initiate divorce twice as often as men and after divorce, women experience less stress and better adjustment in general than do men. The reasons for this are that (1) women are more likely to notice marital problems and to feel relief when such problems end, (2) women are more likely than men to rely on social support systems and help from others, and (3) women are more likely to experience an increase in self-esteem when they divorce and add new roles to their lives (O'Connell Corcoran, *Psychological and Emotional Aspects of Divorce,* 1997).

Tracing the above-mentioned reasons in Shoba's decision to leave Shukumar, clarifies her motivations and the reason why she has been looking for an apartment and had found one. In fact, she is looking for a permanent relief from the stresses caused by the stillborn child and 'the trivial information' on his physical appearance provided by her husband.

On the whole, 'a temporary matter' may seem temporary to the husband and not to the wife who 'notices marital problems'. Small things to Shukumar are the excuses to pass the time in the temporary darkness, but for Shoba the same trivial truths are the building blocks of her motivation to lose interest in her married life (Smith 2011). And as O'Connell's study reveals, Shoba is 'more likely to experience an increase in self-esteem' by her decision to leave Shukumar (1997). Therefore, the new 'diaspora identity' along with a search for a new and independent self turns 'a temporary matter' to a serious decision and a permanent situation in the life of Shoba and Shukumar.

WORKS CITED

Lahiri, Jhumpa. *Interpreter of Maladies*. Mariner Books. "My Two Lives", Newsweek. 2006-03-06. Retrieved on 2008-04-13.

——. *Works and Style*. en.wikipedia.org/wiki/Jhumpa_Lahiri

O'Connell Corcoran, Kathleen. "Psychological and Emotional Aspects of Divorce". June 1997.

Smith, Nicole. Short Story Analysis and Themes Summary of "A Temporary Matter". www.articlemyriad.com. December 6, 2011.

10

Elizabeth Dalloway's '*Chinese Eyes*': Virginia Woolf and the Age of *Japonisme*

Noriko Kubota

'Lily Briscoe's Chinese eyes' referred to in *To the Lighthouse* became a particularly well-known phrase after Patricia Laurence used it in the title of her book, *Lily Briscoe's Chinese Eyes: Bloomsbury, Modernism and China,* which was published in 2003. However, it is to be noted that Virginia Woolf also had given the same 'Chinese eyes' to Elizabeth in *Mrs. Dalloway,* issued two years before the publication of *To the Lighthouse.*

Elizabeth Dalloway, the daughter of the heroine Clarissa, was described as having 'Chinese eyes'. She was said to be 'an oriental mystery' different from the other Dalloway ladies who were generally 'fair haired' and 'blue-eyed'.

> Was it that some Mongol had been wrecked on the coast of Norfolk (as Mrs. Hilbery said), had mixed with the Dalloway ladies, perhaps a hundred years ago? For the Dalloways, in general, were fair haired; blue-eyed; Elizabeth, on the contrary, was dark; had Chinese eyes in a pale face; an Oriental mystery; was gentle, considerate, still. (*Mrs. Dalloway* 135)

Here, Clarissa is having a rest on the sofa and, in a sort of reverie, she sees her daughter standing at the door. So this dreamlike, meditative state helps Clarissa to achieve a truer image of her own daughter. However, even though it should be admitted that Clarissa only remembers Mrs. Hilbery's saying, it may have sounded a bit incongruous and abrupt for readers in the 1920s. It may have been unrealistic for them to imagine that a ship-wrecked Mongol mixed with blue-eyed fair-haired British women a hundred years ago. The people at that time would have thought it an obvious racial trespass which they preferred to ignore, because in this passage the 'Chinese eyes' serve as a harp antithesis of the authentic English tradition which a 'fair-haired' and 'blue-eyed' beauty represented. So, what significance does the passage convey to the readers? Is it Woolf's deliberate challenge of the colonialist conception of the age? What is the meaning of 'Chinese eyes' used in these two novels by Virginia Woolf? It is the aim of this paper to examine Virginia Woolf's interest in the East represented in 'Chinese eyes' and also in relation to that, to consider the meaning of her interest in *Japonisme*.[1]

Before Woolf's interest in *Japonisme* and the East in *Mrs. Dalloway* is further examined, I would like to make a brief survey on *Japonisme* in Britain, and its influence upon Bloomsbury Group. The first half of Virginia Woolf's life, that is from the 1880s through 1910s, coincides with the Age: of *Japonisme* in Britain. *Japonisme* is a keen interest in Japanese art and also in things Japanese, and it swept Europe after Japan had opened its country and resumed trading with other countries in 1854. Towards the end of the nineteenth century, not only artists but also ordinary people were attracted by Japanese prints called Ukiyo-e, Hokusai manga[2] porcelain, lacquer textiles and furniture. Regarding furniture, Anglo-Japanese style was very much in vogue during the 1870s through 1890s in Britain.

Japanese influence on Western painting have been often referred to the depiction of typical Japanese subjects such a fans or kimono robes, in Western paintings. More attention, however, should be paid to the Ukiyo-e style of suggesting space, which is different from that of the perspective of traditional Western paintings. While Western paintings since the Renaissance period aimed to construct a three-dimensional world on a two-dimensional canvas, the emphasis on this two-dimensional plane with bold, clear outlines is a characteristic of Ukiyo-e prints. It was an entirely new mode of seeing things, which offered a totally innovative way. *The British Museum Glossary* points out that *Japonisme* suggested "new angles of vision and an entirely different treatment of perspective." In its explanation of *Japonisme.*

This was an important influence upon Western art of this period. The Bloomsbury Group paid attention to *Japonisme* from the early days. One of the key Bloom bury figures Roger Fry organized the well-known exhibition 'Manet and Post-Impressionists' in 1910 in Grafton Gallery, London, and through this exhibition Post-Impressionism was introduced to Britain.

Furthermore, Roger Fry was a well-known critic who was deeply interested in Chinese and Japanese art as Denys Sutton pointed out (Sutton 37). Among the Bloomsbury Group, the painter Duncan Grant was particularly inspired by *Japonisme* and he painted a series of works evoked by things Japanese.[3]

Virginia Woolf also shared the same interest in *Japonisme:* when Virginia and Leonard Woolf published *Two Stories* from the Hogarth Press[4] as the first publication in 1917, the book was bound by Japanese paper. According to Mark Hussey, "It was bound in Japanese grass paper, some copies in dull blue some in an overall red and white design," (Hussey 133). It may be plausible to say that their choice of Japanese grass paper for the book binding of their first publication reveals their interest in thing Japanese since all the publishing work including book-binding during the first few years of Hogarth Press was done manually by Leonard and Virginia. Thus, the Bloomsbury Group can be said to be at the cultural front of *Japonisme* at the beginning of the twentieth century.

Regarding Virginia Woolf's writing career, her attention to *Japonisme* can be seen from the early days. One of the earliest examples is "Friendships Gallery" written in 1907.[5] In this short work, Japan is mentioned in Chapter Two, and Chapter Three was entirely devoted to an episode set in Japan.

"Friendships Gallery" was a tribute to Violet Dickinson (1865-1948), who was a friend of Virginia's, and acted as her surrogate mother and mentor. Although it was written in a comical mode with satirical burlesque elements in parts, it was meant to be a biography of Violet Dickinson. As Ellen Hawkes explained in her introduction to "Friendships Gallery", Violet Dickinson travelled around the world together with a friend, Nelly Cecil. They visited Japan in 1905 and afterward gave Virginia a "full report of their impressions" (Hawkes 271). So their experience in Tokyo can be thought to be the source for the third chapter of "Friendships Gallery," a Hawke has pointed out (Hawkes 271).

"Friendships Gallery" was "typed with a violet typewriter ribbon and bound in violet leather" (Hawkes 272) and was presented to Violet in August 1907. It is a typescript version "with holograph corrections and in other unidentified hands," according to Kirkpatrick (Kirkpatrick 422), so Virginia Woolf surely thought that it was not completed yet or may have had no direct intention to publish it at that time. The work had been long forgotten and was found by chance among the books and papers of Violet's brother, Oswald Eden, after his death in 1955 (Hawkes 272). It was printed in *The Twentieth Century Literature* in 1979 but it took more than a century until it was published in a book form: "Friendships Gallery" was contained in the sixth volume of *The Essays of Virginia Woolf,* which came out in April 2011.

The original version of "Friendships Gallery" preserved in the Berg Collection in the Public Library, New York, is a short story of about fifty pages, and Chapter One begins with Violet's birth and follows her progress as a society lady. What the narrator emphasizes in the first two chapters is Violet's uniqueness and unconventionality. When she was born, she is described as follows:

> ...she was the cleverest child
> the noisiest child
> the child with
> the finest lungs in the Parish.... ("FG" 275)

Furthermore, Violet grew up to be "as tall as the tallest hollyhock in the garden before she was eight;..." ("FG" 276). These exceptional physical characteristics of Violet imply that she is incompatible with conventional society and the people around her try to suppress her but cannot.

Chapter Two, which is entitled "The Magic Garden," deals with her conversation with a gardener. Violet is staying "at H___d, where her friend Lady R__t C__l lived,..." ("FG" 285). The abridged words are Hatfield (House) and Robert Cecil, as Ellen Hawkes notes), and there she encounters a gardener as unexpectedly as she may encounter 'fawn' or small dear. They immediately begin conversation.

> He explained the best way of treating roses, and how to lay on manure; he was dogmatic on the grafting of Pyrus Japonica, and contradicted the lady flatly without apology on the matter of Cyrus Asiatica, remembering that he knew more than she did. ("FG" 286)

'Pyrus Japonica' is also known as chaenomeles or Japanese quince, but interestingly, it seems that the author uses the rather difficult Latin phrase on purpose to have a pun with 'Cyrus Asiatica', which increases comical and vivid impact. At the same time, however, 'Pyrus Japonica' retains a somewhat heterogeneous impression in this context. As the narrator describes that Violet was "sitting on the most famous terrace in Europe, with the oldest oak trees in front of her, and the smoothest turf, and behind her the finest Elizabethan grey stone,..." ("FG" 285), and the reader easily recalls that Hatfield House used to be the abode of Queen Elizabeth I in her youth. 'The oldest oak trees' evokes the figure of Orlando sitting under the oak tree and 'the smoothest turf' reminds the reader of the turf, excluding women in *A Room of Ones Own*. In that essay the turf of a Cambridge college, which had been smoothly mowed for hundreds of years, was a symbol of male-oriented English society. So this scene implies that Violet is at the very centre of English tradition, of English society, but at the same time she encounters the heterogeneous outside world when she hears about 'Pyrus Japonica' and 'Cyrus Asiatica'.

The gardener himself serves as an important indication. He talks frankly and earnestly to Violet:

> In short he [the gardener] stood there for half an hour telling her of his wifes (sic) dyspepsia, how caustic is poison for tumours, how a drop warms the innards, how he would think over her words, and how if ever she came their way he would be proud to give her a cup of tea, "not spirits" he said with a wink and show her how to treat phylloxera with paraffin. ("FG" 286)

The passage is a vivid description of the humorous heart-to-heart conversation between two people beyond class barriers, but for that reason, it implies a violation of the class distinction for the people at that time. The gardener is described as follows:

> Freedom gleamed in his eyes while he spoke; and he waved his shears towards the house as men waved bloodstained bayonettes once before the Bastille. ("FG" 286)

A gardener talking freely with 'a real lady' ("FG" 286) is compared to people in one of the most decisive scenes of the French Revolution. Of course, it is true that there is a comical exaggeration in the description of the enthusiastic gardener, but at the same time one cannot deny that Virginia Woolf is fully aware that there is a distinct subversive image of the gardener for the reader at the beginning of the twentieth century. The comparison of the gardener waving his large pair of shears, (which is a long, metal tool for cutting) with people waving bloodstained swords at the symbolic venue of the French Revolution means that the conversation of people beyond the class barrier is itself a revolutionary act. 'Pyrus Japonica' mentioned in Chapter Two serves as a clash-like encounter with different cultures and also serves as both a destructive and constructive power because 'Pyrus Japonica' becomes a contact point of two different cultures for Violet who talks enjoyably with a gardener, however it might sound harsh and heterogeneous for conventional people.

The function of 'Pyrus Japonica' continues to the next chapter. Chapter Three is subtitled 'a story to make you sleep,' it is set in Tokio [Tokyo]. The story is written in the mode of a folk tale, beginning with a familiar 'once upon a time' phrase, and 'Tokio' is described as "the most beautiful city in the world" ("FG" 293). It is a fantasy story of "the two Sacred Princesses" who "came sailing over the sea on the back of a whale" ("FG" 295) and about a series of miracles which took place during their stay. The name of Violet is not mentioned in this chapter, but the impact of unconventionality seen through the heroine in the previous chapters is similar in Chapter Three. So, the two Princesses easily overlap with Violet and her friend.

The consistent mode of Chapter Three is deliberately constructed as a kind of slapstick comedy with destructive power. However, under the surface of outrageous incongruity, some animated power exists. In this chapter many things are erected, changed, destroyed, reborn and then disappear. So, the dynamic motion represented in Chapter Three can be attributed naturally to Violet herself. On the Princesses finally leaving 'Tokio', the image of Violet and her friend returning back to Britain after their stay in Japan is overlapped. Tokio, the capital of Japan, offers Violet a new activity ground where she may develop her unconventionality and destroy the bondage imposed upon her, as Constantinople offered Orlando a place where she or he achieved a new vision. The slapstick comedy which took place in Japan implies Violet's unconventionality which the traditional British society cannot nurse. So, Chapter Three is not a mere extra to the biography of Violet Dickinson, but it reveals an essential part of Violet's life.

Thus, Woolf's interest in Japan and *Japonisme* began early and continued alongside her writing career. Another case of Woolf's interest in the East is seen in the novel *Jacob's Room*, published in 1922. Here Woolf refers to the effect of Japanese paper flowers, which magically open up on being placed in small bowls of water.

> About this time a firm of merchants having dealings with the East put on the market little paper flowers which opened on touching water. As it was the custom also to use linger-bowls at the end of dinner, the new discovery was found of excellent service. In their sheltered lakes the little coloured flowers swam and slid; surmounted

> smooth slippery waves, and sometimes foundered and lay. Lake pebbles on the glass floor. Their fortunes were watched by eyes intent and lovely. It is surely a great discovery that leads to the union of hearts and foundation of homes. The paper flowers did no less. (*Jacob's Room* 70)

There are no words which denote Japan in this passage, but 'little paper flowers' are Japanese as the editor of the book explains that they are "Japanese paper flowers, used to decorate the fingerbowls at parties" (*Jacob's Room* 171). So, Woolf subtly turns the readers' attention to Japanese culture. Woolf also refers to (Japanese) paper flowers in "Oxford Street Tide," an essay which was published in *Good Housekeeping* magazine, in January 1932. In *Jacob's Room,* it is to be noted that the paper flowers are contrasted with real flowers, and emphasis is put on the transient lives of "their artificial relations" (*Jacob's Room* 70). It is a witty paradox that artificial flowers have shorter lives than natural flowers, but through these Japanese paper flowers a new perception is suggested, different from conventional perceptions.

Virginia Woolf's interest in *Japonisme* can be seen specifically in her short story entitled "Mrs. Dalloway in Bond Street" written in 1923. Interestingly, there is a description of a woman's physical posture likened to that of a figure on 'a Japanese fan'. The scene is set in a glove shop and the comparison is as follows:

> There was only one other customer, sitting sideways at the counter, her elbow poised, her bare hand drooping, vacant; like a figure on a Japanese fan, thought Clarissa, too vacant perhaps, yet some men would adore her. ("Mrs Dalloway in Bond Street," *Shorter Fiction* 156)

The word 'like' of 'like a figure on a Japanese fan' shows that a Japanese fan was such a familiar object in Britain that it was used figuratively.

Lastly, I would like to mention that Woolf wrote a book review on Arthur Waley's translation of *The Tale of Genji.* The original tale is the oldest Japanese novel written at the beginning of the eleventh century, a thousand years ago. The book review came out in 1925, the same year that *Mrs. Dalloway* was published.

Thus, *Japonisme* was familiar to Woolf from the early days of her life and it can be said that *Mrs. Dalloway* was partly based on Woolf's interest in *Japonisme*, although there is no specific reference to Japan as such in this novel.

Contrary to this, there are references to China or things Chinese in this novel even before we encounter Elizabeth's Chinese eyes. The following passage is about the scene when a car had a flat tyre.

> The car had gone, but it had left a slight ripple...; when the sentence was finished something had happened. Something so trifling in single instances that no mathematical instrument, though capable of transmitting shocks in China, could register the vibration. (*Mrs. Dalloway* 21)

Here, China represents some distant place, far away from Britain.

The reference to Chinese things is seen in the following scene where Peter is walking in London, having coming back from India after five years and every object seems fresh to him:

> Admirable butlers, tawny chow dogs, halls laid in black and white lozenges with white blinds blowing, Peter saw through the opened door and approved of. A splendid achievement in its own way, after all, London; the season; civilisation. (*Mrs. Dalloway* 61)

The formal name of 'chow dogs' is chow chow and it originated in China, and the name itself is, according to *Britannica,* "apparently derived from an English term used in the 19th century to refer to cargo from the Orient" (*Britannica* 'chow chow'). The word China is not mentioned in the citation, but the name 'chow chow' or 'chow dogs' itself sounds very Chinese, and the note suggests a breed strongly connected with Chinese origin. The name is repeated in the next page again as if the author intends to emphasize the word. From these references, Woolf paved a way to connect her readers to China, and Elizabeth's Chinese eyes are the culmination of Chinese things in this novel.

In *Mrs. Dalloway,* Elizabeth is supposed to be a new type of a woman with a clearer vision for her future, treading on her own way herself. However, returning to Elizabeth's passage again, the mixture of a shipwrecked Mongol with Dalloway ladies may evoke harsh, historical memories of the Mongol invasion of Eastern Europe in the thirteenth century, even though the modern Mongol and the Dalloway ladies may have been in love with each other a hundred years ago. It is a tricky passage embracing misapprehension, and such harsh uneasiness reflects the situation surrounding Elizabeth. It is like a clash-like encounter of two cultures but eventually the value of the East is fused into the West just as Pyrus Japonica was grafted into the English soil by a gardener from Hatfield House, and Japan offered a new angle of vision to Violet in "Friendships Gallery".

Virginia Woolf juxtaposes seemingly contrasting things in *Mrs. Dalloway* and tries to integrate them. When Clarissa feels a sense of union with Septimus, a person who killed himself, it can be said to be an attempt to integrate life and death, sanity and insanity. Thus, Elizabeth's Chinese eyes symbolize the possibility of the integration of different cultures.

At the end of *To the Lighthouse,* Lily with 'Chinese eyes' finally obtains her 'vision,' which she has endeavoured to achieve over ten years. Lily, who became the moral successor of Mrs. Ramsay, has achieved what Mrs. Ramsay could not. It means that her 'Chinese eyes' is not a mere physical description; the phrase denotes her mode of seeing things. It implies that Lily obtained her long-sought vision as she saw things through Chinese eyes. Here, again the detachment from the Western tradition, which is represented through the figure of Mr. Ramsay, a distinguished scholar of philosophy, is emphasized, though covertly.

Virginia Woolf, as Leslie Stephen's daughter, is said to be born and reared at the heart of British tradition, and in fact she did not travel outside of the West. However, her criticism against logo-centric British society made her pursue what the West had lost or ignored. Thus, it is plausible to say that Woolf's interest in the East, represented in her interest in *Japonisme* and in Chinese eyes, is an attempt to solve this challenge and to attain a new sense of perception.

NOTES

1. The artists who were influenced by *Japonisme* were, to name a few, Monet, Renoir, Cezanne, Vincent van Gogh, Paul Gauguin, and Henri de Toulouse-Lautrec in France, James McNeill Whistler, Walter Crane and Aubrey Beardsley in Britain, and also Alphonse Mucha in the Czech Republic and Gustav Klimt in Austria. It can be said that an essential influence of Impressionist and Post-Impressionist paintings was Japanese art, in a number of ways.

   Van Gogh repeatedly mentioned Japan and Japanese art in his letters. He says that "All my work is based to some extent on Japanese art" (Letter 640) in his letter to Theo, his brother. In the Van Gogh Museum in Amsterdam, one room is allocated to his 'Japonaiserie' paintings, alongside with 'Earl Works' and 'Paris Works and Pointillism'. Also in a recent exhibition of an Gogh held in London from January 2010, entitled "The Real Van Gogh: The Artist and His Letters," emphasis was placed on the strong relationship of Van Gogh with *Japonisme*. The exhibition consisted of nine sections to show Gogh's main aspects an artist, and 'Japanese prints' is one of the categories and considered to compose the essence of Van Gogh.
2. Hokusai Katsushika (1760-1849) was a Japanese Ukiyo-e artist. Hokusai Manga is a collection of his sketches of various subjects such as landscapes, fauna and flora and people of everyday life. It is said to have given an enormous influence on Western art.
3. A few examples are "Still Life, the Sharaku Scarf" and "James Strachey" (1910).
4. Hogarth Press was founded by Leonard Woolf and Virginia Woolf in 1917.
5. In 1907, Woolf also wrote a book review related to Japan. She contributed a review on Charlotte Lorrimer's *The Call of the East,* a book on Japan and China to *Times Literary Supplement.* There Woolf was very much interested in the perception of Japanese people.

WORKS CITED

Hawkes, Ellen. Introduction to "Friendships Gallery". In "Unpublished Virginia Woolf". *The Twentieth Century Literature.* Fall 1979.

Hussey, Mark. *Virginia Woolf A to Z.* New York: Facts on File, Inc., 1995.

Kirkpatrick, B.J. and Stuart N. Clarke. *A Bibliography of Virginia Woolf.* Fourth Edition. Oxford: Clarendon Press, 1997.

Laurence, Patricia. *Lily Briscoe's Chinese Eyes: Bloomsbury, Modernism and China.* Columbia: University of South Carolina Press, 2003.

Lorrimer, Charlotte. *The Call of the East.* London: Gay and Bird, 1907.

Van Gogh, Vincent. *Vincent Van Gogh: the letters.* Ed. Leo Jansen et al. London: Thames & Hudson, 2009.

Woolf, Virginia. Review of *The Call of the East. TLS,* Friday, April 26, 1907: 131; Issue 276.

——. *Jacob's Room.* 1922. London: Penguin, 1992.

——. *Mrs. Dalloway.* 1925. London: Hogarth Press, 1963.

——. Review of *Tale of Genji.* Vol. I, by Lady Murasaki, translated from the Japanese by Arthur Waley. *Vogue,* July 1925, Vol. 66, No. 2, 53, 80.

——. "Friendships Gallery" (1907). In "Unpublished Virginia Woolf." *The Twentieth Century Literature.* Fall 1979.

——. "Mrs. Dalloway in Bond Street." *The Complete Shorter Fiction of Virginia Woof.* Ed. Susan Dick. San Diego: Harcourt Brace Jovanovich, 1989.

——. *The London Scene: Six Essays on London Life.* New York: Ecco, 2006.

11

Single by Choice or Circumstance: Women in Indian Popular Fiction

Neeta Shukla

Chick lit is a genre that centers on the lives of urban class women written in a lively and playful manner. In the late 1990s the genre gained immense popularity in the West having movies and serials based on the novels. Chick lit is generally not taken as an off shoot of the romance novel, even though many novels have romance central to them. The heroine's relationship is not bound to just one man but to other people in her life too, who could be family or friends. The female protagonist's womanhood is the matter of concern in the plot. The term appeared as early as 1988 as college slang for a course titled "Female Literary Tradition" and Cris Mazza and Jefferey Deshell used the term as an ironic title for their edited anthology *Chick Lit—Post Feminist Fiction*. The genre was defined as a type of post-feminism or second wave feminism that went beyond female as fiction to include love, courtship and gender. The collection emphasized experimental work, including violent, perverse and sexual themes. Works such as Helen Fielding's "Bridget Jones's Diary" and Candace Bushnell's "Sex and the City" are examples that help establish contemporary connotations of the term. The success of Bridget Jones established chick lit as an important trend in publishing. *The Girls' Guide to Hunting and Fishing* by Melissa Bank is regarded as one of the first chick lit works to originate as a novel (actually a collection of stories), though the term was in common use at the time of its publication (1999).

There is well-known band of Indian writers whose writings cannot be neglected for they have a huge readership and have established themselves as writers in the world. The pioneers like Arundhati Roy, Jhumpa Lahiri or Kiran Desai have etched Indian Writing on the international map by winning the much-coveted literary awards. Shobha De writes in a style that deals with modern life cocktail and parties, bold socialite scenes and four-letter words that shocked the Indian reader when they first appeared in print. Today, expletives are commonplace in corporate corridors, entertainment rooms, and college and school circles. There is a general expectation from writers that matters addressed by them should have social relevance. Modern-day writers are bringing in their experiences of international travel, describing graphically the culture shock, how they have made the adaptations and brought change in their value system. Taking into account the demand and supply of modern literature for women, chick lit is considered serious business. What started off as genre specific romance writing for the liberated, modern woman has today become an area that addresses everything from the universal search for love, balancing a career, family issues to psychological problems, growing up, marriage, kids and jobs. Light-hearted fiction writing for the modern Indian women is a relatively new phenomenon. Many women writers like Swati Kaushal (*Piece of Cake*), Anuja Chauhan (*The Zoya Factor* and *Battle for Bittora*), Advaita Kala (*Almost Single*) and Rajashree (*Trust Me*) have tasted immense success with their young, single, modern Indian woman protagonists who are lively, peppy, unconventional and independent. These women have an innate 'Indianness' that every woman here can identify with. Contemporary Indian popular fiction that narrates 'desi' cosmopolitan stories has been mirroring the changing man-woman relationship in a more open and accepting urban India. When the globalised 1990s began to creep into 'desi' books, the theme of love became wider and the books began to include more complex motifs with "emotional riddles, tangled relationships and even same sex love". In the decade of 2000, the thrust of stories became younger in years as dark passionate secrets came tumbling out of cup-boards and the complex relationships (that have always been there in a particular class in the urban areas) became open.

Being single is nothing out of the ordinary for a woman in the present scene. Socio-economic situation after liberalization has made women economically sound and her emergence as an independent individual. But the term 'single' has brought in a host of inchoate meanings that arise from the diverse discourses of the family, free market, development, consumerism, behavioral psychology, feminist movement among others. The single woman is regarded as any one or a combination of the following: unfortunate, lonely, vulnerable, incomplete, frustrated, frigid, man-hater, woman-lover, self-indulgent, promiscuous, predatory, unpredictable, non-conforming, subversive, free or liberal. In a patriarchal context, the whole range of reference is over determined by the absence of a male figure. Her singleness becomes her primary attribute and she is regarded single not because she does not have friends, family and males in her life but because she does not have a legitimate sexual partner. The different modes of singleness include the widow, the divorcee, the separated or deserted woman and the unmarried woman. The unmarried woman is not appreciated as the other figures of women are. The unmarried single woman is an enigma or unthinkable especially in our context where marriages are to a large extent arranged and not a matter of individual choice. Single is thought to be a state achieved almost by chance and in most cases rarely by design. In the modern world, however, this state gestures towards a reordering of relationships, reorganization of notions of intimacy and a fundamental subversion of the family model. To accept them as single means to accept that they are free to act for themselves. But it is a well-known fact that women in this country are seldom free and are always under the guardianship of their father, husband or other relations. The women, who are single, in most cases, never chose to be single out of choice, even though they have strong political opinion on the institution of marriage and are not at all enamored by the idea of marriage.

They never think of it as an ultimate aim in life and it is something that could have happened and their life gone on a different path but the lack of it also does not trouble them. The women instead engage in personal development and need their own time and space for this. Personal space has become very important and also the philosophy of 'live and let live'. The thrust is on quality time which has become an important mantra in today's life. Personal liking over anything, be it caste or status, gets priority and women get into relationships on an equal footing. Chick lit depicts the life of such predominantly young, single, urban women and details their life, loves, trials and tribulations. But the themes in the novels have also gone beyond love and marriage to individuality and fame, love-hate relationship with parents, the arranged marriage circus, female bonding and friendships, homosexuality in India and the struggle to be modern yet Indian. This new writing has become an amazing commercial and publishing success, progressing from just being a trend acquired from abroad, rather it has become a cultural phenomenon cutting across sections of race, religion, culture, age, color, and even sex. The entry of an Indian protagonist on the chick lit scene came much after the best sellers in America and Europe had made their mark. Indian-American characters in chick lit emerged in America in the early 2000s with protagonists following a progressive lifestyle in America. Kavita Daswani wrote *For Matrimonial Purposes* (2003) followed by *Everything Happens for a Reason* (2004), *The Village Bride of Beverly Hills* (2004), *Salaam Paris* (2006), and *Indie Girl* (2007). All the novels have protagonists who started their stories from a life grounded in India but then because of their marriage they found themselves settled in America where their stories orbited around the marriage issue and the way they dealt with it. Arrange marriage is central to them and there is a struggle between the modernity around them and their Indian upbringing. Anjali Banerjee's *Imaginary Men* (2005) shows Lina Ray—a matchmaker in San Francisco with a very traditional Indian family who finds an Indian boy before her life takes a horrible turn and things go awry. In her next novel *Invisible Lives* (2007), Anjali portrays the story of Lakshmi who runs a sari shop in Seattle and "was born with a magical ability to perceive secret longings in others". She too has to make a decision between a marriage arranged by her father and her feelings for an American chauffeur. Then Sonia Singh introduces the problems of Indian women oscillating between values and change in *Goddess for Hire* (2004), *Bollywood Confidential* (2005), and *Ghost Interrupted* (2007). Likewise, Poonam Sharma, author of *Girl Most Likely To* (2007) and *All Eyes on Her* (2008) does the same. She introduces a desi flavor to her works, with her novels discussing similar dilemmas as those of her fellow writers, the daily struggles of career and dating, juggling between personal demands and pressures of family and evolving as an Indian American. But the most sought-after Indian Chick Lit are the three novels by Kaavya Viswanathan, namely *How Opal Mehta Got Kissed, Got Wild*, and *Got a Life* (2006). The popularity of all these books by all the authors lies in their protagonists' presumed Indian-ness and their authors' popularity happens for the same reason. Swati Kaushal's *Piece of Cake* came out in the year 2004 which delineates the story of the protagonist, a twenty-nine-year-old woman, Minal Sharma, who is the Associate Products Manager at International Foods. She has to put up with her mother's attempts to get her married through matrimonial advertisements in newspapers; shield her career from a cowardly boss, as also from the office's in-house femme fatale who poses a threat to her promotion, and a new colleague who turns out to be a peeved competitor from her childhood hell bent on sabotaging her career; she has to choose between an amorous radio-jockey younger to her in age and a successful, selfish and uninteresting oncologist. The novel became a best-seller, encouraging Kaushal to write again and she came out with *A Girl Like Me* (2008) that narrates the travails of an Indian teenager who returns from Minnesota to settle to a life in India. Rupa Gulab's 'Girl Alone' introduces the particular girlish apprehensions of Arti, the emotionally insecure, intellectual snob who is also cough-syrup addict and an avid reader of T.S. Eliot's poetry and finds that rock bands have a calming effect on her. On one hand, she works hard to find professional satisfaction while on the other she has to find a decent man in Mumbai who shares her interests and appreciation for Woody Allen and D.H. Lawrence, and with whom she can make a life. Her worst fear is that if she is not able to find the right man then she has to marry the man selected by her mother. Rajashree's *Trust Me* narrates the experiences of Paro, a girl from Amravati who works in the film industry and gains first-hand knowledge about black money, casting couch and immoral actors. Advaita Kala's *Almost Single* (2007) asks the question, "Is there any such thing as a perfect relationship?" and immediately connects with all women in a relationship or who are looking for a relationship. Focused on Aisha Bhatia, twenty-nine years old Guests Relation Manager at the Grand Orchid Hotel, Delhi, the novel records the predicaments of the young, savvy girls and their gay friends as they hope for love in the city. Chick Lit novel by Smita Jain *Kkrishnaa's Konfessions*, tells the story of Kkrishnaa an impulsive, spirited, stubborn and enterprising *primetime* script writer who is distressed by her inability to write so she goes around looking for inspiration and in the course of this she witnesses a murder, has to steal and seduce, and also spend a night in jail. Meenakashi Reddy Madhavan in *You Are Here* (2008) portrays the character of Arshi a twenty-five-year-old woman who goes through many complicated relationships including one with her American step mom, a two timer ex-boyfriend, and an insufferable boss. Such array of people in her life baffles her and she yearns for solace through alcohol and comfort through physical relationships. Anuja Chauhan's *The Zoya Factor* (2008) tells about a plain looking advertising executive Zoya Singh Solanki's journey with the Indian Cricket team to the ICC World Cup Championships. In spite of all misgivings, she is declared the official goddess of lucky charm for the team. In Chauhan's second novel *Battle for Bittora* (2010), twenty-five-year-old Jinni lives in Mumbai, works as an animator and is very satisfied with her happy go lucky and unconstrained life. This only lasts till her bossy grandmother ends all this and makes her contest the upcoming Lok Sabha elections from their sleepy hometown, Bittora. Her resistance goes unheeded and she soon ends up swathed in cotton saris and frumpy blouses, battling the heat, an irresistible opponent with whom she has had previous association. Almost all the novels discuss the insecurities, apprehensions, desires, pain, dilemmas and tussles in the life of the protagonists.

Why people read these books is because through them the reader wants to find out how the protagonist deals with the problems in the books, the dilemmas they face in their everyday life. Women ask why female dilemmas should be any less universal than male problems. The answer to the question starts with Jane Austen, who, it's been suggested, is the great-great-grandmother of "chick lit". Since then such writing as written by Jane Austen feature upwardly mobile young women and their capricious predicaments in the world of modern romance (and modern-day shopping) and are customarily based in the best neighbourhood in the best cosmopolitan cities. The protagonists are down to earth, erring and painfully aware and critical of themselves in an alluring and irresistible manner. Almost all the novels have the women committing errors of judgment because of excessive pride or prejudice in making out the men in their lives and most do not end up with their match as Elizabeth does in *Pride and Prejudice*. Sometimes, there is a Wickham-like character crossing and misleading the protagonist and causing havoc in her life and maybe breaking up her chances of settling with her Darcy. She works hard at the relationships, but it is only after she fails to connect with the man she is in relationship with that she goes looking for the lesser desired one. The friends too are of no help they are either the married ones who are self-righteous or the single ones who are sailing in the same boat. The female friends are as confused as the protagonist, some because they are maybe undergoing problematic relationships themselves or others who think they are strong and insist on playing the part of a feminist. Despite many complications easy romance and playful dating is what carries the story forward. The protagonists are women of the world and abreast of world issues and familiar with well-known women like Oprah, Julia Roberts, Jane

Fonda and Madonna and are on the same wavelength in their worldly knowledge as any other educated woman of any part of the world. The fact remains that the reader identifies with the protagonist, laughing with her than at her and comes to accept her own flawed-self just as the imperfect character she finds in the book. A feeling of shared camaraderie and intimacy makes the books appealing and popular. The books recount the experiences of one woman, however fictional, that are accepted and understood by many others. Chick lit tries to ratify the readers' feelings as natural and brings about consolidation of a particular group of women because of their ability to reflect everyday reality of women.

Hence, chick lit represents contemporary young women as far as individuality, femininity, career and relationships are concerned, and exposes insights about their lives as they get around their expectations of career and relationships. Women use these popular cultural texts in making sense of their own social experience and construct congruity between the underlying message of the chick lit novels and their own conditions of existence. By construing the different ways in which chick lit tries to challenge cultural expectations about women as buyers, readers and writers, chick lit does open up spaces for ruminating over the contradictions inherent in contemporary feminine personalities. Concerned with the culture and lives of young urban women, the books mainly delineates the lives of modern, cosmopolitan, single women in their 20s and 30s who place great emphasis on their dating relationships, careers and shopping and their everyday struggles with work, home, friendship, family or love. These are young women working in the corporate sector, media and publishing houses, fashion magazines, hotels, PR firms, etc. Almost all are written in a self-deprecating, funny, first-person voice. Taken as a whole, these works provide an interesting examination of images of women and their concerns in contemporary popular culture, while at the same time entertaining their readers. Indeed, the difference between chick lit novels and their literary antecedent is the ability of the modern protagonists to laugh at themselves while simultaneously the literature treats women's issues with wittiness and insight. In terms of desire, sexual play and experience, chick lit heroines seem to differ from the naive and artless heroines of traditional romances. Unlike traditional romances, contemporary chick lit doesn't always end in marriage, and the heroine's active social life outside the man-woman relationship plays just as important a role in her life. Chick lit for this reason reaches to a wider group of women who are not just looking for romance, but the various issues and situations women face when fending for footing in a commercial world. There is a certain typical nature to most chick lit novels that indicates the popularity of it and because of this the novels are adapted to the standards laid down by commercial requirements. Truly, the content of chick lit novels may be formula-driven but the writers have given creative modifications to these formulas. Chick lit is criticized, stigmatized and rejected, but nobody can deny that today it is a publication wonder and social critique. The genre has a long historical connection and actually reflects a powerful cultural interplay. Also, studying the notion of femininity shown in present popular fiction and the chick lit fiction can make us understand how the discourse of marriage, sex, feminism, money unfolded in the years between Jane Austen's *Pride and Prejudice* and present-day novels. The women in the novels and the readers of the novels show how they have found a space to scrutinize similar feelings and experiences of their daily lives regarding gender roles, relationships, sexuality, career and marriage within the framework as exhibited in these popular cultural writing. The situations and dilemmas faced by the young women characters in the stories of chick lit novels have come to be accepted as normal and of those apprehensive women who are dissatisfied with their bodies and their relationships, who seek approval about their female body and show anxiety over career betterment. For instance, many chick lit heroines turn to other magazines and programs that give information to look better and beautiful. Latest magazines and self-help books have a stronghold on the heroines' life. By sharing the details of her problematic relationships, her job, and failed attempts to reduce her consumption of alcohol, cigarettes and calories, she gains women's empathy. To emphasize their individuality and freedom young contemporary urban women adopt drinking, socializing, dating and indulge in the pleasures offered by shopping. The protagonists, therefore, are not only the contrivance of their authors, but they also are an imitation of their reading audience. This couples the stories immediately to their readers by appealing to them to find similarities with the characters and situations described, and to note that they are talking of their own lives, the manner how personal and social problems are managed. It does not seem wrong to say that the women who read these books are a lot like the women in them, young, quite successful but a wee bit insecure, have a propensity for romantic alliances and demonstrate professional weaknesses, look for drama and entertainment and also go to books and magazines for guidance. Chick lit serves two purposes, it is functional and relevant as it emulates women's lives as well as is entertaining. Women use these popular novels in making sense of their own social world and experience and try coping with their contemporary, urban lifestyles where they are torn between the contemporary modern atmosphere and the traditions that still asks of them to maintain a conventional demeanor. The women readers welcome the chick lit texts according to their needs; these texts work for them and are of use so far as it helps them to stand up to the bargains and challenges that their daily lives involve. The female readers establish purpose implicit in the chick lit novels and their own conditions of existence. The manner in which the dilemmas and complications are handled is humorous and this is what makes these books pleasing for readers. They playfully deal with the aspects of contemporary women's lives and relationships in regard to men and the competitive urban world. In today's world, where women are expected to be smart and ambitious as well as stylish and chic, these books are close to heart and easy to relate to without being sententious. The debates on chick lit reflect the conflict over the issue of portrayal of women, gender and sexuality. The conflict on chick lit is ongoing and probably due to the depiction of women's liberation as her entry into the masculine world, her image, identity, sexuality to go hand in hand with the ever-expanding consumption of commodities, while the need for social change to improve women's lives takes a back seat. These books do not claim to bring social reform rather they serve to represent the lives of women as they are, the battles they face daily both inside and outside their self. Women are under enough pressure caught up in between the contemporary modern lives and the prescriptions that still expect them to maintain a traditional femininity; they do not want to worry about what the feminists will think when they want to read something entertaining and easy to relate to. Besides, chick lit deals with issues essential to feminism, like the pressures on women about their identity through how good they look and then how they balance work with intimate relationships. Somewhat paradoxically, it provides readers a humorous break from the demands of being smart, fashionable and sexy all at once, while it also satirizes what chick lit represents. The pleasures, entertainment and meanings raised in chick lit reading are many; it is like they are offering room for cultural manipulation. The practice of reading chick lit raises the platform for opposition as well as compliance to structures of power operating in society. The market promoting chick lit books for profit, using strategic selling techniques and luring readers through formulaic styles are all part of the chick lit reality, but when looked beyond these, one can consider chick lit as an important representation of modern women and issues that they face.

WORKS CITED

Bushnell, Cadence. *Sex and the City.* London, Abacus: London, Reprint, 2004.

Chauhan, Anuja. *The Zoya Factor*. Noida: HarperCollins India, 2008.

——. *The Battle for Bittora*. Noida: HarperCollins India, 2009.

Daswani, Kavita. *For Matrimonial Purposes*. New York: HarperCollins Publishers, 2003.

——. *Everything Happens for a Reason*. New York: HarperCollins Publishers, 2004.

——. *Salaam Paris*. California: Plume Books, 2006.

Ferriss, Suzanne. Young, Mallory. *Chick Lit: The New Woman's Fiction*. New York: Routledge, 2006. Web.

Gulab, Rupa. *Girl Alone*. New Delhi: Penguin Books India, 2005.

Jain, Smita. *Kkrishnaa's Konfessions*. New Delhi: Westland Limited, 2008.

Kala, Advaita. *Almost Single*. Noida: HarperCollins Publishers and The India Today Group, 2007.

Kaushal, Swati. *Piece of Cake*. New Delhi: Penguin Books, 2004.

Lakshmi, Rama. "India's Cheeky Chick-Lit finds an Audience." *The Washington*, November 23, 2007.

Mazza, Cris, Jeffrey De Shell. Eds. *Chick Lit: Postfeminist Fiction*. New York: Fiction Collective 2, 1995.

Madhavan, Meenakshi Reddy. *You Are Here*. New Delhi: Penguin, 2008.

Rajashree. *Trust Me*. New Delhi: Rupa and Co., 2006.

Singh, Sonia. *Goddess for Hire*. New York: Avon, 2004.

——. *Bollywood Confidential*. New York: Avon, 2005.

——. *Ghost, Interrupted*. New York: Avon, 2007.

Sunaina Kumar. *The Rise of Ladki-Lit*. The Indian Express, October 8, 2006.

"Chick Lit", Wikipedia [22/02/07], "Wikipedia. What is Chick Lit"?, Chick Lit Books [22/05/07].

12

Towards Constructing Dalit Aesthetics

Jaydeep Sarangi

It was out of varna system that, it was said, caste system was born. One of the most torturous aspects of Hindu social system for Dalits was untouchability. It was further a matter of great shock and surprise that the system of untouchability was supported and justified by some Hindu 'religious' scriptures such as *Manusmriti*. In regard to caste system, at one point, we may consider that the problem of untouchability is really a class-struggle between caste Hindus and untouchables, and this seems to be a never-ending conflict. Untouchability was born some time about 400 A.D. It is born out of the struggle for supremacy between Buddhism and Brahminism which has so completely moulded the history of India.

Nowhere, in the history of mankind can one notice inequality which is more intense and pernicious than the practice of untouchability. And hence, untouchability was such an abominable stain that it would not matter even if some lives were sacrificed to wash it out. One of the historical periods during which Dalits were tortured to utmost degree on the basis of the notions of untouchability was the period of the Peshwas, the Brahmin rulers, who operated from Pune in Maharashtra. About this torturous period in the lives of the Dalits, under the rule of the Peshwas, in the Maratha country, the untouchable was not allowed to use the public streets if a Hindu was coming along, lest he should pollute the Hindu by his shadow. The untouchable was required to have a black thread either on his wrist or in his neck as a sign or mark to prevent the Hindus from getting themselves polluted by his touch through his mistake. In Poona, the capital of the Peshwa, the untouchable was required to carry strung from his waist a broom to sweep away from behind the dust he treaded on lest a Hindu walking on the same should be polluted. In Poona, the untouchable was required to carry an earthen pot, hung in his neck wherever he went, for holding his spit lest his spit falling on the earth should pollute a Hindu who might unknowingly happen to go that way.

It has been pointed out that Kautilya's *Arthashastra* also suggests that the disadvantaged be kept disadvantaged. In his *Arthashastra*, at one point, Kautilya is reported to be suggesting to the advantaged people that the untouchables should not be allowed to inhabit a certain place for a long time. In case they stay for a long time at one place, they should be immediately driven away.

In Kautilya's times also, the untouchables were not only expected but also forced to follow all the norms prescribed by religious, social, cultural writings/documents composed by the caste Hindus who were decidedly against the downtrodden and hence their writings were also deliberately written against the interests of the disadvantaged. The word 'Dalit(a)' comes from the Indo-Aryan root dal, and means 'held under check', 'suppressed', or 'crushed', or, in a looser sense, 'oppressed'. Maharashtrian Dalit activist and poet Namdeo Dhasal made it a symbol of pride to fight against social injustice. He said:

> Yes, I do feel that the fight to eradicate caste has to be fought by Dalits and caste Hindus together carrying forward the tradition of Adi Shankara, which got broken somewhere in between.

The usage of the term 'Dalit' seems to have originated from the Arya Samaj and their dalitoddhara ('upliftment of the downtrodden'). The Arya Samaj began the All India Shraddhanand Dalitodwar Sabha to specialize in the upliftment of the Dalits. As we all know, when the word dalit is pronounced, it brings with it all negative, pessimistic and similar types of associations. In short, it brings with it associations of darkness, hopelessness, helplessness, etc. But Baburao Bagul is one of the rare writers and thinkers who looks at this term from a positive angle and thereby, he sees in this term adumbrations of optimism, hope, light, etc. and defines the term from this angle. His definition of this term runs as follows:

> Dalit is the leader of the present times. He is a centre of the whole revolutionary upheavals of today.... A Dalit means a revolutionary and a right change.[1]

Dalit literature in India is subversive, or structurally alternative to the models prescribed by traditional Hindu aesthetics precisely because they are literatures of sociological oppression and economical exploitation. Dalit literature is essentially a shock to the traditional senses. A sound piece of Dalit literature is militant in texture and aggressively blunt in meaning. It challenges codified language (because it has so far been used and manipulated only by the dominant, discriminating powers), it challenges assumptions, it challenges age-old world-views. Its temporal and political designation does not give justice to the artist whose intentions may subsequently be ignored. It is an aesthetics of pain, and a prolong longing; a powerful aesthetics of resistance. The poems "Touch" by Meena Kandasamy amplifies, illustrates, and carries on this struggle for power and autonomy by the women poets. Apart from her expert use of language, she has a sincerity of feeling and an honesty of experience that most of the women poets of India lack. For Meena Kandasamy, the young Tamil poetess, poetry is about empirical truth and experience and she writes and reflects from where she is:

> We: their daughters.
>
> We: the daughters of their soil.
>
> We, mostly, write.[2]

Her poetry is at best of private sensibility. Her consciousness is firmly yoked to the world around her, a world characterised by ecstasy and pain, love and despair. "Touch" contains a sparkling 'Foreword' by Kamala Das where the renowned poetess acknowledges the 'superiority' of Meena Kandasamy's 'poetic vision'. Meena follows the psychological tradition of Sylvia Plath and Langston Hughes a 'fabric rare and strange'. Women's fixed role as caregivers was ideologically determined by their biological capacity to bear children and that was through a fixed set of codes represented by 'categorizers' as Kamala Das has expressed in her poem, "An Introduction". Meena Kandasamy regards her poetic corpus as a process of coming to terms with her identity and consciousness: her 'womanness, Tamilness and low/outcasteness', labels that she wears with pride. Meena has honed her sociological awareness of what it means to be a woman in a caste-ridden social groupism in Tamil Nadu (a southern state in India).

Her poetic self-gasps in darkness to search for her emotional root proclaiming it as, sap is her heritage. Sap is liquid in a plant that carries food to all its parts. It is a source of vitality for the poetess to voyage within. Her confessional mode is not as radical as we find in Mamang Dai, Archana Sahani and Kamala Das. She explores wide range of subjective possibilities and relates them to her own identity and sociological formulation.

Therefore, her poetry that arises not out of mere profound reading and knowledge, but out of active engagement. *Touch* is rich with varied dexterity that explore the states of mind and genuine feminine sentiments.

Today, English-speaking Dalits and tribals are less disrespected; therefore, empowered by English, Dalits can take their place in the new globalized world. English broke the stranglehold of Sanskrit, Persian and Arabic teaching, a privilege of only the elite castes.

Dalit literature is included in the syllabi in a number of universities worldwide. Measures are being taken to introduce Dalit literature in the syllabi of Indian literature. Dalit studies, as a discipline is yet to stamp its imprint as a distinctive field of study. It entails a disjunction between academic activism and a deficient theoretical foregrounding. History, Sociology, Political Science will be the major disciplines that will have to incorporate and assimilate areas of Dalit studies. The Social Sciences have yet to comprehend, interpret and incorporate the struggles of the Dalit and marginalized communities into the academic discourse. Most Dalit intellectuals will advocate the rewriting of history and sociology from the perspectives of Dalits to qualify as disciplines to be taught at the post-graduate levels. But one is sure the area of studies will evolve its own character as it develops after being included in the university.

The importance of Dalit studies can be re-emphasized not merely from the perspective of Dalits but also non-Dalits. One of the major objectives of Dalit studies should be to sensitize the non-Dalits with the issues and concerns of the Dalits. Dalit studies will act as a bridge between Dalits and non-Dalits in promoting greater understanding in society—past and present. As of now Dalit studies is in an amorphous state. This exposes the 'casteness' of the establishment.

Like Dalit writers in India, African-American writers in the US have given expression in their writings to the protest against the established order of society that discriminates one man from another on the basis of caste, colour and religion. Dalit writers as also African-American writers envisage a society that is based on new order, a society that values the principles of liberty, equality and fraternity. Dalit literature is quite similar to the literature of Blacks in USA or Negros in Africa. But it has some specific characteristics also, which are not found in Black or Negro literature. These are the opposition of caste-system and untouchability. Blacks and Negros have faced racial discrimination; they were not untouchables like the Dalits in India. This is the reason that Dalit literature is more aggressive, powerful and sharp-edged than the literature of the Blacks and Negros.

Dalit theology is an out-and-out theology about the downtrodden, "the theology which they themselves would like to expound". One of the major generators of the Dalit theology is the Dalit experience of torment and ache. The theology has a twofold function. Firstly, it acts in harmony with the aim of liberation which is an emancipation from both the religio-cultural and socio-economic bondages. Secondly, the theological movements also possess a lot of psychological dimensions which are of equal importance.

'Dalit' as a concept and category has its value, idea, meaning, culture and identification with human dignity. It opens up new possibilities besides rendering critical understanding. It is no more a mere substitute for erstwhile ascribed categories, used in academic exercise. The very emergence of this concept envisages a culture of resistance and assertion of the subordinated. Posing a challenge to the existing order, it propels the initiatives for the creation of an alternative paradigm as well as reconfiguring the contours of everyday materiality.

Dalit authors presently are able to show not only the hostile circumstances in which Dalits live, but also their struggle for emancipation from caste. However, non-Dalit authors such as Premchand (a high-caste Hindu) and Khushwant Singh, are authors based more on a benevolent level as opposed to one urging change and abolishment of caste. Religion has role-played a decisive part in the writings of both Dalits and non-Dalits.

Dalit literature represents a powerful, emerging trend in the Indian literary scene. Given its overarching preoccupations with the location of Dalits in the caste-based Hindu society, and their struggles for dignity, justice, and equality, this literature is by nature oppositional. Dalit literature poses a major challenge to the established notions of what constitutes literature and how we read it.

Thus, Dalit studies have to consciously address the subconscious of not only the oppressed but the oppressor as well. Caste is a state of mind having its roots in religiously codified laws. Caste is undeniably an everyday materiality. In India, for centuries caste continues to be the core principle on which people have been organized. Further, a set of beliefs and practices were created through which caste inequalities are maintained. Most of the cultural forms are essentially those acquired, accumulated, and stored in the subconscious state of a person. It is easy to engage with the conscious but too difficult to engage with the subconscious. Therefore, Dalit critical theory has to proceed from the critical findings arrived from the process of conscientization.

There are efforts to explore Dalit consciousness in other creative arts like painting, theatre and music, etc. There are *Dalit Natya Munches* in existence. There are a number of Dalit folk artists, singers, musicians and painters who are doing their best to express Dalit feelings and raising the voice against inequality and exploitation through their art forms.

The main concern of Dalit literature has been to introduce the socio-economic and political, religious backwardness and exploitation of Dalits, to give voice to the voiceless and sense to the senseless and at the same time to warn the privileged classes to give their due rights to Dalits and treat them as equal human beings. It is in the interest of development, progress and prosperity of the society. We must value the freedom and human dignity of Dalits.

We can conclude that Dalit is not a caste but a realization and is related to the experiences, joys and sorrows, and struggles of those in the lowest stratum of society. It is a symbol of change and revolution. Dalit literature conscientized Dalit masses for assertion, protest and mobilization. It is an evidence of a profound change taking place in Indian society.

NOTES

1. Bagul, *Dalit Sahitya: Ajache Krantividnyan* (*Delhi Literature: Today's Science of Revolution*). Nagpur: Buddhist Publishing House, 1981: 208-81.
2. Meena Kandasamy. "Their Daughters", *Quarterly Literary Review*, Singapore.

13

A Critique of Global Dalit Identity in Narendra Jadhav's *Outcaste: A Memoir*

Banibrata Mahanta

> Damu was not a leader...but he refused to define himself by circumstances and aimed at shaping his own destiny.
>
> Damu had no formal education...yet he steered his children to educational heights and inculcated in them the spirit of excellence.
>
> Damu was not a guru...but he taught his children to believe in themselves and retain human dignity.
>
> Damu was often humbled...yet he maintained, 'Goats are sacrificial offerings, not lions'.
>
> Damu was an ordinary man, they said...but he did an extraordinary thing: he stood up against the tyranny of the caste system. (*Outcaste*, xi-xiii)

"Every sixth human being in the world today is an Indian, and every sixth Indian is an erstwhile untouchable, a Dalit".[1] This is how the narrative of *Outcaste: A Memoir* begins. It is the story of Damodar Runjaji Jadhav (Damu) and his wife Sonabai (Sonu), reconstructed and translated from the diaries of Damu by their son, Narendra Jadhav, who also added to it the oral recollections of other family members and friends. The original Marathi version, *Amcha Baap Aan Amhi* (*Our Father and Us*) published in 1993, was a direct rendition of the diaries of Damu. The English translation (which I attempt to analyze in this paper), published by Viking in 2003, has significant additions—parts of the memoir are written from the point of view of his wife, Sonu. Her voice, sometimes corroborating and adding details to, and sometimes providing a counterpoint to Damu's story, adds to the narrative complexity of the memoir. The English version also has contributions by Jadhav himself, as well as his daughter Apoorva, thus making the text a family memoir that straddles three generations.

The present paper attempts to analyze the construction of Dalit identity in *Outcaste* in terms of the social, cultural, economic and political changes that affect as well as facilitate the structuring of this idea in India which progresses from colonial realities to independence and beyond, and also relocates from indigenous to globalized realities. These two processes are not simultaneous but staggered, and give rise to the complexity inherent in the memoir: the early part of the memoir grapples with the configuration of Dalit identity in pre-independence India and the welfare state model in independent India; the later part moves onto the era of globalization, where translocal connections lead to an ecumenical socio-cultural dynamism which significantly alters the idea of Dalit identity. The paper attempts to identify the basic grammar that goes into this construction, and in the process finds that the Jadhav family's identity is based on their publicly recognized capabilities and is possible because of global realities, and is rather individual. The paper also attempts to assess the practicability and implications of the positioning of this identity.

I

The publication of the book coincided with some important political and literary developments in the country. The most important of them was the opening up of the economy. The New Economic Policy (NEP) was formulated and implemented in 1991 by the then Finance Minister, Dr. Manmohan Singh. The NEP was formulated as a way out of the economic and political crisis that weighed the country down. Fiscal and current account deficits, domestic and foreign debt, and the lack of foreign exchange reserves were the economic aspects of the problem. These were compounded by the political events of the time like the assassination of Rajiv Gandhi and the fall of two governments one after the other, followed by a minority government holding office. It was this combination of circumstances that led to a host of new developments. Under pressure from the International Monetary Fund and the World Bank, the government adopted the policy of liberalization, privatization and globalization. This led to relaxations in trade, removal of restrictions on private sector players and on foreign investments, privatization of the public sector, and a host of other measures that made it evident that the vision of an interventionist, welfare state as envisaged by Nehru had given way to the demands of the market. The democratic socialist republic that Nehru had thought would empower people by ushering in secular modernity and in which the state would play a proactive role was now history. In its place we now had an open economy that allowed multinational companies and international players in various fields to actively explore, invest in and even generate market in the country.

It is largely this context that created the market to sell various commodities in the country, including books. The entry of multinational publishing houses was part of the process, as was the fact that these publishing houses also targeted sections of the populace that would relate to them and to the titles that they would publish. The entry of these publication houses coincided with a spurt of interest not just in Indian Writing in English, but also in Indian Literatures in Translation, and also, significantly, Dalit writings, written in English as well as translated from the *bhashas*.

Dalit writing as a category has existed for quite some time now, but it is only in the last two decades or so that we have seen a phenomenal growth in the publication of English works and translations of autobiographies, memoirs and fiction by Dalit writers brought out by mainstream publication houses. In 2003, activist Ravi Kumar and journalist S. Anand came together to establish 'Navayana', the first publication house in India devoted exclusively to caste issues. The reason for these developments is twofold. One of course is the massive readership as well as visibility that are assured once a work is rendered into English. Chandra Shan Prasad, author of *Dalit Diary* observes:

> English is the only tool that can connect the Dalits of India; and, being the language of modernity, it can connect people around the globe to the Dalit experience. (quoted in Das, online article)

The other reason is the growing interest in Dalit writing in the context of the internationalization of the caste question. Post-1990s, Dalit intellectuals, activists and theoreticians have consistently been able to raise the issue of untouchability at international forums. Since 1998, they have been giving visible presences at conferences in Malaysia, in London, the World Conference against Racism held at Durban, South Africa and the Dalit International Conference at Vancouver. The Vancouver Conference held in 2003 also advocated that Dalit literature should henceforward be a subject of study and research in educational institutions, both in India and abroad.[2] Jadhav observes:

> There is widespread interest in Dalit writing now, all over the world. The upsurge is not because it is politically correct but because people want to know more about the underprivileged sections, about the lives of these whom they knew so little. (qtd. in Anand 31)

It is quite evident that the global interest in Dalit literature and the issue of caste has been one of the reasons for the spurt in recent publications in this field, and the publication industry has catered to this demand. And the story of Narendra Jadhav's book is an example of how this has happened. The runaway success of the rough and earthy Marathi version led Jadhav to plan the English version. But the English version was not merely a translation of the original. While the earlier version was based solely on Damu's diaries and oral recollections, and was often crude and had a local flavour, the English version was more sanitized, and also had significant portions written in, which would appeal to the more sophisticated and urbane tastes. In fact, the narratives of Sonabai, Jadhav himself, and his daughter Apoorva are all later additions. Jadhav himself admits:

> I wrote this book during my stay in Washington DC for four years, with a global readership in mind. That is precisely why the social context, which was implicit in the Marathi book, has been fully spelt out in the English version. (qtd. in Anand 30)

The book was published in French as *Intouchable* (2002), and later in English by Viking. The success of the book prompted Simon and Schuster to re-publish the book in 2005 as *Untouchables: My Family's Triumphant Journey*. Since then, it has been translated into fourteen foreign languages. In 2002, Narendra Jadhav was invited to the literary festival Les Belles Étrangères, where he shared the dais along with stalwarts like U.R. Ananthamurthy and Mahasweta Devi. The popularity as well as the history of the publication of the book substantiates the arguments that I have attempted to put forward.

Of course, who would understand the dynamics of the current world order better than the author himself! Narendra Jadhav is a global citizen in the true sense of the terms. His early life was lived in a crowded chawl in Mumbai, and he received his initial education in Chhabildas Boys' High School. From there he went to Indiana University for his Ph.D. There, he received the Best International Student Award, as well as the Award for Outstanding Contribution to Economic Theory. He joined the Reserve Bank of India in 1979 and served there in various capacities including being the Head of its Department of Economic Analysis and Policy. He was also associated with the IMF in an advisory capacity. Jadhav is also the author of three books on economics. In 2006, he became the Vice-Chancellor of the University of Pune. He was also Member, Planning Commission.

II

The story of *Outcaste* is the story of how Damu and his wife Sonu struggled against the claustrophobic confines of the society that they were born into, and were able to negotiate an identity that was independent of what was thrust upon them from birth. Damu was born a Mahar in the Ozar village of Maharashtra. But at an early age he had the opportunity of going to Mumbai, where he received some education, and when he was just twelve years of age, he also participated in the social reform movement launched by Ambedkar. Ambedkar's message impacted the adolescent Damu intensely, and also shaped the way Damu lived his life from then on. Forced by circumstances to go back to the village to perform his duties as an untouchable, Damu was unable to come to terms with the ignominious treatment that was meted out to untouchables in his village. The years spent in the city had brought "touchability into his life, along with an awareness of his rights as a human being". He tells his wife:

> I can't take it any more Soney.... I can't take it.... We must have self-respect. We must have dignity as human beings. How can I take to begging from door to door?... Have you seen how [the upper castes] throw the food? I don't want rights as a dog. I want my human rights. (18-19)

After a showdown with the village authorities, Damu is mercilessly beaten. It is then that he decides to go back to Mumbai with his wife, so that he could live a life of dignity, freedom and self-respect. Damu relies on the teachings of Ambedkar, who, to him, is no less than God himself:

> When Babasaheb spoke, everyone listened. He urged the untouchables to do away with the humiliating and enslaving traditions of village duties like carrying away dead cattle.
>
> "It is utterly disgraceful to sell your human rights for a few crumbs of bread", he said.
>
> "We will attain self-elevation only if we learn self-help, regain our self-respect and gain self-knowledge", Babasaheb said.
>
> What touched me the most were his thoughts about raising a family.

> "There will be no difference between parents and animals if they do not desire to see their children in a better position than their own."
>
> What a man! What a leader! (22)

Damu, taking the teachings of Ambedkar to heart, works relentlessly to secure the future of his children, and inculcates in them the values that make them stand out in the world. Damu struggles relentlessly through tough times, with Sonu at his side, never giving up or compromising on his ideals, and ultimately, he has the satisfaction of seeing his children establish themselves in the world. The eldest, Janardhan, joined the IAS. Damu's next son, Sudhakar worked for Gulf Air in Dubai. Dinesh retired as Mumbai's deputy municipal commissioner. Both his daughters are graduates and are happily married to established professionals. Narendra, the author, is the youngest of the siblings.

The story of the Jadhavs started in 1915, with the birth of Damu, and continues into the third generation. The story of Damu and his family is also the story of the Ambedkarite Movement. In fact, all the chronological markers in the story, right from Damu's birth to the present-day, are in terms of events in the history of the Dalit movement. Significantly, however, there is no reference in the memoir to any event in the nationalist struggle, not even to 1947. The references to Mahatma Gandhi occur only in the context of his differences and negotiations with Ambedkar and the British in the context of Dalits. The only visible presence in the text is Babasaheb Ambedkar, and that too in the context of the Dalit movement, and not the Indian freedom struggle. An overabundance of such instances seems to suggest that this is deliberate, and intends to suggest that the lives of early Dalits like Damu and Sonu and even modern-day Dalits like Narendra Jadhav and his siblings is a process that has gone on at some distance from the nationalist struggle.

The identity that is negotiated by the Jadhavs is a process that starts with the caste that Damu is born into—the Mahars.

From there, in contact with Ambedkar, Damu and Sonu start calling themselves Dalits:

> Truly, we sensed a change in the way we carried ourselves. We proudly proclaimed ourselves Dalits, with our chin up, and we looked everyone in the eye. We began to lose our former servility, associated with being born in a low caste. (178)

The movement from the social regimentation of the village to the relative anonymity of the city led to freedom from ostracism. However, it was a partial freedom, in that the caste system was so deeply entrenched in the minds of the people of the country that it would come up in the most unexpected ways. The author too was not immune to these incidents, and they occurred with him, and even in his own psyche. However, the author takes a significant step forward in the construction of identity. He undergoes a cathartic transformation. He says:

> Yes, I do come from the Mahar caste.
>
> Yes, my father was an illiterate lowly employee doing menial jobs to earn a square meal for the family.
>
> Yes, my forefathers were required to wear clay pots around their necks to keep their spit from polluting the ground, and the brooms were tied to their rumps to obliterate their footprints as they walked.
>
> Yes, as village servants, my forefathers were mercilessly forced to run...human pilots, foaming at the mouth under the scorching sun, to herald the carriages of government officials.
>
> So what?
>
> Have I not reclaimed my dignity through my achievements?
>
> Why should the caste into which I was born count now? (207)

Jadhav argues for dignity and a position in society based on achievements—his visibly accepted competence—and not on the basis of the fact of his birth. He has no qualms about the fact that he and his family belong to the Mahar caste, and have been subjected to a lot of torture in the past. But he claims space as a human being and a professional, something which makes caste redundant.

Jadhav's daughter Apoorva, who has written the epilogue to the memoir, goes a step further. Born, and for the major part of her life, brought up in the USA, Apoorva talks of how her life in USA makes the question of caste a non-issue:

> No one reminds me that I am a Dalit. I mean, that's who I am—take it or leave it.... I am just Apoorva, not tied down by race, religion or caste. My ancestors carried the burden of being a Dalit and bowing down to demeaning tasks even after India's independence. I have the torch they have lit for me and nothing can stop me. (262-63)

Apoorva articulates clearly what her father does not: that the fact that they are Mahars has no bearing on their lives in the global space that they inhabit. An Indian by descent, but a citizen of the USA, she is an individual in a way that Damu could only aspire, and her father could tend towards, but never quite achieve. It is an achievement, and simultaneously, a rupture from the past. This point is aptly summed up by Dileep Padgaonkar:

> It is young Apoorva, Jadhav's young daughter, who reveals in the epilogue what emancipation truly means: it does not matter one whit to her that she is a Dalit for, in a resurgent India, she has no reason to flaunt that tag or to suppress it. She has become what her forebears had always aspired to be: just normal people who are neither aggressive nor apologetic about their identity.

This is the Dalit identity that Jadhav establishes, and it is global in its perspective. Significantly though, Jadhav locates the epilogue/conclusion in the global metropolis, and not in the village or the slum, where the distinctions of caste still operate. Though Padgaonkar's observation is positive, this resolution is, therefore, not applicable collectively. Examining the linkage between the individual and the process of globalization, Anand Teltumbde says:

> Democracy assumes community and existence of pluralist groups, but neoliberalism dismisses them and atomizes the population into discrete self-seeking individuals. This conception clearly favours business because it eliminates the concept of collective identity and thereby emasculates labour.
>
> Democracy was built on the nation-state. Globalization seeks to remove power from the nation-state and puts it in the global arena thus crippling the nation-state in meeting the democratic aspirations of its people. Today we experience that year-by-year over the last couple of decades the reality of the democracy is being weakened despite the loud talk on its glory.

The issues raised by Teltumbde are the very issues that I use to frame the production of the text. Globalization operates both ways. Jadhav's solution seems operative on the level of the individual, but the larger question is—Can this be a solution to the Dalit predicament on a collective plane? Can the majority really aspire to the kind of Dalit identity that Jadhav establishes? And at a more basic level, is it really worthwhile to think of a modernity that answers to globalization? There are some basic facts to be considered in this regard.

The first and foremost fact is that of the governmental policy of reservation for the Scheduled Castes and Scheduled Tribes that has contributed significantly to their upliftment. Dalits have got jobs in the government sector. At the same time, the policy for reservation in education has given an impetus to the growth of the Dalit middle-class, which in turn has provided important leadership to the Dalit movement. However, there is no reservation for Dalits in the globalized market. If anything, privatization generates scope for eliminating reservation through the backdoor. And considering that the buying power of majority of the Dalits is limited, privatization means that a significant chunk of the Dalit general population will be left out. This is particularly true in the case of education, which if commoditized, will lead to exclusion of Dalits. This is already happening in the field of information technology where a large number of private players means that Dalits are unable to take full advantage of (or are getting left out from) one of the most robust economic sectors of the country.

The gains for the Dalits have been small and insufficient in the context of the Indian state. However, the NEP seems set to wipe out even these little gains. It may thus be argued that to speak of Dalit advancement in terms of globalization would be a contradiction in itself. However, things are not that simple either. It is not easy to dismiss neo-liberal globalization outright, as the "new social movements in India and elsewhere, would be ineffective without global linkages and solidarity" (Parajuli, 283). Various other social movements like the environmentalist, feminist, tribal and agrarian movements have realized the potential of such linkages and implemented them successfully. An example of how successfully such linkages could be exploited is the struggle against the Narmada Dam projects—involving 3,000 small dams and 165 big dams—under the charge of the Indian Government and funded by the World Bank. It was transnational activism at its most effective. Intellectuals and non-governmental organizations from India and across the world supported local activists and could successfully pressurize the World Bank and the Indian Government to halt the project (Khagram, 2002). This combination of a local-global networked campaign accessing a variety of political opportunity structures, both national and international, left an important lesson. This was a lesson not lost on the Dalits. Acting transnationally could bring domestic dividends.

The National Campaign on Dalit Human Rights is a transnational body of Dalits that operates from the local to the global levels. The NCDHR realized that globalization was a contradictory phenomenon and was prepared to make the most of it. As the General Secretary of the NCDHR asked rhetorically, "when you [India] internationalize your trade, when you internationalize your business, when you internationalize your market", should you not be "internationalizing your problems also? We've got every right to do that" (Interview, November 2004). This is exactly what the various international conferences being organized and attended by the Dalit diaspora is attempting to do. The problematic of Dalit identity *vis-à-vis* globalization is thus not easy to resolve.

Outcaste presents a story that is real, but a resolution that remains beyond most, and is hence limited in its potential. The Dalit identity that it attempts to fashion, right from its conception to its resolution, elides, to a large extent, the complex social realities of India. The initial parts of the memoir, though located in India, do not really take cognizance of any political development during that time except the Dalit movement. In the latter part, when the narrative moves into the global space, the resolution offered is practicable to only a limited section of Dalits who are urban and upwardly mobile because they have (probably) been able, in their lives, to bring into play the advantages accruing from the pre-globalization welfare state model. Rural realities of a post-welfare state economic model are thus not within the scope of the narrative. At the same time, if we attempt a comparative positioning of the movement of the memoir from the earthy realities of Damu's quest to the detachment of Apoorva's epilogue, we find a movement away from indigeneity. We realize that the resolution is more personal than communal, a resolution situated in global space being beyond the reach of the majority of the present-day Dalit community.

NOTES

1. These lines are from the "Preface" to *Outcaste: A Memoir*. All subsequent quotations from this text are referred to with page numbers only.
2. The first Dalit Literary Conference held in India in 1958 defined what constitutes Dalit Literature and passed a similar resolution: "Resolution No. 5—that the literature written by the Dalits and that written by others about the Dalits in Marathi be accepted as a separate entity known as 'Dalit literature' and realizing its cultural importance, the universities and literary organizations should give it its proper place" (Dangle, 242).

WORKS CITED

Anand, S. *Touchable Tales: Publishing and Reading Dalit Literature*. Pondicherry: Navayana, 2003.

Corbridge, Stuart and Harriss, John. *Reinventing India: Liberalization, Hindu Nationalism and Popular Democracy*. Oxford: OUP, 2003.

Dangle, Arjun, Ed. *Poisoned Bread: Translations from Modern Marathi Dalit Literature*. Hyderabad: Orient Longman, 1992.

Das, Anupreeta. "Dalit Writing Makes its Mark". http://www.csmonitor.com/2005/0815/p1501-lire.html. Online. 25 January 2009.

Jadhav, Narendra. *Outcaste: A Memoir*. New Delhi: Viking, 2003.

Khagram, Sanjeev. "Restructuring the Global Politics of Development: The Case of India's Narmada Valley Dams." *Restructuring World Politics*. Eds. Sanjeev Khagram, James Riker and Kathryn Sikkink. Minneapolis: University of Minnesota Press, 2002: 3-23.

Padgaonkar, Dileep. "Look back in languor". http://www.outlookindia.com/fullprint.asp. Online. 22 September 2003.

Parajuli, Pramod. "Power and Knowledge in Development Discourse: New Social Movements and the State in India." *Democracy in India*. Ed. Niraja Gopal Jayal. New Delhi: OUP, 2001: 258-87.

Teltumbde, Anand. "Globalization and the Dalits." http://www.ambedkar.org/research/GLOBALISATIONANDTHEDALITS.pdf. Online. 7 March 2006.

14

The Subversion of Panopticism in Bankim Chandra Chatterjee's *Anandamath*

Panchali Mukherjee

Panopticon had been discussed by Michel Foucault as a disciplinary structure in *Discipline and Punish* (1977) and also in an interview entitled "The Eye of Power" (1980). "The Panopticon is an architectural device described by the eighteenth-century philosopher, Jeremy Bentham, as a way of arranging people in such a way that, for example, in a prison, it is possible to see all of the inmates without the observer being seen, and without any of the prisoners having access to one another" (Mills 45). A panopticon may be defined as:

> A perimeter building in the form of a ring. At the centre of this a tower, pierced by large windows opening on to the inner face of the ring. The outer building is divided into cells each of which traverses the whole thickness of the building. These cells have two windows, one opening onto the inside, facing the windows of the central tower, the other, outer one allowing daylight to pass through the whole cell. All that is then needed is to put an overseer in the tower and place in each of the cells a lunatic, a patient, a convict, a worker, or a schoolboy. The back lighting enables one to pick out from the central tower the little captive silhouettes in the ring of cells. In short, the principle of the dungeon is reversed; daylight and the overseer's gaze capture the

> inmate more effectively than darkness, which afforded after all a sort of protection. (qtd. in Mills 45)

Michel Foucault analyses the particular way of organising the spatial arrangements of prisons, schools and factories to attain maximum visibility and argues that a new form of internalised disciplinary practice occurs wherein an individual is forced to act as if she/he is being constantly surveyed even when she/he is not. Thus, this form of spatial arrangement entails a particular form of power relation and restriction of behaviours.

The main tenet of Michel Foucault's 'Panopticism' is that discourse can be effectively used to control and/or modify ideology/ies in a particular space usually for the benefit of a particular governing class or organization which in turn renders the role of an 'active agent' that displays coercive power to be unnecessary.

The idea of the 'Panopticon' which has been described above as a surveillance technique that forces an individual to internalise a particular disciplinary practice even when the individual is not being constantly surveyed leading to a particular power relation and restriction of behaviour can be observed in the colonial subjects. As a result, literature produced in a colony does not enjoy the same autonomy as it does in a sovereign country. Colonialism brings about a compulsion of choices as in the colonies the colonizers do not allow even moderate expressions of free thinking on the part of the colonized.

Bankim Chandra Chattopadhyay (1838-94) who in addition to be a Deputy Magistrate and a Deputy Collector in the Government of British India was also a writer, poet and a journalist. He wrote the novel *Anandamath* (1882) primarily in Bangla which was later translated into English. The novel was produced during a tumultuous time in history. The author who was a colonized subject had written this novel when India was under the yoke of British colonialism and despite being employed in the British administration he espoused the cause of freedom. This novel is said to be based on Indian nationalism or rather Hindu nationalism and is considered to be the pioneer of the anti-colonial movement in India. India was gradually rising up for a freedom struggle to attain independence from the British rule and the Indians required an ideological basis for their freedom struggle which was provided by this novel. The novel is not only political but also historical. It is set in Bengal in the background of the 'Sannyasi Rebellion' in the late eighteenth century and the famine that took place in 1770 thereby portraying the aftermath of the famine. The novel begins with an introduction to a couple Mahendra and Kalyani who are in the grip of a severe famine in the Padchinha village and are without food and water. They decide to move to the nearest city for survival. During the course of the events, Kalyani gets separated from Mahendra. She runs with her infant through a forest in order to avoid the man-hunters till she loses consciousness on the bank of a river later to be rescued by Satyananda, a Hindu monk. Satyananda takes care of her and her infant till she is reunited with her husband. On the other hand, Mahendra has joined the brotherhood of the monks who serve the nation. Kalyani wants to kill herself to relieve Mahendra from his worldly duties. Satyananda joins Kalyani to help her. But before he can help her the British soldiers arrest him as the monks are fuelling a revolt against the British rule. When Satyananda is being led away he spots another monk in ochre robes and indicates to him with the help of a song that a lady is to be rescued. The other monk deciphers the song, rescues Kalyani and the infant and takes them to a hideout of the rebel monks. Mahendra also takes shelter in the hideout of the rebel monks thereby resulting in his reunion with Kalyani. The leader of the rebel monks shows the three faces of Bharat Mata or Mother India thereby indoctrinating him in their ideology. The influence of the rebel monks is on the rise and their ranks swell as a result they shift their headquarters to a fort which is attacked by the British. Heavy fighting ensues and the rebels fight bravely making the British take a tactical retreat. The sannyasis chase the British, finally to be trapped. The British artillery opens fire on the rebels inflicting severe casualties. Some of the rebels capture the British cannons thereby firing back on the British lines. The

British are forced to fall back, and the rebels win their first battle but the struggle continues. The story ends with Mahendra and Kalyani building a home and Mahendra continuing to support the rebels.

The novel although set in 1770 portrays the historical conditions of the nineteenth century when the Indians had begun to feel the urge of freeing their land from the foreign rule thereby beginning a freedom struggle against the British rule. The Indians in the novel are shown to resort to guerrilla warfare as the British forces are stronger in terms of resources than the Indian forces. Warren Hastings wants to establish control over India, so the task is given to Major Edwards. It is thus described as:

> Edwards realized that it was no European campaign. The enemy had no army, cities, capital or forts, and yet everything was under their control. When the British encamped in a certain place, they were in charge for the time, but as soon as the British forces left, *Bande Mataram* rang out from all sides! The newcomer was unable to discover from where his enemies issued like ants at night, burning any village that was under British control, or despatching instantly any small contingent of British forces that came their way. (219)

Thus, the novel conveyed the idea of guerrilla warfare against the English to the Indian masses as the English forces were more powerful and organized compared to the Indian rebels. The novel directly or indirectly tries to motivate the Indian masses to end the foreign rule.

When this novel was produced, India was under the British rule which was a foreign rule. The novel is grounded in a powerful anti-colonialist ideology that is evident here. The famine of 1770 killed many people. In 1771, though there was rain and there was a good growth of crops but there were no people to buy them as a result the tenants couldn't pay their taxes to the zamindars and the zamindars were unable to pay the revenues to the king. Thus, the zamindars' lands were confiscated. The common people joined the order of the 'santans' to rebel against the ruling class of Muslims as the king's men were held responsible for their plight. The British sent their forces to quell the rebellion, but it was of no avail (1888-90). This example portrays the plight of the colonized people who are ruled by foreign powers such as the Muslim and the English that brings about misery and deprivation on the colonized thereby offering an insight into the colonial political set-up. This example questions the efficacy of a foreign or a colonialist rule thereby suggesting implicitly the throwing off of the foreign or the colonial rule.

The novel also questions certain religious practices such as polytheism in the Indian society of those times which have a direct influence on the Hindu way of life. The healer tells Satyananda:

> To worship three hundred and thirty million gods is not the Eternal Code. That's a worldly inferior code. Through its influence the real Eternal Code—what the foreigners call the Hindu rule of life—has been lost. The true Hindu rule of life is based on knowledge, not on action. And this knowledge is of two kinds—outward and inward. The inward knowledge is the chief part of the Eternal Code, but unless the outward knowledge arises first, the inward cannot arise. Unless one knows the gross, one cannot know the subtle. (229)

The historical, political and social condition in which the novel was produced makes it a manifesto of freedom, nationalism and progress through social and religious reforms. These ideas are espoused in the novel to make the Indians aspire for a life based on liberty and progress.

The fact that when the novel *Anandamath* was written and published by Bankim Chandra Chattopadhyay India was a colony of Great Britain and as mentioned above Bankim Chandra was an employee employed in the British Government in India the metaphor of a 'panopticon' is used in this case as a technique of surveillance used by the colonizers, the British, on the colonized, the Indians, to maintain the paradigm of power with the British doing the supervision leading not only to the subjection and normalization of the Indians but also in the internalization of the gaze of the colonizer which in turn results in the disciplined behaviour of the colonized or in justifying and accepting the colonizer's supremacy and in the creation of model subjects. The literature that is produced from the colonies during the period of colonialism usually embodies the discourses that modify the ideologies of the masses through consensus and not coercion thereby benefiting the governing class by justifying their rule as well as by maintaining political control and order.

The novel *Anandamath* a landmark text in terms of providing the ideological basis to the Indian freedom movement and inspiring the Indian freedom struggle belongs to the corpus of literature produced by a colonized territory of the British. The novel raises genuine concerns regarding the yoke of British colonialism and implicitly tries to subvert the justification of the British rule by questioning its efficacy. But this subversion is done obliquely, and it is stated that the British rule should end after maximum mileage is extracted from it by the Indians. When the healer appears before Satyananda in the monastery of the Santans, *Anandamath*, he tells him to give up warfare and to allow people to undertake agricultural activities rather than continuing with it as the Muslim rule has ended but Satyananda argues that the British are yet to be uprooted to which the healer comments that the British being very knowledgeable in the outward knowledge will instruct the indigenous people which will help them to attain an understanding not only of the outer knowledge but also of the inner knowledge. This in turn will help them to understand the "Eternal Code" (*Anandamath* 229) based on the Hindu rule of life thereby making them wise, virtuous and strong. Until then the English rule should remain intact. The English should rule over the indigenous people as friends and moreover, the indigenous people represented by the Santans do not have the power to fight the British and win over them. Thus, the healer advises Satyananda to change the course of his life by going to the Himalayas with him (*Anandamath* 228-30).

Bankim Chandra Chattopadhyay in his novel subverts the metaphor of a 'panopticon' that is in place as a result of British colonialism in India and the Indian subjects have internalised the ideology of the British related to the 'White Man's Burden' thereby justifying their rule. This novel indirectly undercuts the idea of the efficacy of a foreign rule over the indigenous people by showing the Santans to be up in arms against the Muslims who are considered to be foreigners ruling over the Hindus resulting in the end of the Muslim rule. This is an oblique comment that holds good even for the British rule but Bankim Chandra Chattopadhyay being a colonized subject conveys the idea of a free Indian nation to the English through the example of the Muslim rule which is shown to come to an end as a result of the Santans. Nevertheless, the author through his novel makes it evident to the British that their rule is temporary and their presence in India will be there till they impart outer knowledge to the indigenous people. This leads to the subversion of the panopticism that the English had put in place to rule India with an iron hand.

Anthropomorphism refers to the interpretation of non-human entities or events in the form of human characteristics. The term has been derived from the Greek word 'anthropos' meaning human and 'morphe' meaning form. The term was initially used to refer to the attribution of human, physical and mental features to a deity. In the mid-nineteenth century, the term came to be used in all the spheres of human thought and action which includes daily life, arts and sciences in addition to religion. It may occur consciously or unconsciously. It is also known as 'personification' in the domain of literature and graphic art ('Anthropomorphism'). Bankim Chandra Chattopadhyay in his political novel *Anandamath* uses anthropomorphism to bestow a national character or identity to a conglomeration of kingdoms or principalities, that is, India. This national character or identity that is bestowed by the author on India through the use of anthropomorphism is to unify the inhabitants of the above-mentioned geographical territory, to inspire them to revolt against the foreign powers who have established their rule in this territory and finally to throw off the yoke of foreign rule that has had a debilitating effect on the country. The technique of anthropomorphism used by the author in the novel not only gives the country an identity of a mother who sustains and nourishes her children, the indigenous people of this country, but also invokes patriotism in the Indian psyche through the idea of respecting the mother, worshipping her and liberating her from the clutches of the alien rulers. It helps the author to resist the effects of colonialism and pre-empt the dream of a free India. In the novel, the monk, Satyananda Thakur, who is also the leader of the rebels takes Mahendra inside a temple in the abbey which is also the abode of the Santans and shows him three forms of the mother representing India. The form of the mother as she was in the past:

> At first Mahendra was unable to see what was inside, but as he peered more and more closely, he could gradually make out a massive four-armed statue bearing a conch shell, discus, mace and lotus, respectively, in each hand, with the Kaustubha gem adorning its breast, and the discus Sudarshan seeming to whirl around in front. (149)

The monk takes Mahendra to the next image of the mother which is her form in the present. It is described thus:

> Blackened and shrouded in darkness. She has been robbed of everything; that is why she is naked. And because the whole world is a burning-ground, she is garlanded with skulls. And she is crushing her own gracious lord underfoot. Alas, dear Mother! (150)

The monk finally takes Mahendra to the form of the mother as it will be in the future. It is described thus:

> Prostrating himself, the monk said, "And this is the Mother-as-she-will-be. Her ten arms reach out in ten directions, adorned with various powers in the form of the different weapons she holds, the enemy crushed at her feet, while the mighty lion who has taken refuge there is engaged in destroying the foe. Behold her whose arms are the directions...." (150)

The three forms of the mother represent the past, present and future of the nation, India. The example brings home the glorious past of the country as highlighted in the glorious image of the mother. The present image of the mother is dark, mysterious and ominous thereby obliquely commenting on the present state of the country that has been laid to waste as a result of our subjugation, exploitation and deprivation by the foreign powers. The final image of the mother represents the future of the country that will be prosperous after its enemies, the foreign rulers, have been eradicated. Thus, anthropomorphism has been used by the author to indirectly indoctrinate the masses with the nationalistic ideology.

'Panopticon' refers to the surveillance of the many by the few which takes place in a colonial set-up whereas 'Synopticon' refers to the surveillance of the few by the many. Bankim Chandra Chattopadhyay through his historical novel *Anandamath* projects both the Muslim rule and the British rule to be alien rules that are to be ended sooner or later thereby establishing the national identity of a free country, India. Similarly, A.S.P. Ayyar in his Indian English historical novels *Baladitya* (1930) and *Three Men of Destiny* (1939) obliquely comments on the political conditions prevailing in contemporary India like infighting among various members of Indian royalty and support provided by some Indian kings and chieftains to foreigners so that they are able to gain a strong foothold in the country. As a result of which the British had been able to strengthen their rule in the country. He also elucidates the role of the traitors in undermining the Indian rulers and helping the foreign rulers in establishing their stronghold. He covertly comments on the plight of India under the British rule by critiquing the rule of the Huns. Bankim Chandra Chattopadhyay urges Indians to put up a united resistance against the British rule in India. He becomes a representative voice of the masses who puts the rulers (Muslims and British) who are a selected few under surveillance. He is able to present a critique of the rulers as well as of the political conditions prevailing in India at that point of time. He comments on the Muslim rule through the mouth of Bhabananda who states that the Muslim rule has just brought misery on them instead of protecting them:

"Everywhere else there's a pact with the king for protection, but does our Muslim king protect us?" (147).

The author hints at the annihilation of the British rule which is also a foreign rule, not immediately but in the future:

> "Muslim rule has been destroyed", said Satyananda, "but Hindu rule has not been established. Even now the English remain powerful in Kolkata." (228)

The author deconstructs the panoptical metaphor by bringing about a reversal of the panoptical polarity as in this case the author representing the Indians becomes the overseer who gazes at the Indians as well as the foreign rulers who are actually the British but ostentatiously the Muslims. Thus, the author replaces the 'Panopticon' that is in place as a result of colonialism by the 'Synopticon' through his novel.

The effects of the subversion of "Panopticism" is traced in Bankim Chandra Chattopadhyay's political novel when he implicitly urges his fellow countrymen to rebel against the British and put up a united resistance against them through the historical example of Sanyasi Rebellion which is placed far away in the historical past so that he could avoid the pernicious consequences of producing a seditious literary work. Nevertheless, the novel had been banned during the British rule. It was only released in the post-independence India. Bankim Chandra Chattopadhyay through the example of the Santans of the Sanyasi Rebellion urges the Indians to rebel explicitly against the Muslim rule and implicitly against the British rule and drive them out of India. The author preaches his ideology of Hindu nationalism through this novel that portrays both Muslims and Britishers to be outsiders who have been ruling the country and the need for their ouster from the seat of power. He shows in the novel that the Santans have achieved their first goal of ending the Muslim rule but they need to wait to realize their second goal of ending the British rule. Bankim substitutes the metaphor of 'Panopticon' with that of 'Synopticon'. In his novel, he reverses the idea of the surveillance of the many by a selected few and replaces it with the idea of the surveillance of a selected few by the many. The author's role is reversed from being an individual who is observed to that of an observer which gives him agency as a colonized subject to change the power dynamics. He effectively observes the selected few like the Muslim rulers and the British rulers, analyses the reasons behind India's loss of freedom and prescribes solutions.

WORKS CITED

"Anthropomorphism." *Encyclopaedia Britannica. Encyclopaedia Britannica Online*. Encyclopaedia Britannica Inc., 2015. Web. 18 Jan. 2015.
<http://www.britannica.com/EBchecked/topic/27536/anthropomorphism>.

Ayyar, A.S.P. *Baladitya: A Historical Romance of Ancient India.* Bombay: Taraporevala, 1930.

——. *Three Men of Destiny*. Madras: Caxton Press, 1939.

Chatterjee, Bankim Chandra. *Anandamath*, or *The Sacred Brotherhood.* Trans. Julius J. Lipner. New Delhi: Oxford University Press, 2005.

Jefferson, Ann. "Structuralism and Post-Structuralism." *Modern Literary Theory*. Ed. Ann Jefferson and David Robey. London: B.T. Batsford Limited, 1986: 92-121.

Mills, Sara. *Michel Foucault*. London: Routledge, 2002.

Rabinow, Paul. *The Foucault Reader*. New York: Pantheon Books, 1984.

Selden, Raman. *A Reader's Guide to Contemporary Literary Theory.* Hertfordshire: Harvester Wheat Sheaf, 1989: 70-113.

15

The Essence of Worldliness: A Reading of Rita Joshi's Campus Novel *The Awakening: A Novella in Rhyme*

Swati Rai

The genre of campus novel has, as its setting, the closed world of a campus and is focused on students, teachers and sometimes academic administrators as well. David Lodge, one of the most famous practitioners of this sub-genre writes in this context: "In English 'Campus Novel' is a term used to designate a work of fiction whose action takes place mainly in a college or university, and which is mainly concerned with the lives of university professors and junior teachers..." (30). The tone of a campus novel is comic but occasionally it turns into mild or harsh satire on academic life. Chris Baldick in *The Concise Oxford Dictionary of Literary Terms* writes: "Campus novel is a novel, usually comic or satirical, in which the action is set within enclosed world of university (or similar set of learning) and highlights the follies of academic life" (30).

The present paper is focused on the satirical portrayal of campus life as depicted in Rita Joshi's campus novel, *The Awakening: A Novella in Rhyme*. The novel deals with the experiences of a Cambridge-educated idealistic lecturer in Delhi, about whom she writes: "From Cambridge cheerfully she came/ to seek at home fortune and fame" (10). Through JR, the protagonist of the novel, the author gives us a grim insight into the state of higher education in the country. The novel deals with the theme of corruption and opportunism in educational institutions and draws attention to the negligence or lack of concern of the faculty towards academics. The larger part of the action in the novel takes place in the campus of a women's college in Delhi. The unbecoming academic setting in modern India is sketched with enormous detail in the novel.

The novelist, in the very beginning, gives a very clear picture of the quandary of the Indian students and the sorry state of affairs in the academic atmosphere of the Indian colleges. Though JR's first impressions are mixed, she is able to understand the degrading academic scenario in her college:

> The scholarships here seems less,
> The library is in a mess,
> The tutorials are redundant,
> Guidebooks are far too abundant,
> Lectures seem to be forcefed,
> What really goes into the head?
> Other's in the Department say
> That students while time away. (14)

This is a powerful sardonic comment on our times, where the campus—the seat of learning, becomes a subject of satirical criticism on students, teachers and the principal of the college.

JR observes that the students in B.A. (Hons.) English are not serious in their academic pursuits. The young girls take up the study of literature for wrong reasons. They have opted English because a B.A. Honours degree in English comes in handy as a matrimonial qualification:

> An English Honours B.A. degree
> Counts well for matrimony.
> An Eng. Lit. type is thought smart
> And so good for the marriage mart.
> Though is there a real connection
> Between marriage and deconstruction?

Logic seems to be defied
By this concept of a bride. (14-15)

One can distinctly feel the ironic bite in the following lines:

In different contexts degrees
Create different pedigrees. (15)

In such an anarchic situation, JR is naturally inclined to feel concerned about women's education and the female situation. Women's colleges were set up to facilitate the higher education of women so that they could broaden and widen their social horizon, and empower themselves by getting equal opportunity of education and employment.

But the Supreme College for Women seems to make a mockery of these cherished ideals. Neither the principal nor the teachers could be seen making any attempt in helping students rise above their view about their subject and education. The principal called SS is driven by selfish intentions and indulges in power politics. Coercion into subservience is part of her administrative stratagem:

On the first day the principal met
The newcomers to the set.
Called SS by her initials
And compared to SS officials
By students whose muttered dissent
Her rigid armour could not dent,
To the new 'recruits' she made clear,
Her word they must respect and fear. (10)

The character of SS offers a contrast to Mr. Daash, a senior lecturer in Ranga Rao's *The Drunk Tantra*, who was a father-figure and pillar of support to students and junior colleagues. SS like a dictator loves to retain her authority like a monarch and abominate trade unionism in the college which poses a threat to her authority:

Trade Unionism she abhors,
Monarchy she adores,

On sycophancy she thrives
And terrorising young lives. (26)

Among other things happening on the campus, the annual drama performance comes as a big prospect for SS to show herself off. SS who is planning for her extension and so she wants to make a notable impression by inviting all the dignitaries to the show. With the senior members of the teaching staff preparing to go on a strike, she singles out the new candidate JR as a soft victim, and almost forces her to assume responsibility of the college Drama Society:

JR begins to demur,
SS stops any murmur:
No protest, you must say yes,
I will not accept anything less,
You are not married, you've got the time,
Teach them drama, teach them mime. (27)

If we compare the character of SS with Mr. Natarajan, the Principal in P.M. Nityanandan's novel *The Long Long Days* we can observe that while the graceful personality of Mr. Natarajan is remembered by his students with tremendous love and respect, SS on the other hand insists that she should be feared and esteemed, little realizing that respect and love cannot be forced and has to be earned. Her relationship with the students is shown in these words:

SS always wants to evict
Students for disobeying orders,
Her strictness on mania borders. (55)

In another very important episode, the author shows how SS, blinded by her power and position indulges in malpractice. JR is shocked to find that the principal, who preaches discipline and morality, indulges in corrupt activities. During examinations, JR is shocked to see that SS unashamedly approaches her niece in the examination room and tells her the answer:

After ten minutes SS again
Returns ostensibly with a pen.

This time JR goes near
Them in an attempt to overhear,
SS is clearly giving clues,
Asking the girl not to have blues. (88)

When JR tells SS that what she is doing is wrong and she can't do it, SS simply glares but moves along. An hour later ET and PR discuss this event of malpractice and misuse of power by the principal. An emergency meeting is called the next day when ET gives a report that she and JR saw the principal help her niece in the examination:

ET (to the Staff) gives a report
(JR interjects for support):
"Miss JR and I yesterday saw
SS help her niece outside our door,
Without teachers the girl was placed
Alone on a desk-SS grace
The corridor twice and supplied
Answers to her niece at her side." (88-89)

It is quite shocking that in the meeting SS straightaway and unabashedly denies having done such an act. It is through her power and position that SS arranges things to prove her innocent. A few flatterer like NV also come out in the defense of SS:

NV speaks in defence of SS:
"JR once more causes distress.
These young upstarts are out to shame
Us, and upset our good name." (89)

Here the author highlights and satirizes another aspect of college life, where teachers are shown, driven by the selfish motives, trying to get into the good books of the principal.

During the enquiry SS highlights the absence of any concrete evidence, the lack of a photograph or a recorded tape of her conversation with her niece, and in turn accuses JR as a creator of conspiracy:

What proof do they have of what I said
To my niece? You can't accuse a Head.
No photographs, no recorded tape
Can their claim support this scrape
Is cooked up what they say I'll deny,
This is all that forms my reply—
All this is just defamatory,
Insolent, inflammatory. (92)

In absence of any tangible proof, SS gets a clean chit along with a note of reprimand. But the Board of Trustees is not pleased by this squalid state of affairs. The principal's demand for extension of her term is rejected and she is asked to proceed on leave without any farewell. At the end, when the principal's post is advertised, it is quite distressing to know that ET, any undeserving candidate is made the principal:

In a strange quirk of fate
ET is chosen and thought first rate. (94)

Here the novelist attempts to indicate the flaws of the selection committee in the modern-day educational institutions because of which the chosen candidates are sometimes not even worthy of their posts. JR's view is therefore right when she feels:

Colleges must awareness breed,
Fight evil, not egos feed,
Can our present dons truly guide
Students to swim against the tide? (95)

After these histrionic events the protagonist JR feels disillusioned with her fraternity and her place in it. She also becomes aware of the irony which permeate higher education. She realizes that everything else has captured the centre stage in teaching profession aside from teaching. This insight weighs heavily on her consciousness and she feels depressed. She therefore makes up her mind to resign from her job because she feels she does not belong to this fraternity:

She explains her predicament thus—
I teach, it should be fine,

But I feel I'm toeing the wrong line,
I'm fighting fights I don't want to fight,
How do I get out of this plight? (51)

This is the moment of her awakening and it dawns upon her that creative writing is decidedly her field and she must devote herself to it:

She must try to heal her gashes,
The phoenix must rise from the ashes,
Creative work she feels will bring
Resurrection, an awakening. (52)

She decides to write a book which will be based on her experience in SC college.

The novel also portrays the faculty with its very strange with conflicting attitudes. None of the faculty member is seen to be academically oriented or concerned with the welfare of the students. JR during her tenure in the college learns about the insalubrious details about her colleagues in the department and gets to know the outlook of individual faculty member. For instance, MW, short for Maid in Waiting, is a weird and strange character. She feels offended at the fact that though she liked men, they never return her compliment:

She liked men but they did not return
The compliment, this made her burn. (13)

She is a discontented cynical woman who savours self-praise and loses no opportunity of condescending her colleagues:

These women, they don't read,
They're teaching only out of greed.
They are just housewives and mothers
But of course there are others—
I'm the poetess of the Staff,
MW ends with a laugh. (13-14)

In the course of her outburst, MW never loses the chance to praise herself. She claims that the girls are enthralled by her, and she lives in a world of self-deception, hoping that her poems will earn her fame and fortune:

Like patients they are etherised,
By me the girls are mesmerised.
My poems will bring me fame,
I'll make my fortune, have a name. (17)

Since she has the habit of denouncing everything and everybody, she tells JR that since the publishers in India are unremarkable, she has sent-off her manuscript abroad for publication:

I've sent off my manuscript,
Publishers here are nondescript,
I'm going to publish abroad,
Here everyone is a fraud. (17)

Apart from MW, there are a number of other peculiar figures in the teaching staff. NV and PR are SS's stooges who always want to be in her good books. NV is MW's aunt and considers her niece much efficient than JR. She never misses an opportunity to criticize JR:

Some of the responses are odd,
All do not her effort laud,
NV, MW's lofty aunt,
Says with a sneering taunt:
No one can with my niece compare—
To do a play does JR dare? (30)

PR is a non-assertive woman. She takes pride in being a devoted wife and feels irresolute and perplexed about everything:

I am feeling weak,
At home my husband is my guide,
Here I walk by SS's side,
Such angry word about SS
Will lead us all into a mess. (70-71)

MT is interested in astrology and often speaks of starry influence and professes to dabble in occult powers:

All the younger Staff come to me,
I predict without a fee.

I read hands, I can read face,
But I believe in God's Grace. (18-19)

ET is the Secretary of the Teacher's Union. She is a large woman who could always be seen eating. PV reads papers at conferences and considers herself a renowned academician. She carries about her air of discontent with the college. Then there is CD who is twice an M.Phil and a Ph.D and is considered most intellectual of the lot. In JD one can trace similarities with the character of Ranjana Malhotra from Anuradha Marwah Roy's *The Higher Education of Geetika Mehendiratta.* Like Ranjana Malhotra she too is renounced by her husband, and she independently carries out the responsibility of her two children. There is another odd character, QT who belongs to high society but whose morals are considered loose.

A women's college is a place where female mind should be progressive and liberated, but ironically, the women in question lack a sense of female fraternity and fail to form any meaningful bond. They are shown to be motivated by selfishness and rivalry. It is very unfortunate to see how mean and ruthless women can be with their own kind. A better understanding of their attitude can seen when they pass derogatory comments on JR's endeavours. For instance, when JR's review appears in *East Ind Times*, ET considers all that as 'faltoo' and advises JR that there is more to life than only the books. According to her, money is far more important as one can buy food with it. She also reveals to JR the futility of her exercise of reviewing books:

By reviewing books what will you earn?
Uselessly why do you burn?
What we know is more than enough—
All they read is that kunji stuff. (47)

According to ET, teachers need not update themselves academically as students are in the habit of reading guide books and so they do not require any scholarly ideas. The protagonist JR laments over the pathetic condition of the academic profession:

Education seems a pretense.
She wonders where she's getting,
What scholarly urge she's whetting,
Universities have not curbed
A society from being disturbed.
Higher selves have not emerged,
In fact they seem to be submerged. (38)

JR feels sad when she compares Supreme College to Cambridge. She is baffled to see the degradation of higher education and the behaviour and attitude of the academicians.

The novelist also points out that the dilapidation is prevalent not only inside the campus, but also in society at large. The author throws light on the sycophantic reverence shown to foreign experts, in the hope of getting an assignment abroad. There is an episode in which the FIC (Foreign Indian Centre) is shown sidetracking a very knowledgeable local academic, Dr. Bhim and choosing an Englishman to deliver a lecture just because he was incharge of some grants:

The Englishman's reading is slight,
To give this talk he has no right,
But all listen obsequiously
They take him very seriously.
He is incharge of some grants
And can aid academics' wants.
So at the end of the talk
Many persons around him flock. (54)

Through this episode the author draws out attention towards the biggest tragedy of our present-day education system. Our education system today has become so commercial and materialistic that people with power and money climb the ladder of success while the truly knowledgeable and sincere people are left behind.

By way of summing up, we can easily call *The Awakening* a powerful campus novella which very realistically captures the grim realities of the world of academia and brings to light a host of unsavory aspects of higher education in India. A range of themes like, an uneasy political context, teacher's movement and the struggles of writers and artists, forms part of the backdrop of the novel. Through an amusing and light-hearted portrayal, the author throws light on the various aspects of campus life and brings home the point that with corruption, and malpractice sneaking into the citadel of learning, the higher education and teaching positions are not sacrosanct anymore.

WORKS CITED

Baldick, Chris. *The Concise Oxford Dictionary of Literary Terms*. Oxford: Oxford University Press, 1990. Print.

Joshi, Rita. *The Awakening: A Novella in Rhyme*. New Delhi: UBSP, 1993. Print.

Lodge, David. Nabokov and the Campus Novel, paru dans *Cycnos*, Volume 24, No. 1, mis en ligne le 20 mars 2008. Web. 10 March 2014. <http://revel.unice.fr/cycnos/index.html?id=1081>

Nityanandan, P.M. *The Long Long Days*. Bombay: Asia Publishing House, 1960. Print.

Rao, Ranga. *The Drunk Tantra*. New Delhi: Penguin Books India Pvt. Ltd., 1994. Print.

Roy, Anuradha Marwah. *The Higher Education of Geetika Mehendiratta*. New Delhi: Orient Longman Limited, 1993. Print.

16
Postcolonial Dilemmas in Laurence's *This Side Jordan*

Neera Singh

Imperialism was legitimized by the European colonizers by expounding anthropological theories which portrayed the peoples of the colonized world as inferior races and, therefore, requiring the 'paternal' rule of the West. The concept of race underlying such anthropological theories placed the White races as superior to the non-White ones inhabiting the countries of Asia and Africa. White culture was seen as civilization and anything non-White was 'non-civilized'. Consequently, the imperial powers went about 'civilizing' these people with a clear conscience, terming their self-imposed task as the "White man's burden".[1]

The twin instruments that helped establish the cultural imperialism of the West were the Church and the Western way of education. While the first, through missionaries, Christianized the native population, the second, through mission schools, westernized them. The two, however, proved counterproductive as the educated colonized, realizing the worth of their own culture, led the masses to resist the Western domination. Thus, much of the 20th century involved long political struggle, and the eventual triumph, of the colonized against their imperial masters. The shift from colonial to an autonomous status represented only a relatively minor shift as neo-colonialism still exists, with the major world powers continuing to run the governments and the economies of their ex-colonies, on the pretext of 'developing' them. Their agenda is furthered by globalization, privatization and by generating transnational capital.

However, the cultural imperialism of the West proved more damaging to the indigenous psyche than did its political and economic exploitation. As the traditional way of life of these people had been disrupted, the now semi-westernized colonials constantly suffered from a nagging sense of guilt at having abandoned the gods and culture of their forefathers. Long years of suffering humiliation and exploitation robbed them of their real identity. They realized they belonged neither to the old nor to the new world, and that they could neither fit in the westernized modern cities nor feel at home in their native villages. A feeling of uprootedness and unbelonging created a fear psychosis in their minds. Ironically, the same sense of fear and insecurity assailed the colonizers too. On the verge of leaving a world where they had been comfortably living for years and now having to return like strangers to their own native land, unsettled and unnerved the colonizers.

Margaret Laurence brilliantly captures these psychological, moral and political dilemmas in her first and only Africa-based novel *This Side Jordan* (1960). One of the most prominent names in Canadian literature, Margaret Laurence happened to be in Africa when the European settlers were on their way out of their adopted land. She was witness to the Africanization of the British colony of Ghana, for the three years she lived there, prior to its independence. Laurence herself belonged to a time when Canada, which had never been an imperial power, was just emerging from its experience of being a colony of the British and French. This greatly helped Laurence to relate sympathetically to the plight of all colonized peoples and to also draw parallels between the African and Canadian situations and characters. Spending seven years in the 'Dark Continent', from 1952 to 1957, Laurence observed the stunting effects colonizing nations can have on the lives and cultures of the people. *This Side Jordan* particularly establishes how a colonized person is injected with complexes, trepidations, fears and insecurities which lead to a "cultural cringe".[2]

My paper is an attempt to show the stultifying effects of colonization on the African psyche by taking Nathaniel Amegbe (the protagonist of the novel) as representing all colonized people.

This Side Jordan has a network of parallel situations and characters. It is a story revolving around two communities: Ghananian and expatriate British; two protagonists: Nathaniel Amegbe and Johnnie Kestoe; and two sets of cultural pasts, which continue to influence the present, and with which the characters must come to terms. On the African side, the protagonist is Nathaniel Amegbe, a teacher at Mensah's Futura Academy. He is the mission-educated son of Kyerema, a drummer to a Chief. On the British side we have Johnnie Kestoe, an accountant employed in the Accra Textile Branch of Allkirk, Moore and Bright, which is an English-centered export-import firm.

This Side Jordan portrays the problems of colonialism and the damage it causes not only to the Africans but also to the British. The English, who know that their days are numbered in Ghana, are confused, resigned and resentful as embodied by Johnnie. In the sanctuary of his club, Johnnie mourns his island home and a lost world of private schools and comfortable security. He feels a mingled attraction and repulsion for Africans, which suggests that he is projecting his own guilt on them. The sense of confusion and insecurity felt by the British colonizer is very aptly expressed in his words: "It's true that I'm afraid of Africa...but—if we're sent home, what shall we do? What will become of us?" (*TSJ* 124).

The story of the novel moves on two levels, each presenting its own dilemmas and conflicts. On the broader level, it concerns the birth of a nation—Ghana, and on the level of the individual personality, it deals with the birth of self-awareness. The birth of the new nation means the death of the old order. It means the death not only of European domination but also the death of the tribal world. To the men still owing allegiance to the old world, whether European or African, the new world is thus an abomination—a monster. Moreover, once the bewildering transition from 'traditional' to 'modern' comes about, the Africans must face the twin problems of freedom and survival, of gaining and maintaining an independence that is both political and inner. According to Clara Thomas, "the Africans, deluded or cynical, ignorant or corrupt, are in various stages of unpreparedness. They must, willy-nilly be ready to take over the problems whose magnitude they cannot even estimate and for whose solution they have neither sufficient training nor sufficient self-confidence, as embodied by Nathaniel."[3] As Victor Edusei, Nathaniel's friend puts it: "You put your faith in Ghana, don't you.... As far as I'm concerned, it's a dead body lying unburied. You wait until after independence. You'll see such oppression, as you never believed possible. Only of course it'll be all right then—it'll be Black men oppressing Black men, and who could object to that?" (*TSJ* 117).

On the personal level, the novel deals with how the individual, despite odds like an identity crisis, the disintegration of personality or the mental conflicts caused by the pulls and pressures of an inherited past and an acquired present, is able to find his true bearings and recover faith in himself. Through Nathaniel, one hears the voice of the colonized and experiences the ambiguity of the situation. One learns through him that Africa had a rich culture, which disappeared when the colonizers came. One also learns about the suffering and humiliation of the African people caused by years of exploitation, and their sense of despair regarding their life. "The past was dead...but the future could never be realized" (*TSJ* 64) is how Nathaniel sums up his agonizing awareness of the situation.

For Nathaniel to find his true bearings means to find out who he really is. He knows that Nathaniel is not his African name. Missionaries who Christianized him give it to him: "And after they had given him a different name they began to give him a different soul" (*TSJ* 242). This makes him unsure about himself and his real identity. He is also tremendously insecure about his situation in life, including his job as a teacher. The root cause for this insecurity, according to Nathaniel is, "his lack of qualification" which "terrified him" (*TSJ* 24). His own inadequacy and a sense of fear always hover very close beneath the surface of his personality. To add to his woes at work, he is made to "grovel apology for every remark that his employer, Mensah, chooses to interpret as insubordination" (*TSJ* 26). With no bargaining power at his disposal, Nathaniel only feels more and more vulnerable. He is also not comfortable with his physical self and this discomfort manifests itself in his physical appearance as well. He lacks the confidence and the pride of conviction to wear his native clothes and, at the same time, he feels uncomfortable and gauche in a badly fitting European suit. At a European party he attends, he realizes that his father would have done better, "he would have worn a Kente cloth and sauntered among these people...and they would have flocked to him...but he, Nathaniel...was not interesting to them because they could see no further than to think he was trying to be like them and not succeeding" (*TSJ* 145). His increasing anger towards the situation is not only easily discernible but it also highlights the fact that he is suffering from an acute crisis of identity engendered by colonialism which in turn has led to inner conflicts that make it difficult for him to cope with the existing situation.

These conflicts surface time and again, especially when dealing with situations involving the Europeans. The feeling of being exploited by the Europeans has engraved itself so deeply on Nathaniel's mind that in any interaction with the Europeans, he feels uncomfortable and ends up getting defensive. In one incident, he over-reacts and refuses to help push Johnnie's car because he is "not a servant, not a slave to be summoned" (*TSJ* 161), but later realizes his mistake of having made too much of a small request which any other person would have agreed to unquestionably with no thought of insult. This realization adds to his already heightened feeling of shame and humiliation.

This Side Jordan presents the struggle and confused despair of Nathaniel who is a product of two cultures pulling him in two opposite directions. He is torn between past and future;

bush and city; between his ancient tribal culture and modern Western ways. According to Clara Thomas, "Laurence focuses on Nathaniel and the multiplicity of the worlds he must live in."[4] Nathaniel is presented as a colonized who is displaced, dislocated and even depersonalized. He lives in the city and his education and migration create opposing pulls between his inherited socio-cultural and religious traditions that he has discarded, and the alien beliefs and values that he has acquired. He has lived in mission schools since he was seven years old and the "stamp of the mission was deep on him" (*TSJ* 28). However, his acceptance of the religious beliefs of the mission priests always cause a conflict in is mind whenever he realizes that his family and village believe in different religions: "Sometimes the old anger stirred and he would not set foot in the church for months. Then out of need or habit he would return, never entirely believing, never entirely disbelieving, doubting heaven but fearing hell" (*TSJ* 107).

A victim of British imperialists, he suffers from a sense of belonging nowhere. He has been uprooted from his village and yet has not been able to accept the city as his permanent home where he feels in exile. "The city of strangers is your city, and the god of conquerors is your God, and a strange speech is in your mouth, and you have no home" (*TSJ* 167), is his distressing thought. Colonialism has made him a stranger in his own home. He has never quite been able to fathom where he belongs. On his own admission, "I was of both and I was of neither. I forgot one way when I was too young to remember everything of it...and learned another way when I was too old for it to ever become second nature" (*TSJ* 243). This is what has been the cause of his fragmented personality.

Nathaniel welcomes the freedom which the new world offers him in the city, yet at the same time he finds he cannot totally reject the old world of the tribe and its values. He, especially, cannot reject his father, the old tribal drummer, and all the things his father believed in without doing violence to his own self. He feels guilty about his father's death and believes that "He, Nathaniel, had damned his father to that eternity. The father had been damned by his son's belief" (*TSJ* 28). But at the same time, while performing the funeral rites for his father, Nathaniel realizes that "He had not forgotten the ways of his people" (*TSJ* 28). This realization is further augmented by the remark of one of his uncles, "They have not stolen your soul Nathaniel, the White priests" (*TSJ* 30). This remark intensifies Nathaniel's mental turmoil as he cannot reconcile himself to the fact that somewhere he is still a tribal at heart, in spite of his rational self believing in the missionary religion. While on the one hand, he admits to himself that he does yearn for his simple village life even now "You do not know that I mourn everything I have lost. I mourn the gods strangled by my hand. You do not know how often I have wanted to go back" (*TSJ* 73), on the other hand, he cannot make himself give up his new faith despite his having tried once in the chapel after his father's funeral: "He stood before the statue of God's crucified son. And he spat full in the thing's face, his heart raging to avenge his father. But it did not work. For he believed in the man-God with the bleeding hands, and he could not spew that out of himself" (*TSJ* 31-32). These contradictory emotions only add to his confusion and agony. Thus, Nathaniel is a tortured man standing between two worlds, and aware of the ambiguity of his situation. As he puts it himself in a conversation with his uncle, "I belong between yesterday and today". On his uncle commenting, "But that is nowhere," Nathaniel replies, "I know...yes, I know" (*TSJ* 106-07).

It is often believed that one has to touch rock bottom before one can begin an ascent. In the case of Nathaniel, this is seen to be completely true. When he reaches the depths of despair, self-loathing, confusion and mental turmoil, it is only then, that he gains a new perspective into his life and makes his decisions. When Nathaniel starts taking stock of his situation, he learns his first important lesson in self-knowledge: fear has held him back but overriding curiosity with its strong element of hope has pushed him on. This moment of epiphany occurs when Nathaniel visits an Evangelist Church. Listening to the confessions made by the members and how all of them were saved by the grace of their god, Nathaniel too confesses to himself and recalls how he has suffered from an acute feeling of guilt because he has not entirely forgotten his old ways while he has adopted the new ways of the mission. As he remembers, "The new name took hold and the new roots began to grow. But the old roots never quite died, and the two became intertwined" (*TSJ* 243). Once he confesses this, the meaning of what the preacher is saying becomes clear to him. He realizes that everyone carries their own private hell and fears within themselves and it is for each person to overcome these and strive for a better life. Just as in the Biblical reference, "Joshua had a big battle to fight and Joshua has a big river to cross. Yes, he was afraid. Nobody ever got to the Promised land without a fight" (*TSJ* 245), Nathaniel too realizes that it is not fear itself that is bad, but the fear of failure that warps a man and causes rifts in his personality. Joshua agreed to try, "That's right God, I'll try if you say so. Yes, Sir, I'll try if you say so" (*TSJ* 246), and things fell into place for him. "The river parted its waters...and the children of Israel crossed over on dry ground" (*TSJ* 246). Nathaniel too decides to try, leaving whatever he may have done behind him and resolves to re-dedicate himself to his life afresh. This unique experience helps him to recover faith in himself and hope for the future.

On the heels of this incident comes another one which helps seal his decision to make the city his permanent home. Aya his wife gives birth to their baby in the city hospital much against the wishes of her mother and aunt who want the birth to take place in the village. Their insistence constantly reminds Nathaniel that he is betraying his people in some way. But now all his apprehensions are laid to rest and he feels "...a terrible longing to stay after all, to stay here in the city where you could feel tomorrow being reached for, where you could believe it might happen so, and to you" (*TSJ* 268). At last he can finally say, "A man must belong somewhere. If it is right or it is not right, I must stay. The new roots may not grow straight, but they have grown too strong to be cut away" (*TSJ* 274).

Nathaniel now understands that in order that he may retain his sense of worth as a human being, he must assimilate the old into the new. He must come to terms with the emotional pull of the old ways, neither succumbing to them nor rejecting them outright. He must stay where he is and take his own uncertain tortured steps into a very uncertain future, to cross like Joshua at last the river Jordan, and return again to his own land and take possession of it and enjoy it as "there must be pride and roots, O my people" (*TSJ* 22).

The Biblical image of being on this side of River Jordan and crossing to the Promised Land on the other side, sets up the expectation of a final transition from the old traditional life to a new life of independence, as a country and as an individual. The Biblical image also refers to a turning point after a long struggle or journey. Nathaniel successfully completes this journey, from his upcountry traditional ways, through mission school to urban Western life. His naming his child Joshua is a metaphor for his own renewed efforts of building a better Ghana.

Nathaniel is finally freed from his ambivalence regarding his identity when he stops despising his inherited past and goes on to accept it. Only then is he able to assert confidently that, "...my home is here, here, here, my home is here at last" (*TSJ* 275). Nathaniel is given the novel's final words to voice the enduring hope that has always been stronger than his fear: "Joshua, Joshua, Joshua, I beg you. Cross Jordan. Joshua" (*TSJ* 282).

This Side Jordan thus places before the reader the problems caused by colonialism. The novel echoes Margaret Laurence's firm belief that individuals can achieve harmony only when they can make peace with their past, ancestors and gods and assimilate the old into the new. This belief is aptly reinforced through the person of Nathaniel Amegbe, who starts with a consciousness of psychic disorder that is overwhelming, but he ends with a fragile, but stubborn grip on a new order and with a degree of hope. In his struggle one can see the struggle of all colonized Africans contending with problems generated by colonialism. And in his hopeful march into the future one can look forward to the colonized, now better-equipped with self-awareness and a correct assessment of their situation, overcoming all odds.

NOTES

All quotations from the novel *This Side Jordan* have been taken from the McClelland and Stewart Publishers' edition. 481 University Avenue, Toronto, Ontario.

1. Coined by Rudyard Kipling the term refers to the supposed or presumed responsibility of the White people to govern and impart their culture to non-White people, often advanced as a justification for European colonialism.
2. A feeling of inadequacy or insufficiency vis-à-vis one's culture and traditions.
3. Clara Thomas, *Margaret Laurence* (Canadian Writers No. 3, New Canadian Library, McClelland and Stewart Ltd., 1968), 28.
4. Clara Thomas, "Morning Yet on Creation Day." *A Study of This Side Jordan, from A Place to Stand On: Essays by and about Margaret Laurence*, ed. George Woodcock (Edmonton: New West Press, 1983), 99.

17

The God of Small Things: The Politics of Language and The Language of Politics

Kalikinkar Pattanayak

The God of Small Things which won Booker Prize in 1997 and sold like hot cakes among the lovers of fiction merits attention for the innovative use of language. Language is the vehicle of communication of thoughts, feelings, sensations, worries and anxieties. It conditions consciousness and vice versa. Politics is the art or the craft of acquiring power. The powerful human emotions; love, hate, pity, fear, and anger that *The God of Small Things*, arouses in the readers are owing to Roy's masterly use of language. As the title of the novel suggests, it focuses on the margin rather than the centre. The novelist discovers the beauty and strength in the elemental human passions like love or lust which she calls 'small things' because they are internal and private; she considers conservatism, patriarchal ideology, caste bias, law and order system in the society to be big things which embarrass her. 'God' is the metaphor for joy supreme. As an artist she attaches importance to empathy, the identification of the self with the other—here lies the godliness which man has been searching all down the ages.

Jason Cowley, one of the five 1997 Booker Prize judges holds:

> *The God of Small Things* fulfils the highest demand of the art of fiction: to see the world, not conventionally or habitually, but as if for the first time. Roy's achievement,

> and it is considerable, is never to forget about the small things in life: the insects and flowers, wind and water, the outcast and the despised. She deserved to win. (http://www.indiaaaj.com/aaj/india/indexI.html?campaign=times of India)

Cowley admits that Roy is gifted with such imaginative power and extraordinary sensibility that she makes the reader see the ordinary things like 'insects' or 'flowers' in an extra-ordinary way—here lies the secret of the popular appeal of the novel. Language, in her writing acquire power because it overwhelms, saddens, puzzle and provokes the readers to examine things that prevail in the society: patriarchal biases, taboos on sexuality, untouchability, public envy and so on, from the new angles. Roy's attitude is iconoclastic; zeal, reformative and writing, original. The interior structure of the novel corresponds perfectly to the exterior structure—that is, the feelings that the characters harbour match the episodes that occur in the novel which has 'a surprise twist ending' (Miller 72). Moon Moon Mazumdar rightly holds that Roy integrate causal unity with unity of sentiment. The purpose of this paper is to discover how Roy's intelligence and artistic acumen result in innovative and creative use of English that empowers the subalterns in the novel to give vent to suppressed feelings like sexuality, the assertion of individuality and above all, the longing to live and love in a natural way despite barricades erected by the society.

The first section introduces the objectives of the paper: it hints at the secret of the tremendous popularity of the fiction. The second section deals with the politics of language. It analyses *The God of Small Things* as a wonderful text. It highlights the uniqueness of Roy's choice of registers (topic-oriented variety of language) and style (the situationally appropriate use of language). The section vividly pictures how Roy's language acquires power and exerts influence upon the consciousness of the reader. Her talent and experience as a screenwriter stand her in good stead. The third section provides clues to the understanding of Roy's psyche. In this section, the major issues of the novel: the suppressed sexuality, the disharmony in family life, the hostile attitude of the society towards the blossoming of latent talents of the individual and so on, are discussed. Like Indian-English poet Kamala Das, Roy emerges as an artist who is disarmingly frank about instinctual needs of woman and man. This section highlights the Indian-ness of the novel because the novelist is very much preoccupied with the problems, crises and attitudes that are deeply rooted in the Indian society. In the last section Roy, the novelist emerges as a great painter in language who has an observant eye and retentive memory to capture the details of what the ordinary people in our society do, behave, dream and imagine. In this section, the portrait of Roy the artist is drawn.

II

The God of Small Things reads like a best seller because the title is catchy like *The Decline of The West;* it sharpens the curiosity of the readers to know the meaning of the phrase. God is the infinite source of power and wisdom. Thus, the title provokes the reader to think over the meaning of the phrase—how to discover God in small things.

John updike comments that like a devotionally built temple *The God of Small Things* builds a "massive interlocking structure of fine, intensely felt details" (quoted in Miller 71). The opening paragraph of the novel can be looked upon as the finest specimen of visual art because in this passage there is an orchestration of colours:

> May in Ayemenem is a hot, brooding month. The days are long and humid. The river shrinks and black crows gorge on bright mangoes in still, dustgreen trees. Red bananas ripen. Jackfruits burst. Dissolute bluebottles hum vacuously in the fruity air. Then they stun themselves against clear windowpanes and die, fatly baffled in the sun. (1)

The colours depicted in the above passage are: black, dustgreen, red and blue. Such a description allows the reader to fly on the wings of imagination to a land where he can enjoy the beauty and bounty of nature. The language acquires poetic grace. This passage is immediately followed by suggestive lines like:

> The nights are clear but suffused with sloth and sullen expectation. (*ibid.*)

The novelist makes a reference to time (night) when a person is torn between desires or expectations. Thus, the opening chapter entitled "Paradise Pickles & Preserves" and the descriptions create an impression that Roy has eyes to see beautiful things and ears to perceive the symphony of sounds. Thus, artistically the words, the phrases and the paragraphs constructed by Roy are excellent. The concluding lines of the novel are equally suggestive and splendid. The heroine's love affair with an untouchable like Velutha is not successful; hence the heroine puts a dry rose symbolic of lost romance:

> Ammu laughed:
>
> Yes, Margaret, she thought. We do it to each other too. She kissed his closed eyes and stood up. Velutha with his Back against the mangosteen tree watched her walk away. She had a dry rose in her hair. She turned to say it once again: 'Naaley'. Tomorrow. (340)

Thus, a perceptive reader feels that Roy has an artistic command over English language. The novel ends with the word 'Tomorrow' which reminds a reader of Shakespeare about *Macbeth* which has a tragic ending. Roy depicts the history of world in suggestive phrases:

> It was an awe-inspiring and humbling thought...that the whole of contemporary history, the world wars, the war of Dreams, the Man of the Moon, Science, Literature, philosophy, the pursuit of Knowledge—was no more than a blink of the Earth Woman's eye. (54)

The whole description is poetic. It provides the intimations of the world of transient existence where the humans are frozen in time. The novelist looks upon the sad happenings of the earth, which are labelled by T.S. Eliot as 'cunning passages' as a 'blink of the Earth woman's eye'. Thus, the narrative becomes masterly feminine—here lies the fascination for reading.

Roy takes delight in word play but such a play is not to be construed as affectation. The child characters read words backwards; they read pots for 'stop'. Roy also splits words and writes in a novel style. She write 'identity' as 'eye-identity'. She herself reveals in her interview with a noted ecological historian:

> My style, my language, is not something superficial, like a coat that I wear when I go out. My style is me—even when I'm at home.
>
> It's the way I think. My style is my politics.
> (Quoted in Arundhati Roy *Critical Perspectives* 25)

Roy unlike many Indian writers is not simply a reporter to the West. Her prose is very often poetic and sometimes incantatory. She uses short sentences, phrases pregnant with meaning.

The novel's artistic success lies in the use of unusal collocation. Roy uses tropes; the tropes are the foregrounded deviant forms of the language. Below are given some striking examples:

> Communism [...] seeped into Kerala like tea from a tea bag. (33)

'Seep' means flowing into or out of something through small holes when it shouldn't happen (*MacMillan* 1285). Roy uses the word 'seep' in context of communism in Kerala because she doesn't appreciate such a political scenario. In the context of Chacko, the heroine's brother the novelist brings the image of whale, a sea animal.

> Chacko lay like a beached whale on the narrow hotel bed. (119)

'Beach' is usually used as noun but Roy uses it as a verb which means, in the above context, taking rest on a beach.

In context of Rahel, the heroine's child the novelist writes:

> Rahel's new teeth were waiting inside her gums like words in a pen. (37)

Roy's imagination, like John Donne, is far-flung, the images are far-fetched. Here Roy, compares 'teeth' with words. I.A. Richards and his scholars will find Roy using concrete 'tenors' and abstract vehicles and vice-versa in metaphorical expressions. Some examples are given below just to prove this point:

> Strange insects appeared like ideas in the evenings. (9)

Insect is a visible creature but ideas are abstract. Hence in the above example tenor is concrete but metaphor is abstract. The reverse is the case in the following example:

> Only that quietness and emptiness fitted together like stacked spoons. (328)

In the above metaphorical expression 'emptiness' or 'quietness' which is quite abstract is compared to 'spoon' which is visible, tangible and palpable.

Roy is adept in the use of oxymorons: 'noisy television silence' (28), 'beautiful ugly todes' (187), 'green heat' (202), 'the mirthless smile' (239). The oxymorons are functional not decorative; in this sense she is strikingly modern.

Roy has an acute sense of humour; many of the descriptions in the novel provoke laughter because the novelist deliberately and dexterously obliterates the distinction between the profane and the sacred; the ugly and the beautiful. The novelist's sole purpose is to engage the attention of the reader. Here is a brilliant passage where the novelist uses figures of speech in an innovative way which provide food for laughter:

> Baby Kochamma lifted her rumpled sari. Rahel studied her baby grandaunt's enormous legs. (years later during a history lesson being read out in school—The Emperor Babur had a wheatish complexion and pillar-like thighs—this scene would flash before her. Baby Kochamma balanced like a big bird over a public pot [...] poor little tiny feet to carry such a load!) Baby Kochamma waited for half of half a moment. Head thrust forward. Silly smile. Bosom swinging low. Melons in a blouse. Bottom up and out. When the gurgling, bubbling sound came, she listened with her eyes. A yellow brook burbled through a mountain pass. (95)

A linguistic analysis of the passage above reveals that Roy uses language in a creative way. She is a minute observer of situations, casual manners of people who become characters in her fiction. Here she is concentrating on the lifting of sari and pissing of one of her lady characters. She is also shedding light upon the way such act is viewed by the niece of the character. The niece is very young and she imagines the legs of her aunt to those of Babur the founder of Mughal Empire—the imagination is far-fetched but not lofty. Roy compares the flow of urine of Kochamma to the 'burbling' of a brook through a mountain pass; the act of pissing, a call to nature is described in a language which, borrowing the phrase from Rousseau, can be viewed as the 'cry of nature' (Shah 77) because the character listens with her eyes. She compares her breasts hidden inside the blouse to 'melons' that were swinging low. She calls her smile silly—such kind of pictorial description is creative but it doesn't instil noble feelings. Perhaps this is the reason why C.D. Narasimhaiah depreciates this novel and calls that this is a curse to creativity. The great critic of Indian English literature perceives the politics of language—the language that can arrest the attention of the readers, specially the juvenile readers.

III

The God of Small Things is an explosive text; it clothes the ideologies of Roy in tricky language. Kamala Das rightly perceives that Roy spits at correct English. To the novelist many things have gone wrong with the society; hence the language she uses deviates from the normal rules of morphology and syntax. In the 1990s the novel was written: perhaps a committed writer such as Roy was probably tired of either nationalist or socialist rhetoric; she weaved a plot and used a kind of language in order to defend a set of human rights that had been ignored by colonialism, democracy and communism.

The novelist deals with colonialism as a psychic experience; she is critical of patriarchal set-up and caste system. She pictures that emigration isn't worth trying; Americanization isn't necessarily an improvement on this split identity of the colonized subject. This negative image of America is pictured through Rahel's experience. Her marriage to Larry Me Caslin fails. Rahel's sojourn in America is criticized by the residents of Ayemenem:

> His daughter's daughter is this. In Amayrica now. (...)
> Oower oower, oower. In Amayrica now, isn't it. It
> Wasn't a question. It was sheer admiration. (Roy 129)

America has been misspelt. The thrice repetition of 'oower' gives a wrong image of the emigration to America.

Roy sarcastically writes about Americanization:

> Look at the way they dressed' Why did Malayalees have Such awful teeth? (...) Going to the dogs India is 191. Soon, Foreign Returnees would be trapped outside the History House, and have their dreams redreamed. (192-92)

The writer indicates that Americanization is as bad as anglophilia—both the trends make the Indians forget their own culture. She hints at the fact that India is going to be neo-colonized by America through the power of the dollar.

In the novel, politics is the old 'omelette and eggs thing' and politicians are professional omeletteers (195). As the cook has to break eggs to make omelettes the politicians define their set of priorities which serve the vested interests, the common people are betrayed; hence the author writes:

> Once Ayemenem office of the communist party, where
> Midnight study meetings were held is a place grown limp
> And old and the red of its flag has bled away. (194)

The representation of communism is an illustration of the dismissive view of political utopia. Comrade Pillai is goaded by the ambition to promote his own interest. This private ambition and prejudice make Pillai resent Velutha the untouchable. But in Roy's imagination Velutha is the real god; he fulfils the private desires of Ammu the heroine. Pandian writes:

> Arundhati Roy's choice for the representation of an untouchable lover as a person entitled to respect, affection and career opportunities interferes with sensitive areas in the traditional organization of the Indian society. From a feminist angle, the assertion of Ammu's female desire

> and agency, materialized in the attitude of choosing a lover for herself, are equally disturbing for the established patriarchal system. (20)

Roy is against establishment; she exposes the evils of existing patriarchal set-up and caste-bias. She dwells upon the female desires—private emotions which are not publicly talked about. She looks down upon this trend. Here is a passage on transgression—a transgression of laws enacted by the society. In our society, the love between a high caste woman and a low caste man is forbidden; so is incestuous relationship. Roy the rebel pictures it boldly in this novel:

> They all broke the rules. They all crossed into forbidden territory. They all tampered with the laws that lay down who should be loved and how. And how much. The laws that make grandmothers, uncles uncles, mothers mothers, cousins cousins, jam jam and jelly jelly. (3l)

Roy is sarcastic about human laws that fix the categories in human relationships: uncles, mothers, grandmothers, cousins and so on. Sarcastically, she compares such kind of human ties to the family of jam and jelly. In the passage above, the language is conversational; the novelist is using verbless sentences like 'and how much'. In fact, love is immeasurable; it can't be measured. Hence, Roy uses ironically like a quantifier, 'much'.

Eroticism in the novel is conspicuous by its presence. Baby Kochamma's desire for union with the Irish Catholic priest is delineated in superb language:

> Baby Kochamma...possessed him in death in a way she never had while he was alive.... In her memory of him, he embraced her. Just her. As a man embraces a woman. Once he was dead, Baby Kochamma stripped Father Mulligan of his ridiculous saffron robes and re-clothed him in the coca cola cassock that she so loved. (Her senses feasted, between changes, on that lean, concave, Christ-like body.) (298)

Baby Kochamma dreamt of having romance—the physical romance with the Irish priest Father Mulligan but he couldn't have it in practical life. Roy the writer has the knowledge about psychoanalysis; hence he pictures the dream of Kochamma in appropriate language. Even if Mulligan was a priest Kochamma wasn't attracted towards his priesthood; she was attracted towards his lovely physical appearance, hence she dreamt in such a manner for dream analysis. Roy's language is apt. Human feelings condition the language a human uses. Kochamma loves coca-cola cassock; hence she dreams of clothing the priest in such a robe.

Baby Kochamma who has failed to materialize her dreams—the dreams of getting united physically with Father Mulligan grows intolerably jealous of Ammu who makes a love marriage and then divorces her husband. Roy pictures the psyche of Kochamma which gets revealed through the language she uses:

> As for a divorced daughter, according to Baby Kochamma, she had no position anywhere at all. And as for a divorced daughter from a love marriage, well, words could not describe Baby Kochamma's outrage. As for a divorced daughter from an intercommunity love marriage—Baby Kochamma chose to remain quaveringly silent on the subject. (45-46)

Roy pictures the Indian society—the conservative set-up in which a divorced woman gets humiliated the expression 'quiveringly silent' is suggestive of Roy's analysis of the psyche of a woman who has failed to love the person she longed for. Roy lends credibility and authenticity to her character sketch. Premananda Kumar perceives that Roy feels that ours is a generation of disillusionment (*The Hindu*, Sept. 6, 1998). Hence, the characters in the fiction are disillusioned, frustrated, very often hopeless and helpless.

IV

"...*The God of Small Things* is a work of fiction but it is no less political than any of my essays" (*The Algebra of Infinite Justice* 196). Roy admits that the fiction has political and literary concerns. Hence, she is to use the language of politics. The fiction reflects the ideology of the novelist on various issues: the woman's point of view in matters of eroticism, power relationship between the boss and subordinate servant, the incest which is the claims of instinct, articulating the marginal, the postcolonial feminisms in the transnational economy, the moral mathematics of physical relationship between the high caste woman and a low caste untouchable, cosmopolitanism and so on. For a good artist language exists in a 'dispersed mode'. It is more of functional, as Aristotle holds, than representational nature. Roy uses language, narrates incidents in such a dexterous way that her ideology reflected in the novel raises disturbing questions in the mind of perceptive readers. In matters of language, Derrida uses the French verb 'differer' (quoted in *Studies in Critical Approaches to Literature* 90) which combines two principal senses: to 'differ' and 'defer'. In the intricate complex of differences, that is, language, meaning is always deferred, put off and scattered. Roy believes in Derrida's conception of language. What and how Roy pictured in her debut novel in 1997 has relevance today. Roy has portrayed the untimely death of the heroine, Ammu and her lover, Velutha in tragic circumstances which evoke pity and fear. Such kinds of descriptions are pictorial, harrowing and models before the writers, reporters and columnists. Today, in the article *Parliament and Patriarchy* Ramchandra Guha pictures the death of a gang-raped girl student of physiotherapy at Delhi:

> ...Although widely used, 'tragic' is too tame a word to describe an event that has shaken a nation. "Horrific" and "barbaric" may be more accurate. As the anger and the outrage slowly stir an apathetic citizenry—and a still more apathetic political class—and as we understand how the barbarism and brutality that manifested itself on that Delhi bus on a single evening is reproduced daily in hundreds of location across the country. (*The Hindu*; December 31, 2012)

The description is sure to haunt the mind and linger in the memory of the readers. Many passages in *The God of Small Things* read like the above where the picture of human cruelty is delineated. Doubtless, Roy will be appreciated for her handling of English language in depicting human barbarism for the years to come.

WORKS CITED

Guha, Ramchandra. *The Hindu* (September, 06, 1998).

Macmillan English Dictionary. London: Macmillan Publishers Ltd., 2002. (http://www.indiaaaj.com/aaj/india/indexI.html?campaign= times of India)

Miller, Winnie. *Life and Works of Booker Prize Winners [1969–2003]*. New Delhi: Dominant Publishers and Distributors, 2003.

Pandian, I.D. *Arundhati Roy: Life and Works*. Kanpur: Bhasker Publications, 2009.

Prasad, Murari (ed.). *Arundhati Roy: Critical Perspectives*. Delhi: Pencraft International, 2006.

Roy, Arundhati. *The Algebra of Infinite Justice*. New Delhi: Penguin Books, 2002.

——. *The God of Small Things*. London: Flamingo, 1997.

Shah, Manoharlal. *Studies in Critical Approaches to Literature*. Delhi: Swastik Publications, 2010.

The Hindu. December 31, 2012.

18

Eco-aesthetics in *The God of Small Things*

Ambika Bhalla

The literary interest in the environment is a recent development and dates from the early 1990s when a new critical approach known as 'ecocriticism' emerged in the USA. The central concern of this movement is the relationship between literature and the environment. The eco-critics generally share the assumption that culture and nature are interconnected. In their view: "Literature does not float above the material world in some aesthetic ether, but, rather, plays a part in an immensely complex global system in which energy, matter and ideas interact" (*The Ecocriticism Reader*). Moreover, the first law of ecology states that "everything is connected to everything else" (*The Ecocriticism Reader*).

This paper is an attempt to trace Eco-aesthetics in Arundhati Roy's *The God of Small Things* (1997). An Ecocritical study views the relationship between humans and nature due to the growing dangers of environmental pollution. It represents an approach that focuses on environmental theme in her fiction. It emerges from the fact that due to the modern activities, the biotic, abiotic and human elements in a given situation undergo degradation. Through the subversive narrative strategies and images of environmental decay, Roy warns her readers against the ecocidal tendencies of humankind. Given that Roy's interest in 'connections' and her warning of the dangers of severing "the link [and] the *understanding*—between human beings and the planet they live on [...] the intelligence that connects eggs to hens, milk to cows, food to forests, water to rivers, air to life and earth to human existence" (*The Cost of Living*) and her vocal support for various environmentalist causes in India, it is surprising that this aspect of her writing has received less attention.

"Nature and culture do not exclude each other but be entangled with each other in multiple ways", writes Cheryll Glotfelty in the introduction to *The Ecocriticism Reader.* It takes as its subject the interconnections between nature and culture. Roy subversively yokes nature and culture together in *The God of Small Things,* where various forms of patriarchal and governmental power are reflected, in multiple ways. She portrays the scenery of the village Ayemenem in her novel very consciously, describing both the picturesque beauty of the landscape and its subsequent degradation through decades of human intervention. The destruction of nature emphasizes and reflects the moral corruption of characters in the larger narrative. The river Meenanchal that runs through the village and the landmark "History House" are focal points in depicting ecological abuse in juxta position with Ammu and Velutha's characters' symbolization of gender and class discrimination in Kerala.

According to Aarthi Vadde throughout her literary career, Arundhati Roy has suggested that narratives of connection are weapons against the bedfellows of global capitalism and state control. Where the latter gathers power from the privatization, domination of nature and the hierarchal separation of human beings, her narratives challenge institutions that wield power through the creation and subjugation of human and non-human others. *The God of Small Things* is her most complex narrative of connection including caste politics, corporate globalization, and ecological collectivity. Roy begins her ecological concern at home, specifically her native state of Kerala that is the setting for her only novel. Kerala has historically been a crucial centre in India's environmentalism versus development debates. It is globally renowned for its beautiful backwaters—a network of rivers, lakes, manmade and natural canals, and estuaries that run between the Arabian Sea and the Western Ghats. The region is known for its rich biodiversity, containing ecotones between freshwater and saltwater ecosystems and two internationally recognized Ramsar wetlands—the Vembanad and Ashtamudi.

In the novel, Roy illustrates the ways that the environmental corruption, characteristic of the 1980s era of United States has travelled across the Atlantic to India by the 1990s. To Mukherjee, this environmental degradation of Ayemenem in 1991 is a direct result of the process of global capitalism and is proved by various situations of foreign economic and cultural domination that are projected prominently. For instance, the first reference to the environmental problems we get in the very first chapter of the novel. In 1991, when the silent Estha goes on long walks along the local Meenanchal river, this is what greets his senses: "Some days he walked along the banks of the river that smelled of shit and pesticides bought with World Bank loans. Most of the fish have died. The ones that survived suffered from fin-rot and had broken out in boils" (13). The novelist is here critical of the hands behind polluting the river and the policy of the government buying with World Bank, both of which will ultimately contribute in making the life of the people miserable. The reader gets another reference to the polluted river in the fifth chapter of the novel where God's own country gets the notoriety of children defecating directly onto the riverbed. "The river would rouse itself to accept the day's offerings and sludge off to the sea, leaving wavy lines of thick white cum in its wake" (125). Furthermore, in the highly sarcastic naming of a chapter of the novel as 'God's Own Country', Roy describes another view of Ayemenem in 1991, this time seen through Rahel's eyes:

> Years later, when Rahel returned to the river, it greeted her with a ghostly skull's smile, with holes where teeth had been and a limp hand raised from a hospital bed.... Downriver, a saltwater barrage had been built, in exchange for votes from the influential paddy-farmer lobby, an alteration that generates two harvests a year instead of one and more rice, for the price of a river. (124)

In spite of the fact that it was June and raining, the river was no more than a swollen drain: "A thin ribbon of thick water that lapped wearily at the mud banks on either side, sequinned with the occasional silver slant of a dead fish. It was choked with a succulent weed, whose furred brown roots waved like thin tentacles under water" (124). The poor and dispossessed had made a slum by its side, adding to pollution. While upstream, "clean mothers washed clothes and pots in unadulterated factory effluents" and "people bathed", downstream at Ayemenem, slum: "children hung their bottoms over the edge and defecated directly onto the squelchy, sucking mud of the exposed river bed" and the net result would be that "on warm days the smell of shit lifted off the air and hovered over Ayemenem like a hat" and naturally, even the History House transformed into a luxury hotel was not exempt from either the stench or the "thick and toxic" water (125).

To screen off the scum and prevent it from encroaching on Kari Saipu's estate a tall wall was built. But nothing could be done about the foul smell that permeated. Thus, it was a smelly paradise. The five-star hotel people called it 'God's own country' in their brochures because they knew that "smelliness, like other people's poverty, was merely a matter of getting used to. A question of discipline. Of Rigour and Air-conditioning. Nothing more" (126). Roy points out how both farming and factories pollute nature. The novel situates the causes of environmental damage squarely in the West. It focuses on the bodies of water and bodies of women as literal and figurative site of pollution: Ammu, Rahel's mother, like the Meenanchal river, is "polluted" in the eyes of her family and community as a result of her affair with the untouchable Velutha.

In Roy's novel, the natural is represented as a wild Eden, a landscape that is lovely and fertile but also dangerous in its transgression of boundaries: when Sophie Mol's body is pulled into a fisherman's boat, for example, the fisherman "thinks how wrong it is for a fisherman to believe that he knows his river well. No one knows the Meenanchal. No one knows what it may snatch or suddenly yield. Or when" (245). The first page of the novel is filled with images of this explosive uncertainty of nature, of black crows gorging on mangoes and jackfruits bursting, while "boundaries blur...brick walls turn moss green. Pepper vines snake up electric poles" (3). In Ayemenem, Baby Kochamma gives up care of her garden for the pursuit of cable television, a technological "advance" that ironically allows the ornamental garden to thrive and become "knotted and wild" (27). Throughout the narrative, the natural world—the plants in the garden, the monsoon rains, and most significantly, the river-push against the constructedness of their confinement and creep into "civilized" spaces.

A few pages later Chacko, Rahel and Estha's Oxford-educated Rhodes-scholar uncle lectures them on history:

> Then, to give Estha and Rahel a sense of historical perspective...he told them about the Earth Woman. He made them imagine the earth—four thousand six hundred million years old—was a forty-six-year old woman...it had taken the whole of Earth woman's life for the earth to become what it was. For the oceans to part. For the mountains to rise. "The Earth woman was eleven years old," Chacko said, when the first single-celled organisms appeared. "The first animals, creatures like worms and jellyfish, appeared only when she was forty." She was over forty-five—just eight months ago—when dinosaurs roamed the earth.
>
> And...everything we are and ever will be—are just a twinkle in her eye, Chacko said grandly.... (53-54)

Chacko's lecture is suited to be intelligible to children. But the essential point is that given the late arrival and monopolization of the Earth by human beings, a lesson in humility towards her and all the living and non-living existence that supports, would be necessary. Beginning to view the role played by the fictional characters in the novel, a few instances of environmental degradation due to the phenomenon of uneven development emerge. At the very beginning of the novel, we come across a world where nature and culture have remained integrated enough for years to perpetuate a stable, abiding and harmonious environment:

> ...by early June the south-west monsoon breaks and there are three months of wind and water with short spells of sharp, glittering sunshine that thrilled children snatch to play with. The countryside turns an immodest green. Boundaries blur as tapioca fences take roots and bloom. Brick walls turn moss green, Pepper vines snake up electric poles. Wild creepers burst through laterite banks and spill across the flooded roads. Boats ply in the bazaars. And small fish appear in the...PWD potholes on the highways. (1)

The visible effects of development activities seem to merge with nature. But there is apparently no lack of harmony between nature and culture. The novel tells about the politics of the state which proclaims to undertake development activities for all but more often than not marginalizes a section of the same society and degrades the environment in various ways. Analyzing the novel itself with "a skyblue day in December sixty-nine (the nineteen silent)...when...[a] skyblue Plymouth... sped, past young rice-fields and odd rubber trees, on its way to Cochin" (35), the comparatively clear environment of Kerala in a bygone era is evoked. But there are two elements to disturb this picture of serenity. The first is the reference to 'old rubber trees', reminding the old colonial days when natural and human resources in India were held to be equally easy to exploit. The second disturbing idea comes a sentence later: "Further east, in a small country with similar landscape (jungles, rivers, rice-fields, communists), enough bombs were being dropped to cover all of it in six inches of steel" (35).

There is every attempt on the part of the invading superpower to destroy life and natural environment and ecology completely. Sandwiched between the global and the historical, Roy's fictional Ayemenem, even in 1969, is a place where natural environment and human culture strike a discordant note mostly, anticipating and revealing a dissatisfaction that surfaces especially when there is an attempt to move forward at a furious pace, breaking off with tradition. To show how human beings arrive at this point in time, looking at Baby

Kochamma's garden and then contrasting it with Velutha's environment would suffice.

> ...Baby Kochamma [had] returned from Rochester [in America] with a diploma in Ornamental gardening... [Her] father gave Baby Kochamma charge of the front garden of the Ayemenem House.... She turned it into a lush maze of dwarf hedges, rocks, and gargoyles. The flower she loved most was anthurium.... Their single succulent spathes ranged from shades of mottled black to blood red.... In the centre of her garden, surrounded by beds of canna and phlox, a marble cherub peed an endless silver are into a shallow pool in which a single blue lotus bloomed. At each corner of the pool lolled a pink plaster-of-Paris gnome with rosy cheeks and a peaked red cap.... Like a lion-trainer she tamed twisting vines and nurtured bristling cacti. She limited bonsai plants and pampered rare orchids. She waged war on the weather. She tried to grow edelweiss and Chinese guava. (26-27)

Baby Kochamma's carefully cultivated garden is a mixture of colours and cultures. Bonsai plants prove the existence of culture or the kind of power that man exercises to control the natural world completely. Similarly, in the red anthurium juxtaposed with the single, oriental-looking blue lotus, there is a deliberate clash of cultures and natural environments belonging to different countries and origins and this is also evident in her attempt to bring edelweiss and Chinese guava together in her garden. The ornamental garden represents a state of existence where both natural and cultural environments have been undergoing corruption.

Opposed to Baby Kochamma is a son of the soil, Velutha, a Paravan or untouchable person, who fosters nature and a natural way of living. He also provides crucial service, taking care of the aesthetic environment of Ayemenem by means of carpentry and by tending to machines. Against the expensive foreign diploma of Baby Kochamma, Velutha, "eleven then...like a little magician. He could make intricate toys—tiny windmills, rattles, minute jewel boxes out of dried palm reeds; he could carve perfect boats out of tapioca stems and figurines on cashew nuts" (74). When Baby Kochamma's "garden cherub's silver arc dried up inexplicably, it was Dr. Velutha who fixed its bladder for her", along with making angel's wings, cardboard clouds, an easily dismantled manger "for Christ to be born in" for her "annual Nativity plays" (75). In other words, Velutha, an untouchable, belonging to the class utterly opposite Baby Kochamma's, succeeds in bringing together the best knowledge of tradition and modernity to improve the environment at Ayemenem.

Viewed through the eyes of Rahel and Estha, Velutha appeared to be a special person because of his 'green' knowledge, or his ability to shape their world in keeping with the natural environment. He was not only, merely by himself, living in harmony with nature even as he continued to work confidently in the Machine age; at the same time, through Rahel and Estha, he was also planting in the next generation the values that made such an integrated modes of life possible. His "little laterite hut, downriver from the Ayemenem House" (78) is a near-perfect instance of eco-conscious living or living in constant touch with one's natural environment. Thus, the commodification of both nature and culture seems to be complete. This was 'God's Own Country' with a polluted, stinking environment, already sold to foreign visitors. It is this state of environmental decay that Rahel and Estha return to.

Roy has searched for ways of redemption and rectification leading to a different and better future in the two different scenes of the novel. The first is a description of baby Kochamma's garden in 1991.

> Recently, after enduring more than half a century of relentless, pernickety attention, the ornamental garden has been abandoned.... The reason for this sudden, unceremonious dumping as a new love. Baby Kochamma had installed a dish antenna on the roof of Ayemenem house...in Ayemenem...now whole wars, famines, picturesque massacres and Bill Clinton could be summoned up like servants. (27)

The way Roy presents this phase of history is to be noted; "...while her ornamental garden wilted and died, Baby Kochamma followed baseball, cricket, tennis, *The Bold and the Beautiful* and *Santa Barbara*" (27). Simply speaking, the cultured gardening is replaced with another system of culture absorbed via the artificial visual and auditory environment generated by means of American soaps and league games. It seems as if all Baby Kochamma has succeeded in doing is to replace the corruption of the natural environment in her garden earlier with the pollution of the cultural space that she inhabits in 1991. The description points towards a regeneration of nature after the prolonged torture that it had been subjected to in the name of culture:

> ...Left to its own devices, [the garden] had grown knotted and wild, like the circus animals who had forgotten their tricks. The weed that people call communist patcha (because it flourished in Kerala like communism) smothered the more exotic plants. Only the vines kept growing, like toe-nails on a corpse. They reached through the nostrils of the pink plaster gnomes and blossomed in their hollow heads, giving them an expression half surprised, half-sneeze-coming. (27)

Roy reveals the way in which nature can stage a comeback and destroy the artifices of culture that had corrupted the natural environment for long. The garden in the novel emerges, like Rahel and Estha's life, as an empty space, but at last free from the corruption effected by artifice and culture a place full of "promise, the space of the possible, of expectation"· In ecocritical terms, it hints at the possibility of something constructive, a positive change in terms of the situation that suggests a balance of power between nature and culture.

In the other instance of Roy's subtle treatment of nature-culture equation, we re-read the description of vines climbing up telegraph poles and fish swimming in the rain-drenched, waterlogged potholes on PWD-made roads on the opening pages of novel. The short-lived poles and roads (signs of human effort, development and culture) that seem to compete with the everlasting elements of nature gradually tend to merge with them to present a picture of a harmonious co-existence of nature and culture.

Roy has highlighted the environmental problem as a major problem in the novel. Very often people would forget about their surroundings to make life miserable for themselves and for their future generations. One gets enough evidence in the novel to prove this point. The necessity to articulate and work consciously towards a better environment had been incorporated in *The God of Small Things.* Roy has subtly and consistently introduced images that suggested a particular orientation in environmental concerns. This work is definitely a critique of development policies and the resulting condition on environment and ecology in our times. She uses her celebrity status to augment the environmental causes that she fights for. Roy's unrelenting distress about issues related to environment makers her readers, as consumers of the earth, more conscientious.

WORKS CITED

Anand, Divya. "Inhabiting the Space of Literature: An Ecocritical Study of Arundhati Roy's *The God of Small Things* and O.V. Vijayan's *The Legends of Khasak*" *Interdisciplinary Studies in Literature and Environment,* Volume 12(2). Oxford University Press, Jan. 1, 2005.

Glotfelty, Cheryll and Harold Fromm (eds.). *The Ecocriticism Reader: Landmarks in Literary Ecology.* Athens, University of Georgia Press, 1996: xix.

Mukherjee, Upamanyu Pablo. *Postcolonial Environments: Nature, Culture and the Contemporary Indian Novel in English.* Houndmills, Basingstoke: Palgrave Macmillan, 2010.

Roy, Arundhati. *The God of Small Things.* New Delhi: India Ink, 1997.

——. *The Cost of Living.* Modern Library, 1999: 101.

Vadde, Aarthi. *Modern Fiction Studies:* Volume 55, Number 3, Fall 2009: 522-44.

19

Negotiating in Between: Rohinton Mistry's *Family Matters* as a Tale of Existential Struggle

Chitra Thrivikraman Nair

It is a psychological fact that human beings have an innate desire to identify themselves with one specific linguistic, cultural or religious group. Such a situation becomes problematic in the case of those groups which are decentred and placed on the margins of mainstream society where even their very existence is called into question. It is, therefore, quite natural that those on the margins experience a sense of "otherness" and so they tend to assert themselves in relation to the dominant culture. In the literary world, several postcolonial writers have essayed to reconstruct the experiences of the minority sects and to seek a space for the articulation of their voices in the contemporary multicultural social order. My paper intends to examine Rohinton Mistry's *Family Matters* as a tale undertaken by its protagonist Nariman Vakeel, and the heroic struggle that he waged in order to maintain the equilibrium of his life intact. Through his individual sufferings, Mistry gets an opportunity to address the broader concerns of familial or communal duties and obligations. The focus here is more on the struggle made by an individual to redefine his/her position within the larger social order, and such an act very often brings an individual into conflict with his family and community.

Family Matters is the third novel by the critically acclaimed Indian born author Rohinton Mistry. It was first published by McClelland and Stewart in 2002. *Family Matters* was also short-listed for the 2002 Booker Prize. The novel is set in the city of Mumbai, where Mistry was born and bred, and tells the story of a middle-class Parsi family living through a domestic crisis. Through the exploration of the affairs of a family, Mistry is able to convey the problems of definition, and the dilemma ensuing out of the strong need have to preserve one's culture against the ideas and practices of the larger cultural order.

Set in the post-Babri Masjid era, *Family Matters* tracks the story of seventy-nine-year-old Parsi widower, Nariman Vakeel. Afflicted with Parkinson's disease, Vakeel leads his miserable life in the company of his two middle-aged stepchildren, Jal and Coomy, children of his wife's first marriage. Nariman's "fading eyesight, tiresome dentures, trembling limbs, stooped postures, and shuffling gait" (*FM* 5) contribute to his personal disabilities and his stepchildren find it extremely difficult to cope with the problems arising out of his fragile health. The problems faced by Vakeel assume universal dimensions, for he stands out as a representative of the older generation. Nariman Vakeel, thus, symbolises the geriatric community placed on the margins of the mainstream healthy community. Not having been able to find solace and comfort neither in Chateau Felicity nor in the Pleasant Villa, Vakeel finds it difficult to carve a space for himself in his family. Mistry has designed the novel with such artistic dexterity that all the characters are portrayed in a realistic light, and that their issues are similar to the ones confronted by human beings in the daily course of their lives.

The sense of insecurity experienced by old people like Vakeel, in fact, exposes a murkier picture of Bombay with its underworld and other nefarious activities. They live in a world of apprehensions, and there is a speedy decline in human values in the matrix of life. Coomy prevents Vakeel from taking strolls outside of their flat on account of the Babri Masjid riots, but Vakeel points out that the riots can be indoors as well. Further, as Jal points out: "Just last week in Firozsha Baag an old lady was beaten and robbed...inside her own flat.

Poor thing is barely clinging to life at Parsi General" (*FM* 5). Like the old people, the Parsis as a religious community live a life on the edge of the multicultural metropolis of Bombay.

As a religious group, the Parsi community is known for their exclusivity, racial purity and cultural superiority. Hence, they are keen on preserving the specific customs, traditions and rituals, and thereby have adopted a position of insularity. They maintain their own standards and taboos in all spheres of life. In *Family Matters,* Mistry's representation of the Parsi community and their rituals is realistic to the core, and it seems as though he categorically refuses to idealise the dogmatic, age-old and orthodox rites and rituals followed by the Parsis from generation to generation. The rigidity of being a Parsi is best exemplified by Mistry through the character of Yezad Chenoy, one of the main protagonists of *Family Matters.* As the narrative progresses, he undergoes much transformation as a result of the experiences he gained from his life. We first meet him as Mr. Kapur's employee at Bombay Sport Goods Emporium, Marine Lines. Though a Parsi by birth, Yezad does not approve of be conservative mindset of the Parsis, and so strikes the readers as a secular-minded individual. Yezad is a truly dedicated husband to Roxana and an affectionate father to Jahangir and Murad. As in the case of a family-oriented individual, problems, mostly financial, crop up in Yezad's life as well. Nariman's illness and bed-ridden state are a source of constant trouble for the family, and in fact, puts the financial condition of the family in jeopardy. So to improve his poor financial condition Yezad desperately proceeds to fool his employer, but it fails. Mr. Kapur simply refuses to be the butt of the game played out by Yezad. His life situation gets worsened when he loses his job. Utterly disappointed, Yezad is stricken with despair and at this juncture, he turns to religion for comfort. Yezad attributes his failure in life to the lack of spiritual values, and henceforth, decides to become religious to the core. Having turned to the fire-temple to derive mental happiness and satisfaction, Yezad becomes an outright fundamentalist, and the readers cannot, but be surprised at his sea-change from a secular rationalist to a religious bigot.

His religious fundamentalism reaches its peak when he cannot tolerate people belonging to other religious communities. By tracking Yezad's transformation from a cosmopolitan to a narrow-minded Parsi man, Mistry throws light on the role played by the socio-cultural circumstances in bringing about a shift in one's outlook towards life.

In detailing the role of the Parsi community against the larger canvas of Indian social life, Mistry also consider it appropriate to cast light on the attempts made by an individual to find a space for themselves in his/her family and community. Very often, the personal desires and interests are subordinated to meet the familial needs. In the novel, Nariman Vakeel's affair with his Christian girlfriend Lucy Braganza does not receive the approval of his parents based on the simple reason that she is a non-Parsi. Vakeel is forced to forsake his individual desires for the better prospects of his family and community at large: "No happiness is more lasting than the happiness that you get from fulfilling your parents' wishes" (*FM* 13). Though Vakeel's orthodox Parsi father marries him off to a widow Yasmin with two children, thoughts about Lucy continue to haunt him:

> Then the evening visits began. To Yasmin, they did not pose a threat at first, or even an inconvenience—the answer was simple. "Just ignore her. There are dozens of people on the footpath—she is one more. When she gets tired, she will go home."

But Lucy on the footpath brought back the past with a force that left him shaken. Holding the window bars, he waited, while Yasmin asked him was he feeling unwell, was something wrong?

> "Nothing," he mumbled, unable to explain the sight of Lucy, standing motionless, her face turned towards his window, had accomplished which they had dreaded—filled him with a torrent of memories from their early days together. First, her family forbidding her to go out with him. Then her brothers warning her that they would beat up her boyfriend if they caught them together. (*FM* 67)

It is religion that stands in the way of fulfilment of relationship of love between Nariman and Lucy. Both have decided to lead a cocooned existence into which they could retreat at their own pace, but unfortunately after eleven years of ill-fated; unfulfilled relationship, Nariman tells Lucy about ending their relationship for "they had been ground down by their families" (*FM* 13). Thus, following stiff opposition from his parents, Nariman concludes that "the traditional ways are the best" (*FM* 16), and in order to uphold the values of his community and to maintain the purity of his race, Nariman marries a woman in spite of her being a widow. Nariman's emotional liaison with Lucy is so strong that he cannot completely erase her image from his mind, but Nariman's parents consider education to be the reason behind Nariman's secular views on his relationship with Lucy: "Modern ideas have filled Nari's head. He never learned to preserve, that fine balance between tradition and modernness" (*FM* 15). The thoroughly conservative outlook of Nariman's parents destroys the innocent love affair of Nariman with Lucy, and through this episode, Mistry, in fact, has shown that love based on a pure emotional attachment should become the order of the day. It can be seen that the strictness of the Parsis in maintaining the purity of their cultural ethos and religious values by not encouraging inter-communal marriages has resulted in a speedy decline in their population. *Family Matters* concludes with an epilogue which elucidates the fact that history repeats itself. Murad, the elder son of Yezad follows the footsteps of Nariman when he falls in love with a non-Parsi girl, thus bringing into question once again the tenants of the Parsi religion with its strict and orthodox rules and rituals which fail "to preserve that balance between tradition and modernness" (*FM* 15). In the end of the novel, we find Yezad not able to accommodate Murad's relationship with a Maharashtrian girl, and terribly shaken, he warns his son: "You can have friends you like, any race or religion, but for a serious relationship, for marriage, the rules are different" (*FM* 482), and further adds that the pure Persian racial origins make the Parsis a unique lot, and therefore, they cannot approve of the mixed marriages which, according to them, will destroy the sacredness and pristine nature of their racial affiliations.

It is important at this point, to focus on the concept of home, a place that offers comfort and stability, and no doubt, it is the family that becomes the centre point of a whole series of experiences and memories. In this respect, *Family Matters* turns out to be successful in bringing out the dilemma faced by each character to make meaning of his/her existence within the socio-cultural and political framework of the nation at large. When Nariman breaks his leg and is bed-ridden, he fails to live up to the satisfaction of his family members. Roxana tries hard to lead a dignified existence with her divided attention to her father and her family, but in the end meets with rebuff following her financially straitened circumstances. Roxana attempts to provide a space for Nariman within her family, but unfortunately Nariman is left without either physical space or emotional space. Nariman's marginalization in the family space offers immense scope for the novelist to cast light on the rot characterizing the Indian society and the Parsi society, in particular. The decision of Coomy and Jal to entrust Nariman under Roxana's care is like a throw from a hot pan to a frying pan. Being an old man beset with osteoporosis, Parkinson's disease and hypotension, Nariman suffers from a lack of space, and in Roxana's flat, he is confined to the space of a small room.

Nariman's marginal existence echoes the diasporic experiences of the Parsi community in India. As a Parsi of Zoroastrian origins, Nariman, like Mistry, is a doubly displaced individual, and as Bharucha observes: "However, Mistry is also a Farsi Zoroastrian and a person whose ancestors were forced into exile by the Islamic conquest of Iran, he was in diaspora even in India. This informs his writings with the experience of multiple displacements" (24). In order to preserve the strong-rooted religio-cultural identity of the Parsis, they follow their rites and rituals on close heels: "For Parsis in the Indian Diaspora, the fact of being a Farsi Zoroastrian is racial and religious identity; then comes the Nationalist identity; then the wider transnational identity" (Bharucha 58-59). Mistry's texts are drawn out of Parsi experiences and in his *Family Matters,* he throws light on the daily rituals of the Parsis which indeed make them a class apart. As Mistry writes:

> The fragrance of frankincense delighted Roxana, for ritual and religion meant more to her than it ever had to Yezad. After her mother's sudden death, her training had been taken over by the Contractor side of the family, and Nariman's heavy conscience had refused them nothing. They had taught for the prayers, performed her navjote, taken her to the fire-temple for every holy day. (*FM* 24-25)

The silver thurible reminds Roxana of her childhood days, and as a true Parsi treats it with the utmost respect, and to her, loban smoke was like "angels and fareshtas floating through the house" (*FM* 25). Certain mythological beliefs related to the Parsi religion are thrown open to the readers through the interrogating nature of one of the boys who wanted to know about the significance of names:

> It [Jehangir] means "Conqueror of the world."
>
> Jehangir was impressed....
>
> Murad came into the front room... "What does my name mean?" he asked.
>
> "You are a boon, a blessing," said his father.
>
> "And Mummy's name?"
>
> "Roxana means the dawn."
>
> "And yours?"
>
> "Guardian angel..."

Their names taken together, thought Jehangir, made the perfect family: they were blessed, they possessed the whole world, they had their own guardian angel, and Mummy's dawn light shone upon all of them. Yet Mummy and Daddy were fighting and unhappy... (*FM* 281).

Mistry has deliberately introduced Parsi characters with Parsi names rooted in Zoroastrian tradition, and this makes them remain as a class as distinct from other different ethno-religious groups. Though Mistry illustrates the Parsi domestic experiences in *Family Matters,* he is not without reservations while discussing the overindulgence of the Parsis in their intimate and emotional attachment with their rites, rituals and beliefs which they deem to the best. The Parsi dislike of cats is made obvious by the novelist, as for instance, when Nariman tells his grandson: "No. No cats. Parsi families never keep cats. They consider them bad luck, because cats hate water, they never take a bath" (*FM* 139). Even though the Parsis harbour a strong disinclination towards cats, they do not kill spiders, and never eat cock's meat: "...you must know that, from the story of Zuhaak the Evil one" (*FM* 162). It is the story of Zuhaak that accounts for the reason why the Parsis do not kill the spider or ate the cock, for "if people ate up all the cocks and killed all the spiders, there would be no one to help us fight all the evil" (*FM* 164), and Nariman attests to it saying that "beliefs are more important than facts" (*FM* 162). Mistry's fiction acts within the framework of religious orthodoxy based on the foundation of a strong personal faith in various rituals of the Zoroastrian religion.

Like any other socially committed novelist, Mistry mixes both the personal stories of individuals and the social stories of contemporary events into the framework of the narrative of the same novel. *Family Matters* is no exception to this, for in it Mistry sets out to document the way in which the Babri Masjid riots had its repercussions on the private lives of the citizens. It explores the covert, yet deep-rooted corruption of political leaders, and how corruption has become both systematic and systemic. As Mistry notes:

> "Corruption is in the air we breathe. This nation specializes in turning honest people in crooks. Right, chief?"
>
> "The answer unfortunately, is yes."
>
> "The country has gone to the dogs. And not well-bred dogs either, but pariahs." (*FM* 31-32)

Corruption coupled with extremist tendencies has persuaded the Parsis and the non-Parsis to think of the possibilities of migration to Western countries. Dislocation and displacement are part and parcel of the Parsi psyche, and to quote V.L.V.N. Narendra Kumar:

> The Parsees prefer the West since it offers unlimited scope for growth and prosperity. Dislocation is part of the Parsee psyche. Exiled twelve hundred years ago, they came to India. Now they are migrating to west in search of greener pasture. Thus there is "double migration" in the case of Parsees. (14)

With a view to improve material prospects, Yezad entertains the idea of emigrating to Canada and the immigration trends can be read as the inability of the Parsis to find a space for themselves in the multicultural fabric of India. Like Yezad, Mr. Rangarajan, a non-Parsi technician who attends on the professor, also thinks of leaving India to some other country in the West, for he strongly condemns the lack of a Mahatma figure in India which boasts of a five-thousand-year-old civilization and a population of nine hundred million people. Instead of Mahatma, what we have now, as Nariman points out, "are micro-mini atmas" (*FM* 54). Yezad's dreams are shattered when he is confronted with the reality that immigration does not provide a solution to his problems, for the life of a Parsi or an Indian in an alien country is miserable and traumatic. He is taken aback at the extreme rudeness of Mr. M.M. Mazobashi, the Immigration Officer, and as Yezad remarks:

> You, sir, are a rude and ignorant man, a disgrace to your office and country. You have sat here abusing us, abusing us, abusing Indians and India, one of the many countries your government drains of its brainpower, the brainpower that is responsible for your growth and prosperity. Instead of having the grace to thanks us, you spew your prejudices and you're bigoted ideas. You, whose people suffered racism and xenophobia in Canada, where they were Canadian citizens, put in camps like prisoners of war you, sir, might be expected, more than anyone else, to understand and embody the more enlightened Canadian ideals of multiculturalism. But if you are anything to go by, then Canada is a gigantic hoax. (*FM* 253)

The arrogant behaviour of the Immigration Officer forces Yezad to retract on his decision to migrate to Canada, for he seems at last to concur with Nariman's observation that "... emigration is an enormous mistake. The biggest anyone can make in their life. The loss of home leaves a hole that never fills" (*FM* 254).

Cast against the post-Babri Masjid era in India, *Family Matters* quite sensitively records the lack of fellow-feelings and fraternal attitude among human beings whether they be Parsis, or Muslims or Hindus. The horrendous and ugly times of the Babri Masjid riots are brought home to the readers through the portrayal of the life of Husain. The events following the demolition of Babri Masjid fanned the flames of communal riots across the country in the early 1990s. Husain is deliberately introduced by the novelist to show how the policy of intolerance followed by the religious communities leads only to chaotic social situations. When the readers come across Husain for the first time, he is undergoing a dark phase in his life, for he has been witness to the traumatic experience of seeing his "whole family burnt in the communal riots. People caught in fanatic religious circles fail to see their fellow beings with a humane outlook, but instead view them as representatives of certain religious or communal groups. As a completely heart-broken and grief-stricken individual, Husain's plight, in fact, urges the readers to ponder over the futility of caste-based and community-based atrocities, and exhorts them to uphold the feeling of unity and oneness among humanity. It is Mr. Kapur who understands the need to be philanthropic and cosmopolitan in his attitude and viewpoint. Though a businessman, Mr. Kapur's humanistic sensibilities extend far beyond his commercial concerns, as is evinced in his appointment of both Parsi and Muslim employees at his shop. But unfortunately, he has to pay a huge price for the liberal views he espoused. Mistry highlights the need to discard fundamentalism in favour of a more tolerant way of life.

As a masterpiece from the pen of Mistry, *Family Matters* is a fine exposition of the eccentricities of the miniscule Parsi, religious community of Bombay in the early 1990s. Mistry is quite sensitive to the issues faced by those on the margins of society such as Nariman whose personal life gets intertwined with the life and times of the society around, and in the process of negotiating his in-betweenness, Nariman's life turns into a tale of struggle to make sense of his selfhood.

WORKS CITED

Kumar, V.L.V.N. *Parsee Novel.* New Delhi: Prestige Books, 2002. Print.

Mistry, Rohinton. *Family Matters.* London: Faber & Faber, 2002. Print.

20

Bharati Mukherjee's Dimple: Exiled Sita?

Gharge Sunita Sunil

Writers like V.S. Naipaul, Salman Rushdie, Kamala Markandaya, Bharati Mukherjee, Vikram Seth, Rohinton Mistry, Amitav Ghosh, Jhumpa Lahiri, Chitra Banerjee, Meena Alexander, Kiran Desai, Aravind Adiga, etc. have enriched the Indian English fiction. They all share the Diaspora consciousness. It is the state of mind and a particular kind of consciousness that generated among the transnational communities (Vertovec). Alienation, nostalgia, dual nature/duality/double consciousness are the indicators of diaspora consciousness. They identify themselves with historical heritage, culture, language and literature of homeland and their new society.

Bharati Mukherjee is one of the Indian diaspora novelists who live with many 'selves'. She is Indian, American, Indo-American, Indian diaspora in USA, and even Canadian. She claims to be American, doesn't like hyphenated identity, and to be called post-colonial. She says "I'm American" of Indian origin (American Dreamer). Her dilemma can be stated as simply—she cannot be both Indian and American; she can be either Indian or American, even when she remains only Indian or American, she is both Indian and American. An activist of civil rights, educator, an author of highly praised eight novels, two collections of short stories and non-fiction works, Mukherjee utilizes her personal experiences in crossing the cultural boundaries.

Her work labels her as the 'grand dame' of Indian Diaspora fiction, mainstream American writer, Third World writer, North American writer, expatriate writer, immigrant writer, Canadian writer, post-colonial writer, transnational writer and the writer of the world like Rushdie. Her work displays her Indian sensibility/immigrant sensibility, the impact of her mother country and its culture. *The Tiger's Daughter* (1971), *Wild* (1975), and the stories of *Darkness* (1985) are expatriate works. Her Canadian aloofness of expatriation reflects in these works. *The Middleman and Other Stories* (1988), *Jasmine* (1989) are immigrant while *The Holder of the World* (1993) and *Leave it to Me* (1997) indicate the transnational phase of Mukherjee's life. Her trilogy consists of *Desirable Daughters* (2002), *The Tree Bride* (2204) and *Miss New India* (2011). These eight novels and two collections of short stories are the markers of Mukherjee's own phases of expatriation, immigration and transnational. In her trilogy, she looks back in the mirror of her past, it is her repatriation.

Mukherjee is Hindu-Brahmin Bengali, Indian upper-class elite by origin, American by migration and naturalized citizen, and Canadian by marriage. She is American not only because she lives in America but her works present and enrich our understanding of plurality of American identities as an exile, expatriate, immigrants and transnational.

Wife, her second novel, is shaped out of a question asked by a visiting Columbia Professor of history, Leonard Gordob, to Mukherjee in Calcutta during her sabbatical year 1973-74—"what do Bengali girls do, between ages of eighteen and twenty one?" (Blaise and Mukherjee, *Days and Nights* 220). Mukherjee's response is her *Wife* which is dedicated to Leonard Gordon. It is the tradition of India that the grown-up daughters have to be married (un)willingly. In her non-fictional work *Days and Nights in Calcutta* (1977), she states about her own trouble, it is—even in India with its woman Prime Minister, women in politics, medicine, law, journalism and labour union, "the average woman molded her life not on their modern example (Mrs. Indira Gandhi, the then P.M. of India) but on Sita and Savitri of ancient Hindu literature. The stories of Sita and Savitri were kept alive by oral tradition" (Blaise and Mukherjee, *Days and Nights* 231). Mukherjee tells a tale of Lord Ram and Sita for her Western readers in this non-fictional work.

Wife (1975) shows her Indian sensibility and the impact of her origin. *Wife* is a tale of exiled (?) Dimple Dasgupta. She is, initially in the novel, a young unmarried girl, waiting for marriage. Marriage according to her will provide her freedom and love. Dream girl Dimple desires—a Neurosurgeon, her would-be-husband. Novel begins with "Dimple Dasgupta had set her heart on marrying a neurosurgeon, but her father was looking for engineers in the matrimonial ads" (Mukherjee, *Wife* 3). Twenty-year-old Dimple waiting for marriage, is worried as the days/weeks/months pass in waiting. It makes her sick and is admitted in the hospital where she dreams. "She became Sita, the ideal wife of Hindu legends who had walked through fire at her husband's request" (4). Being Indian she does like to be an ideal wife like Sita from *Ramayana*. Sita, the wife of Lord Ram, is the model for her. Sita is the epitome of female purity and virtue. She follows her husband in exile and is abducted by Ravan. She is released by her husband, but she has to admit I submit herself into 'Agnipariksha' and despite 'Agnipariksha' the rumors make Ram to exile her second time. Upon their reunion she calls her mother (Earth) to accept her. She doesn't follow her husband—Ram.

Ramayana portrays the ideal characters like—ideal lither, ideal servant, ideal brother, ideal king and ideal wife. The ideal royal couple, Ram and Sita, is the age-old model for Indians. It is the cultural consciousness of Indians. As an Indian Dimple expects herself to be Sita, an ideal wife. So she doesn't dream of love but role of an ideal wife "a good wife, a docile wife..." (9).

After all Dimple's father has found Amit Basu, a suitable boy for Dimple. He is an engineer. She is Indian in her values, so she accepts the traditional marriage proposal, which she thinks "would bring her freedom, cocktail parties on carpet lawn, fun-raising dinners for noble charities...love" (3). She marries Amit but feels "as someone going into exile" (15). She tries to change herself and accepts—"marriage teaches the virtues of sacrifice, responsibility and patience and wife has obligations to the husband" (27). She has been trained to please. Amit, her husband al so "expected her, like Sita, to Jump into fire if necessary" (2).

Bharati Mukherjee doesn't like women around her, in 1973-74's India, to follow Sita and Savitri. She portrays Dimple as pulled and pushed by the Indian values. Dimple ruthlessly aborts her baby for migration. "She did not want to carry any relics from her old life" (42). They migrate to America for better life/job/economic progress, where at first they live with Mr. and Mrs. Sen then in the Mookherji's flat where Dimple wants to turn American like Leni, Milt and Ina Mullick, her new friends. In Sens' apartment, she has seen "a framed batik wall hanging: king Ram & his court...a bonfire and a short, voluptuous Sita hip-deep in pale orange flames..." (53). Dimple doesn't trust Amit, who appears shabby in America, "seemed unreal to her" (97). His jobless, so Dimple "was bitter that marriage had betrayed her, had not provided all the glittery things she had imagined...a man without a job wasn't a man at all" (102). She is changed, transformed in America, "kept seeing herself through Ina's eyes" (103).

The final part tells about her psychosis which is grown out of the pull and push of Indian and American values. She is totally confused in the new world. "She ranked her husband, blender color TV, cassette tape recorder, stereo..." (113). He is not more than an electronic object for her who doesn't provide her fantasy but small material comforts.

The outer world is dead for her "she had not seen or done anything since coming to the States except sleep and cook" (114). She couldn't live with people who don't understand about Durga Puja, she is caught into inertia, exhaustion endless indecisiveness. She thinks of different ways of committing suicide. "Love is dead" (116). She is alien to herself. Her loneliness in migration is the basic reason of it. Loneliness is grown out of her incapability to assimilate into the new world and culture. It is due to language problem. But she is tempted by American value. She involves in Milt Glasser. So she thinks now "If fate had assigned her not Amit but some other engineer, she might have been a very different kind of person" (126). As an Indian how could she imagine the 'other' in place of her husband? Once she desired to be an ideal wife like Sita. Now she wishes someone other than Amit as her spouse. It is Mukherjee's stance to display the change in Dimple. Amit can't feed her reveries. She turns to T.V. as her only friend. She can't keep up with the people like Ina, Leni, Milt. She just likes to watch T.V.

Milt makes her feel American "he was, to her, America" (174). She likes Milt Glasser (191) with whom she can talk about all sorts of things. He is different from Amit. She now thinks of killing Amit. Amit has no idea how close she has come to betraying him. She has seduced Milt. Eventually, Dimple murders Amit—"She brought her right hand up and with the knife stabbed the magical circle once, twice, seven times. Then he saw the head fall off" (212).

To the Hindu girl-child Sita is an exemplary figure. The lesson is "The wife's role is one of self-abnegation" (232). Sita's loyalty is tested by the blandishment of the evil king Ravan, by the ignorance and cynicism of the subjects of Ayodhaya and by unimaginative nature of Ram's devotion to his people. But Sita never hesitates or questions. The story of Savitri also tells that it is a wife's duty to follow her husband no matter what the destination is. Savitri's wifely devotion made Yama, the God of Death, to revive Satyavan, to restore him to Savitri. Mukherjee observes, in the words of Pramila Venkateswaran, "The women hold one common value: serving the husband as the primary duty of the good Indian wife" (Nelson 29). Indian woman equates her husband with God, who provides identity. Marriage and motherhood are still seen as a woman's ideals in India.

Mukherjee has heard and enacted these stories in her childhood and played the role of Satyavan. Mukherjee, after migration, is against all these odd matters of her tradition in which women are born to suffer. Women are taught to cover their heads in the presence of older men and speak softly and never look boldly into their eyes. Women have to go through all the pain of labour and then the child carries the name of the father. To be a widow in Hindu-India is to lose all social status. Bharati praised the woman like Bitto, a widow but loved another man instead of worshiping the memory of the dead husband. That is the real transgression to have new life with new pattern. But villagers killed both of them—Bitto and her lover. "Mukherjee chooses to wed the Hindu imagination to the American" (Nelson 41). So, Mukherjee draws the portrait of Dimple, an Indian who is exiled like Sita, in USA by following her husband but is caught into two cultures and unable to escape from it. But she turns bold enough to murder her husband instead of committing suicide. She rebels against the stereotype role of a wife in India. Mukherjee doesn't like to follow tradition blindly. She makes Dimple to pose the questions like—am I happy? If not, achieve it. Her happiness is in self-assertion, for which Dimple has taken a step forward. But she is neither an ideal happy Indian nor American enjoying the freedom and individualism. America makes her aware of self-assertion but does not provide the correct path to travel. In this course of self-assertion, she is alienated.

In the words of Fakrul Alam, the major theme of *Wife* is "The plight of an Indian wife torn between the need to play the role society expects of her and her need for self-expression..." (Alam 37). Dimple likes to be an ideal wife/devotional wife like Sita, the model of innocence, purity, devotion, chastity, who follows the husband. But her migration turns her into a psychotic by double oppression, being a woman and an expatriate. She feels the pains of oppression but is not clever enough to make sense out of situation and break out. She breaks out in her psychosis. She loses her identity, an ideal Hindu wife. Her only available outlet was suicide, but in America she is transformed into an Indian expatriate in America.

She murders her husband. Bharati calls it "misguided act of self-assertion...misguided Americanization" (Edwards 24) and calls it "a wounding novel" (Mukherjee, *Days and Nights in Calcutta* 268). The duality of her mind, as an Indian and American, makes her swing between two extremes—collective and individual, the opposite cultures. Mukherjee wants to present her Sita a bold instead of a submissive, docile, ideal Hindu Bengali wife like Sita in *Ramayana*.

WORKS CITED

Alam, Fakrul. *Bharati Mukherjee*. New York: Twayne Publishers, 1996. Print.

Blaise, Clark and Bharati Mukherjee. *Days and Nights in Calcutta*. Minnesota: Doubleday & Co., 1977. Print.

Edwards, Bradley C. *Conversations with Bharati Mukherjee*. University Press of Mississippi, 2009. Print.

Mukherjee, Bharati. *Wife*. Boston: Houghton Mifflin, 1975 (First Edition). New Delhi: Penguin Books (India), 1987 and 1990. Print.

Nelson, Emmanuel S. ed. *Bharati Mukherjee: Critical Perspectives*. New York: Garland Publishing INC, 1993. Print.

Vertovec, Steven. "Conceiving and Researching Transnationalism" in *Ethnic and Racial Studies*, Vol. 22, No. 2, 1999. Web.

21

Basavaraj Naikar's *Light in the House*: A Hagiographical Novel

Meenakshi Sundaram

Light in the House is a commendable effort by the author to document the scattered and uncollected events of the saint's life.

Basavaraj Naikar's book *Light in the House* is a hagiographic account of the life of one such saint. It details the life of Sharif Saheb of Shishunala (1819-89), a saint poet of the stature of Kabir, born to Imam Saheb and his wife Hajjuma of Karnataka, by the grace of Hazaresha Khadari, whose shrine the childless couple visited with the greatest purity of heart and devotion of mind. Despite his Muslim antecedence, the boy Sharif began to take interest in Hindu scriptures from a tender age and mastered the mystic literature of Virasaivism and the Saranas. The book traces the gradual development of the saint from his childhood, through adolescence to a final period of mature wisdom. In all these stages, the saint exhibits a consistency, comprehending all but inkling particularly towards none. His receptor was the revered Govindabhatta, who took an instant liking to the boy despite stiff opposition from his other Hindu disciples. With the passage of time, the two, the preceptor and the disciple became inseparable. Modern prejudices need not be deterrent to the understanding of hagiography, which is fundamentally different from either history or biography. In the study of the mortal life of a saint, it is not the life of a saint that is of particular interest to succeeding generations, rather it is the ability of the saintly mind to transcend religion, which elevates him in the common man's view. Sharif Saheb's sainthood lies, not in the fact that he was a Muslim, who embraced the Saiva faith, rather it lies in the fact that he transcended religion towering over it like a Titan. *Light in the House* is a commendable effort by the author to document the scattered and uncollected events of the saint's life. Sharif Saheb exhibit equanimity of mind which is illustrative of the fact that he believed in the fundamental unity of all things. This is apparent in almost all his words throughout the text, which reflect one worldview made up of several complementary ideas pertaining to several major philosophies. Only the highest mind could have possessed such a comprehensive view of human condition, while lesser mortals view the world in parts. Sharif Saheb viewed the world in its entirety. Existence for him was not confined to isolated philosophies; his religion was a higher one, the religion of humanity. It is precisely this catholicity of view, which places him in the corridors of the greatest.

Sharif Saheb as he came to be called became a wandering minstrel, as itinerant singer, singing of karma, Omkara and Sunya. His secular bent of mind adheres to no particular philosophy but revels in their fundamental unity. His songs remind one of the Tiruvachagam or the sacred utterances of the great Tamil poet and seer Manikka Vachagar whose songs are an illustration of the great south Indian system of religion and philosophy called the *Saiva Siddhantam*. Medieval Indian Literature is best presented by the ecstatic verses of the Sufi saints and the saints of the Bhakti Movement. Stalwarts of this movement like Kabir and Nanak shunned caste-ism, religious intolerance and the accompanying evils and effected a harmonious bridge between the erstwhile warring groups.

Kabir among other was the best blend of the Sufi and the Bhakti strains as is reflected in his verses. Sharif Saheb's songs, like the verses of the saints of those great movements are an effusion of the best and highest philosophies of the time, their transmission coming straight from his heart to the hearts of the listeners. There is nothing sectarian in these songs which stir up the divine within the listener, elevating his heart to a rare degree of purity:

> This is the song of meditation
> On Gurugovinda.
> This is the song of Omkara Pranava.
> This is the song of the Lord
> Of Shishunala.
> This is the song that dispels
> The vices away from you. (*LH* 45)

It was Sharif Saheb's conviction that any action done in the name of Allah and Allama was *namaz* and to this effect he sang:

> Let us get the sheep of karma butchered
> Chant the guru's *mantra* and boil it.
> Let us take the consecrated food of awareness
> To the mosque wherein resides the lord.
> Let us climb the big stairs there
> To the mosque of knowledge divine
> Wherein resides the Lord of Shishunala. (*LH* 63)

Sharif Saheb was always accompanied by a disciple by the name of Basappa, who belonged to the community of potters. The reference to Basappa and the community of potters may not be accidental, for the twelfth century saw an active movement initiated by a Brahmin called Basaveswara, who called for a revolt against the hegemony of Brahmins, despite being a Brahmin himself.

Light in the House is a melting pot of several faiths, a dexterous blend of the Islamic, Saivite and Buddhist ideas. Govindabhatta, the preceptor puts a question to the young Sharif about his father which elicits the response:

> A soul is born countless times and at each birth it has a father. Thus a man has several fathers. I therefore wish to know which of these fathers you refer to. Do you want to know my physical father or spiritual father? (*LH* 37)

Sharif continues in the same vein:

> The physical father gives us birth and brings us into the world of mortality and bondage, whereas the spiritual father enlightens our soul, releases us from attachment to the mortal life and gives us spiritual liberation. (*LH* 37)

According to the Saiva theory, all existence is transformational, and Siva is ever ready to retrieve souls from the bondage of matter. Sharif Saheb was a non-dualist in his philosophy and it is a fact well worth noting that non-dualism merely means that the divine element is so pervasive that it cannot be differentiated from the world. Non-dualism does not necessarily imply oneness, rather it means inseparability. The subtle difference between oneness and his mother regarding the nature of his relationship to Govindabhatta:

> I am the wife, this is my husband. Our souls are married spiritually. (*LH* 107)

While Sharif Saheb does not deny the misery of the human condition he affirms the idea that slipping down into the mortal world, meaning giving into the baser self is relatively easy, but hoisting oneself up again is possible only when one has the right values in life and when one craves for divine grace:

> But Shiva is full of grace and is waiting through successive aeons to receive the recognition of the soul and his adoring lovers. A personal tie binds the soul to God. The grace of God is the road to freedom. It demands childlike trust in Shiva.

Sharif cannot bear separation from his Govinda Gurunatha. On his part the guru too craves the company of his disciple. The bond between them is inexplicable to their own-selves and bewildering to others. Sharif is so immersed in the devoted service of his guru that he has no thoughts of anything else. The light of knowledge that he is in quest of is to be found only in the sanctuary offered to him by his guru. He tells his mother:

> I shall therefore go into his spiritual gymnasium where I shall burn to ashes the taint of mortality and live in

> the service of Lord Shiva. I shall follow that path from which there is no return. (*LH* 54)

In his well-known work, *The Dance of Shiva,* Ananda Coomaraswamy says:

> Where and what is the burning ground? It is not the place where our earthly bodies are cremated, but the hearts of his lovers, laid waste and desolate. The place where the ego is destroyed signifies the state where illusion and deeds are burnt away; that his crematorium, the burning ground where Sri Nataraja dances, and where he is named Sudalaiyadi, Dancer of the burning ground.

Shiva is the supreme reality in Shiva thought, the beginningless, causeless, flawless Doer and Knower of all things, freeing individual souls from the sea of bondage. Shiva is Sacchidananda, embodying the eight attributes of self-existence. Shakti is his instrumental cause and he operates through her. The *Saundarya Lahari* or the *Waves of Beauty,* a famous literary work in Sanskrit, is traditionally ascribed to Adi Shankaracharya. Part I of *Saundarya Lahari* begins with the affirmation:

> *Shaiva Shaktya yukto yadi bhavati shakta prabhavitam na chedevam devo na khalu kushalaha spanditumapi.* (Shiva is enabled to create only when he is united with Shakti; without her, he cannot move an inch. (Translation mine)

This metaphor runs throughout the powerful statements made by the saint in all his daily transactions. Another equally powerful metaphor which occurs consistently in Sharif Saheb's words is that of the body as a temple of the Living God. This view is subscribed to by almost all the major religions of the world.

Shiva is often referred to as Pasupati, a name of Rudra-Shiva in the *Atharvaveda* meaning the Lord of Cattle. The name has also been interpreted as the 'Lord of Creatures'. He is the lord of numberless soul who are like cattle. He is the potter, the individual soul, his clay. Notwithstanding the Saiva element, Sharif Saheb's simple statements have an inextricable train of Buddhist thought embedded in it, although he does not profess to be a Buddhist. This precisely is the charm of this unassuming and endearing saint. He professes no single faith, yet he spouts the best ideas of all. Although Saivism was in many ways opposed to Buddhism, there are several points of similarity between the basic ideas of Hinduism and the Buddhist stand. Both strive for salvation of the individual, which results in the cessation of the cycle of innumerable births and deaths, the difference being that Hinduism talks of the expansion of the self to its fullest degree and Buddhism believes in the complete dissolution of the self. This is the Buddhist theory of Anatta or non-self. In Hindu thought, the expansion of the self to the fullest degree ends in its final union with the universal-self. In the Buddhist theory, there is no expansion to its fullest height, rather there is a contraction of the self to its lowest degree wherein dissolution and non-existence become possible. This is *nirvana*. This idea is reflected in Govindabhatta's words, "One should abolish the 'I'..." (*LH* 155). A considerable portion of the text is tempered with Buddhist thought. Paradoxical though it may sound, in the Buddhist way of life, one rather strives to shrink and in that shrinking lies the reward of being freed from the endless tangle of births and deaths. Rather than the idea of becoming fulfilled, there is in Buddhism the idea of emptying, in place of merging, there is the idea of withdrawing to a level where one becomes conscious only of emptiness, the *Shunya* referred to in Sharif Saheb's song (*LH* 45). Becoming one with the great emptiness simply means that the imprints and impressions of earlier states of existence which the Hindus call *samskaras* and which the Buddha referred to as *sankharas,* have been wiped out sufficiently to result in a cessation, a *nirvana*. Anatta is, thus, the Buddhist theory of non-self a negation of the idea of self.

This draining oneself of the idea of self, the complete emptying is captured beautifully in the book. Sharif Saheb's preceptor, Govindabhatta is nearing his end, meaning the end of his mortal existence and undergoes an agitated spell of vomiting. Sharif Saheb refers to this as the guru's *prasada* and gratefully cups his palms to receive it. Seeing that none of the other disciples wish to have anything to do with the disgusting stuff, Govindabhatta weakly tells Sharif to throw it away in a place which nobody treads:

> "Which is the place which nobody treads? Where shall I throw this phlegm on the earth, into the water or into the sky? Even if I threw it into one of these places, it is trod by some human beings or birds or worms or beasts, which might be the place, which is not trod by anybody? O now I understand. Now I understand. My spiritual father has granted me everything. I shall throw it into a place where nobody can desecrate it." Then Sharif Saheb suddenly quaffed it. (*LH* 156)

One longstanding argument against the Buddhist theory of Anatta or non-self has been that if Buddha's silence on the question of self is to be understood as there being no self, what or who can be said to experience the *karma* and what or who takes rebirth? Herein lies the solution to the riddle by Buddha's thought. The self in Buddhist thought is an error of human judgment, a superimposition by the conscious, thinking mind of something which has no substance. It is a vanity which leads to the forging of inextricable bonds. What is true is that in the course of a series of births and deaths, all that is residual is merely an amalgam of impressions which contracts itself and frees itself from all bonds and having fully reduced itself to a point where it has no attachments and no affinities, not even the consciousness of a name or a form annihilates itself. It is an expression of this philosophy that Naikar brings out in Sharif's words, "my soul defies any kind of naming" (*LH* 129).

Existence in both Hinduism and Buddhism is transformational. The scene of Sharif's own exit from the world is strongly reminiscent of the Buddha's *Mahaparinirvana* or the great passing. Sharif Saheb tells his disciples: "You have a big bundle with you. Please give it away to me" (*LH* 166).

In his discourse known as '*Bhara Sutta*' meaning burden, Buddha spoke of the five aggregates, namely form, meaning, perception, fabrication and consciousness which were burdens carried by human beings: "A burden indeed are the five aggregates and the carrier of the burden is the person. Taking up the burden in the world is stressful. Casting off the burden is bliss" (*Bhara Sutta*). Sharif's warning to a young man called Fakirappa who desires to enjoy the pleasures of worldly life reflect the Buddhist thought and the Buddha's concept of life as all or sorrow:

> Then note down, young man. After marriage, you will have four daughters totally. When the first daughter attains sixteen years of age, you will marry her off to a young man of Malligavada village. She will fall a prey to evil habits. She will commit suicide on a New Moon Day and bring you deep sorrow. You will marry off your second daughter to a man in Rottigavada village. She also will go astray and bring deep sorrow to you. The other two daughters will be born blind in course of time and have your leg broken and suffer limitlessly. Finally you will die of starvation. This is the chart of your further life. Now tell me, young man, do you want to get married even after knowing your future? (*LH* 149)

Naikar's book offers food for thought. Written in the form of a novel, this hagiographic work avoids any intellectual discussion of philosophy. Although it is a serious and scholarly study, yet the text is streamlined to cater to the lay individual. The working of miracles by the saint takes on the garb of a highly intuitive mind in constant communion with the powers that be. Added to this is the rare charm of the saint's songs which makes the work extremely readable and a rewarding experience. It is an effort to shape the record of the past keeping in mind contemporary goals. The past thus offers a hope to the turbulence of the present. Legends pertaining to saint's function as established paradigms for human behaviour in the present time. The idea of universal brotherhood, so central to human peace and prosperity is not such a distant thought after all if one would only look within and adopt an attitude of self-abnegation. In this age of dissonance and discord, the book opens a fresh pathway for time seekers after knowledge. Simplicity, clarity, symbolism and allegory jostle with one another in Naikar's work. *Light in the House* has an edge over other works of this genre in that it is an effort to promote the higher values of life. Unlike other authors of Western, hagiographic writings who have at times felt the need to tactfully alter the past in order to accommodate an established contemporary view, Naikar's book is an objective description of a saint without the embroilment of ideologies. Nowhere does it appear that the past has been constructed, in fact the text has very little to do with the particular historical period it deals with. Just as the saint has transcended religion, the text has transcended the temporal. Naikar has winnowed the grain from the accompanying chaff and presented only the salient, meticulously doing away with all that is superfluous. Sharif Saheb is a unified presence in a divided world.

The book is also a reflection of the Jain theory of Anekantawada. Anekantawada comes from the root word Anaya, which means that a particular statement is made from a particular position and so it cannot be exhaustive. This theory, applied to *Light in the House* has several important implications.

WORKS CITED

Bhara Sutta: The Burden (SN), Trans. from the Pali by Thanissaro Bhikkhu. Access to Insight June 8, 2010. http//www.accesstoinsight.org

Coomaraswamy, Ananda. *The Dance of Shiva.* New York: Sunwise Turn Inc., 1918: 61.

Mishra, Prabhu Dayal. *Soundaryalahari: Tantra-Drishti Aur Soundarya-Srishti.* Varanasi: Vishvavidyalaya Prakashan, 2007: 1.

Naikar, Basavaraj. *Light in the House.* Delhi: Authors Press, 2009: 168 (abbreviated as *LH*).

Radhakrishnan, S. *Indian Philosophy.* New York: Macmillan, 1930: 728.

22

Womanism and Alice Walker's *The Color Purple*

Nidhi Arora

> And I wanted to explore the relationship between men and women and why women are always condemned for doing what men do as an expression of their masculinity. Why are women so easily tramps and traitors when men are heroes for engaging in the same activity? Why do women stand for this? (Alice Walker)

Such deep penetrating thoughts really troubled Alice Walker during her portrayal of victimized women characters in her fiction. By raising the issue of violence against women in the African-American society, Alice Walker has tried to gain the foreground in American Fiction. In her novels, she has projected her women as victim to fully responsible protagonists. In spite of being badly treated by men, her women try to assert their status in society. Violence though is a negative term, yet it helps Walker's women to think positive about themselves.

Historically, African-American literature started with slavery; along with slavery came humiliations and tortures, which led the frustration among black men. They wanted to turn against whites but were failed since whites were the masters and blacks were the slaves. However, black men found their black women as soft targets to release their frustration and started taking out their frustration upon black women. Thus, black women had to live a traumatized life not within the four-walls of home but socially, where they had been living in white's land also treated as an object for sexual gratification.

Though later Feminist Movement made them aware about themselves, yet American and African-American fiction had till 19th century, assigned only stereotyped roles to the black women. In American-Fictional world, black women appeared as mammies who were strong, fat, nurturing and uncomplaining. The Harlem Renaissance, which began around 1920s, brought a considerable change in attitude towards black women and their characters in literature. The image of tragic mulattoes no longer dominated and was replaced by a diversity of physical and psychological types. Though black male writers like Ralph Ellison, James Baldwin and Richard Wright tried to project the real character of black women, yet they were unable to do justice with the same.

Female African-American writers added a new chapter to the delineation of black women in literature. Black women writers like June Jordan, Maya Angelou, Alice Walker, Toni Morrison began to project the intensity, complexity and diversity of the experience of black women. The focus here shifted to black women as individuals, struggling towards their freedom and selfhood.

Whereas Maya Angelou exposes the black women's position within the family and mentions the impact of rape on a young black girl and also talks about inter-racial marriages, Tony Morrison presents the trauma of black women's life. She universalizes the oppression where blacks torment blacks, whites oppress blacks, and women are against women, etc. The picture of black women's life that emerges from her novel is indeed harrowing. "Bluest-Eye" is a story of a young girl Pecola, whose inability to understand or adjust to the ways of the world around her and the consequences thereof. Her own family being full of quarrel and violence, the child seeks and gets love from prostitutes. *Sula*, another novel appears to criticize the feminist doctrine of unconditional freedom. The theme of universal operation is re-iterated in *Song of Solomon*. In *Tar*

Baby, Morrison has effectively shown the relationship between the genders, has reached an impasse. The novel also denounces the possibility of a white and black cultural amalgamation. In *Beloved*, Morrison turns back to the history of slavery. Here, she delineates the psychological and emotional effect of slavery. In *Jazz,* Jazz music represents an original African-American response to the need of community cohesion.

Though Toni Morrison, in her novels, has explored various possibilities for African-Americans, yet the fabrics of her texts do not show any radical solution to the multiple problems of the blacks. On the other hand, Alice Walker not only has given a voice to the violence against women but also made them winner in the battle against violence. She has given strength of womanism to her women to make them strong emotionally as well as intellectually.

Alice Walker made the black woman struggle her primary concern and it has her special identifying mark. The motivation behind this seems to be a craving for same personal identification. In her interview with John O'Brien, she says, "I believe in listening...to a person, the wind, the trees, but especially to say black women whose rocky road I am still travelling."[1] She shares their burden of oppression and their empathy, which is evident in all her writings. As Dobash, R.E. and Dobash, R. said, "The problem lies in the domination of women the answer lies in the struggle against it."[2]

Alice Walker first presents her women as victims of violence, then they try to assert their status in society and finally they get victory over violence. This is a speciality of Walker's novels. Towards the end her women realize the need of self and of the identification with the present American society. What particularly distinguishes Walker in her role as a chronicler for black women; that is, she sees the experiences of black women as a series of movements from the men in their lives to the growing developing women whose consciousness allow them to have control over their lives.

Walker creates a fiction wherein oppressed black women can experience self-recoveries and victory over violence without a dialectical process without political efforts, without radical change in society. Greatly influenced by the political events of the sixties and the changes resulting from the Freedom Movement, Walker's characters are coming just to the edge of a new awareness. Alice Walker herself is a real-life prototype of the emergent black women.

During 1960s, the feminist movement emerged as the resistant against the dominant patriarchal system. Women discovered that they were forced to bear a secondary status to men in every occupation. The goal of feminism, according to Faye Powell, "became to eliminate, sexist oppression imposed by patriarchal society...and discriminations against women on the job, in the home and in all areas of women's lives".[3]

From this feminism comes the awakening in black women section also. They realized that being a victim of differences based on race and gender they have been suppressed for an interminable time. Black women now try to give a voice to these long-silenced women and trying to prove its legitimacy in a world which determines their status by their blackness and womanhood. Since the late sixties, black women writers have written, as political gesture, trying to prove their individuality in a society that considers them non-existent. They raised their voices against this injustice; they are now in a position to change all the misconceptions, and confusions regarding the black women. These writers deny the image of black women as portrayed by a white female writers and black male writers. They have brought a personalized knowledge of their own life and experiences into literature.

Walker prefers womanism to feminism because it sounds stronger and more exclusive. Womanism is more emphatic in the case of black women writers than feminists, who are mainly interested in the rights of individual women. Many black women writers, lesbians and non-lesbians, project lesbian relationship as a sensitive bond between two women, who have been deprived of love and have been physically misused by men. Most of the black women writers like Alice Walker, welcome these lesbian visions in her writings and in her definition of womanism, which she coins to express the distinctive black and female experiences. She refuses to accept the label of feminist since it is "tabooed and invested...with negative stigmata".[4]

Since Walker has given that word womanism to show the spirit of black women against injustice, thus, to understand Walker's point of view, the term womanism needs to be discussed. Walker defines the term womanism in various ways. The word womanist derives; "From womanish" (opposite of girlish, i.e. frivolous, irresponsible, not serious) and it means "A black feminist of color...usually referring to outrageous, audacious, courageous or willful behavior responsible in change."[5]

According to the interpretations, a womanist dares to do what a feminist would not even think of, since she has the requisite qualities of being outrageous, audacious, courageous and willful. Walker gives yet another definition of womanism:

> A woman who loves other women, sexually and/or non-sexually appreciates and prefers women's culture, women's emotional flexibilities...and women's strength... sometimes loves individual man, sexually and/or non-sexually committed to survival and wholeness of entire people, male and female.... Traditionally universal,... Traditionally capable.[6]

The black women's intrinsic strength makes them graciously accept the friendship of males. It advocates a female bonding, however, at the same time, this opens to form a relationship with males on equal terms. Since it encompasses both male and female, womanist is universal in its concerns. The other distinctive quality of womanist is that it is traditionally capable. Alice Walker says in an interview with David Bradley, "My tradition assumes I'm capable...."[7] In the same interview, Walker specifies the need for a different work, "One that is organic that really comes out of the culture, that really expresses the spirit, that we see in black women it is just womanism."[8]

Walker's yet another definition of womanist describes the black women perfectly. A black womanist "Loves music...loves dance, loves the moon. Loves the spirit, loves love and food and roundness. Loves struggle. Loves the folk. Loves herself. Regardless."[9] Walker's women took all these lessons as a strength which makes these women, a fighter and the winner.

Almost all of Walker's female characters come to womanism after such catastrophic events and finally become winners. Walker's women are docile but not absolutely helpless. To aid the black women in their struggle for survival, the black women writers need to discover a matriarchal matrilineal link with their past, their racial female ancestors. The black women draw strength from the foremothers and form a nexus with their tradition. Alice Walker finds the literary and non-literary foremothers, right down to their own literal mothers, are a source of strength and nourishment.

Walker herself realized the gift of the past when she became a writer and the stories she had absorbed from her mother flowed from her pen. The historical legacy of creativity inherited from the foremothers has to be expressed in some way because it becomes the duty of black women to give the proper due and recognition to their matrilineal heritage. This is what Alice Walker has termed as sisterhood.

The black women struggle to live and as Claudia Tate points out Walker, "She ways the struggle with self-confidence, with courage and conviction and her principle strategy is herself conscious affirmation of black womanhood."[10] Walker's novels bear testimony to the black women's self-affirmations.

Although Walker's women are full of human failings and weaknesses, yet what is striking is their striving for a dignified survival against all injustices and odds. The social conditions prevent them from extricating themselves out of the impossible situation. Walker's early women are helpless and give in, but not the new women, who are aware of themselves as their changed social environment. The strength gives them the impetus need to survive. Bettye Parker Smith writes about Walker's women, "The distinctive feature of these women is that tremendous quality with which they carry their sufferings."[11]

Gradually, black women have realized that for all their fighting and disagreements, the black men are able to get along, very well together. As Bettye Parker Smith points out black men: "Their ability to enjoy and maintain a unity is element of beauty in their strength."[12] Such togetherness among women can lead extra help in strengthening the women individually and collectively. Walker's women learn this gradually when they find that there is no apparent reason for the distrust they have for each other. Barbara Christian applauds women's insight, "Women however see the possibility of empowerment for black women if they create a community of sisters that can alter present-day unnatural definitions of women and men."[13]

Walker suggests through her novels that once women adopt the step against injustice men will automatically follow them. Walker opines that female protagonists establish cordial and friendly relationship with men and everything else even with nature. The relationship between the men and women is initially very turbulent. The men following the old system of patriarchal values are not able to understand the free spirit of the black women. They are not able to accept the women in any other role. It is only after that, men accept and understand womanist ideals, giving enough space to the women for growth that they are able to form a relationship with the women in equal terms.

II

The Color Purple, Alice Walker's prize-winning novel is a vivid account of womanism. Though the novel begins on a note of passive submission by Celie, Alice Walker makes sure to end it on a positive note. However, the liberation comes only after the great struggle and her sister's strength and wisdom, Walker successfully brings out the fact that the black women seem to find no way of men's behavioral pattern, which is violent and undignified. She strongly believes that refinement can come only through self-education. Women are particularly the victims of inhuman male domination. The scenario can change only through the indomitable will of the black women. In *The Color Purple*, Celie comes out of the seemingly universal patriarchal condition through her self-education, which is different from literacy.

Celie is victor in *The Color Purple*, on the other hand, it is more impressive because Celie has won against the flesh and blood representatives of patriarchy, i.e. people like stepfather and her husband. Besides, Celie is not alone in her struggle, as Shug Avery a fellow sufferer and whole community of women are helping her tremendously. What puts the novel in a class of its own is that the story has been told by Celie in her own inimitable language. Alice Walker has specially used the epistolary form to provide the necessary outlet to a young traumatized girl's suppressed feelings and creativity.

Many women in the course of the novel, tell Celie to fight for herself. Her sister Nettie tells her "You got to fight". Even Mr__'s sister Kate tells her "You got fight them, Celie" Mr__'s ill-treatment of Celie makes Nettie said, "you ought to bash Mr__ head open". In spite of all these advices, Celie is scared, not because she cannot do it but because she does not know how to go about it. This has to be taught to the virgin Celie and she is shown all this by Shug the bad woman. Ironically, the tramp-Shug teaches Celie how to regain her self-respect and self-love.

Celie's husband thinks of the ill-treatment and cruelty meted out to the women as the normal fate of women. No male comes forward to help Celie rather her silence makes the men passive oppressors. It is only because of the woman, who comes forward, first singly and then collectively that Celie's change of fortune is possible.

Alice Walker's message seems to be clear enough i.e. until women come forward to help their own sex, they cannot get out of the self they are forced in. Like Alice Walker's other women, Celie has the capacity, the patience, to endure. She is the winner towards the end. This is mainly possible because of the inherent strength and resiliency that she possesses. However, the act, which completely makes Celie winner, is Shug's standing up for her against Mr__. Gradually, Celie learns that there is more to her than being just a drudge or a slave. Shug and Celie meet when their morale is at its lowest. Celie is trapped in a loveless marriage and Shug comes to the town after an unsuccessful singing tour and is seriously ill. The care that Celie takes of Shug during her illness is amply repaid by Shug when she nurtures Celie's self-esteem and heals her emotional wounds. Thus, a lifelong bond is established between the two women, which is both physical and emotional.

To become self-possession person, Celie must overcome her sexual revulsion and learn to love her own-self. Once again, Shug helps her by showing her how lovemaking could be a beautifully shared act. Celie learns to love her own body under Shug's careful fuselage. Her recovered self-esteem awakens her lost desires and this in turn, makes Celie aware of the deficiencies in her marriage with Albert. She voices her aches, anguish and anger for her lost innocence and lost year that have been stolen from her by an uncaring brutal male. Rudolph Byrd rightly observes, "Until we can speak in our own voices the doors leading to the self, the world, and the spirit remain bolted forever."[14]

Shug's act of returning Nettie's letter to Celie makes it possible for the latter to repossess her lost-self. Celie's struggle towards independence is helped by the various relationships she forms with the other women. By returning the letters and by making her love her own body; Shug teaches Celie to find God in her own self, and to accept all feelings, positive or negative, as her own. Shug arouses a sense of pride in Celie when she sings a song, she has written just for her. For Celie it is the "First time somebody made something and name it after me."[15] Celie realizes that she must be somebody if she is a subject of a song. Her aroused self-esteem finally allows her to overcome her dependence on Albert and takes her life into her own hands.

Celie not only overcomes her dependence on man but also starts questioning the phallocentric foundations of her beliefs about God. During one of her discussions with Shug, Celie realizes that the God she had been praying and visualizing was the white men's God, who never listened to the blacks and definitely not to women. With Shug's help, Celie deconstructs the phallocentric discourse and decides, to get rid of men's race. Celie and Shug in this instance become the mouthpieces of their author and her womanist visions; like true womanist Shug, and Celie decide to find God in everyone and everything.

It is the moment of triumph for Celie and Shug too, when the former asserts her belief in her own-self by declaring to the astounded Mr.___Albert and the male congregation, "I'm pore, I'm black, I may be ugly and can't cook, a voice to say to everything listening. But I'm here."[16] She decides to go away with Shug and starts a new life. The career she chooses for herself is typically feminine. However, at the same time, her swing shows her disregard for gender identities when she makes pants that can be worn by both men and women. Finally, Nettie's revelations about their father remove that last mark of shame that was left on Celie's psyche and she becomes pure, ready to love again.

However, Celie's sisterhood extends to sexual love for Shug. Both are initiated into a vision of sexual spirituality, which is nature's essence as symbolized by the color purple. Celie does rise from a close poverty and deprivation to a human way of living and this improvement stems out from the inner growth. In *The Color Purple*, "the relationship between Shug and Celie is at the centre of the novel and is presented as a natural strengthening process through which both women, as well as the people around grow".[17]

Celie's last letter rewards the broadened insight she has gained during her journey towards self-realization. The frightened fourteen years old girl has grown up into a mature independent woman. Celie has come long away from her first solution to a nobody God to a body. And lastly her pantheistic vision of looking for God everywhere, as her last letter shows, "Dear God. Dear stars, Dear trees, Dear peoples. Dear everything."[18] This is an evidence of Walker's womanist vision. This all-enveloping unselfish view of the world transforms Celie into a true womanist.

Celie's fairy godmother is Shug who helps her throughout her struggle. Walker has a message to convey through Shug. Shug articulates Walker's thought and brings all the women together in a shared sisterhood. She knows that despite the content jealousies and bickering among themselves women are sisters. Shug's discourage on God is an eye-opened for Celie as well as for the readers. The imposed figure of God is so impressive that one automatically visualizes God as a white old man with blue eyes. Shug realizes the real purpose of going to church, which is to share God, not find God. Shug initiates Celie into the pantheistic vision of God, who is present everywhere and in everyone, she dislocates God and neutralizes him to it. Moreover, she also tells Celie that one should accept both good and wicked feelings, because God loves both types of feelings. Shug's theory that God becomes angry if one passes by without noticing the color purple in nature is thought provoking.

In the world of women in *The Color Purple*, Walker's men are delineated to strengthen the inner power of women. Alice Walker employs animal imagery in order to bring out Celie's feelings of revulsion towards the men. Celie thinks of them as frogs and snakes. Except Odessa's husband Jack, all other men in the novel are brutal. Albert whom Celie call Mr.___is a man who says nothing before his mistress but ill-treats his wife. Basically, Albert is a black man, who could not even stand up to his father to marry Shug. Celie highlights this trait in his character when she remarks: "I notice his chin black. Not much, chin there at all. I have more chin, I think."[19] This is how from his black character Celie learns the inner strength. Celie's success in life helps Albert to think for his own cowardice as well as his cruelty. At the end of the story, Albert is the changed man, capable man, capable of loving and sharing freely. As a gesture of his new womanhood, he joins Celie on the Portico in the act of sewing. Both Albert and Celie share a new relationship, one that is based on equality and a new understanding of themselves as human being.

The female body of sisterhood helps women in *The Color Purple* immensely in their struggle against the adverse circumstances. Apart from this factor, what assures the women from despair in the novel is that they can express themselves creatively in one way or the other. Each woman in the book has a talent, which sustains her through all her trials. Shug and

Mary Agnes are singers, while Celie expresses her creativity by designing unisexual pants. What saves Celie, moreover, is her act of writing letters and telling her own stories through them. Black women are for beneficences of a rich oral tradition, which has come to them through their mothers. Walker's "women go beyond the womanist ideals to become traditionally universal".[20]

Thus, Alice Walker through her coined term 'womanism' tries to give strength to all victimized women who are her primary concern and would like to bring them back to the dignified life. In one of her interviews with Jim Hanley Walker says, "Dreams as important as any message you'll ever receive."[21] She wants to enlighten that spark of self-realization in suffering women, so that they start imagining things. In the process, they will start dreaming about their life and could gain their self-respect, self-identity and self-dignity. However, to achieve that stage it is must for all suffering women to have the conversation with themselves. This is how Alice Walker's womanism gives strength to all women individually and makes them feel complete women in themselves. This article is a small step towards highlighting Alice Walker's contribution towards suffering women.

NOTES

1. O-Brien, Interview with Black Writers, N.Y., 1992: 199.
2. Richard Newman and Sawyer Marica, *Everybody Say Freedom*, Plume Book, 1996.
3. Powell, Faye. "African-American Feminist Issues: An Overview", *IJAS*, 20.1 (Winter 1990): 2.
4. C. Hernton, Calvin. "Who's Afraid of Alice Walker? *The Color Purple* as a Slave Narrative." In *Sexual Mountain and Black Women Writers: Adventures in Sex, Literature and Real Life*. New York, 1987: 30.
5. Walker, Alice. *In Search of Our Mother's Gardens*. N.Y., 1987: XI.
6. *Ibid.*
7. Bradley, David. "Alice Walker and Her Works." *New York Times Magazine*, Jan. 8, 1984: 39.
8. *Ibid.*, 33.

9. Walker, Alice. *In Search of Our Mother's Gardens*, New York, 1987: XII.
10. Tate, Claudia (Ed.), *Black Women Writers at Work*, New York, 1983: XXIII.
11. J. Parker-Smith, Bettye. "Alice Walker's Women: In Search of Some Peace of Mind", In *Black Women Writer's (1950-1980): A Critical Evaluation*, New York: Anchor, 1984: 478.
12. *Ibid.*, 481.
13. Barbara, Christian. "Alice Walker: The Black Women Artist as Wayward". In *Black Feminist Criticism Perspective on Black Women Writers*, N.Y., 1981: 181.
14. Byrd, Rudolph P. "Sound Advice from a Friend; Words and Thoughts from the Higher Ground of Alice Walker". Callaloo. 16, Spring-Summer, 1983: 128.
15. Walker, Alice. *The Color Purple*, New York: Pocket Books, 1982: 11.
16. *Ibid.*, 75.
17. Barbara, Christian. *Black Women Novelist: The Development of Tradition, 1892-1976*, Greenwood Press, 1980: 184.
18. Walker, Alice. *The Color Purple*, New York: Pocket Books, 1982: 249.
19. *Ibid.*, 50.
20. Walker, Alice. *In Search of Our Mother's Gardens*, N.Y., 1987: XI.
21. Walker, Alice. *The Originals: Alice Walker: A Portrait in the First Person*/Interview Jim Hanley; Produced by Jim Henley and David Lee. Chicago, III. PMI/Films Inc.

23

Alexithymia, Gender Difference and Institutionalized Sex Inequality in the Novels of Elfriede Jelinek and Toni Morrison

Neeru Tandon and *Kavita Tiwari*

Analysis of prevailing gender power differences and alexithymia in the society is incomplete without discussing the works of two Noble Laureates: Toni Morrison, the Afro-American novelist and Elfriede Jelinek, the Austrian writer. "*Alexithymia* is a personality dimension that involves both *cognitive deficits*, including difficulties in recognizing, describing, and distinguishing feelings from bodily sensations of emotional arousal, and *affective deficits*, including difficulties in emotionalizing and fantasizing" (Bermond et al. 2007).

The first and dominant approach analyses the emotional irresponsiveness of men towards emotional/physical/social needs of women. Second approach examines the disastrous difference in the power practices in society. The guiding principle of this article is the integrated study of socially imposed constraints, reinforcement of traditional gender roles, structured gendered relationships and oppressive patriarchal society with a least emotional response to the declared subordinate status of women. In patriarchy, male privilege has been associated with control over power and production, circulation of pleasure and representation of desires. Social patterns have been designed to accommodate male preferences and modes of gratification. Female sexuality has been relegated to a marginalized position to disallow pleasures and gratification; the woman's body has been inscribed or 'imprinted' by 'his story'. In all the cultures, woman has always been subjugated by 'male gaze' and power practices.

Austrian writer Elfriede Jelinek won the Noble Prize for Literature in 2004. All her writings *Lust, Women as Lovers, The Piano Teacher, Wonderful, Wonderful Times* and *Greed* are full of tireless fury with the human race. The Noble Prize in Literature 1993 was awarded to Afro-American writer Toni Morrison. Morrison's consciousness is the consciousness of victimization. It is an apprehension that one is victim because one is African-American, female and stereotyped as a female gender and similar is the approach of Austrian Noble winner Elfriede Jelinek. Her heroines are a study in a female psyche alienated due to lack of compassionate relationship. This research also revitalizes the existence of those who have been silenced, absent and denied an individual voice. She portrays her woman not only as a prey but also as a woman whose sexuality is considered dangerous, outrageous and a version of identity and self-worth. Their alternative values directly contravene patriarchal and paternalistic control of men, who ignore, restrain and forbid their women to practice any kind of control over their own bodies. Jelinek's exploration of women's sexuality reveals an area related to creative energies, the claiming of identity and the recognition of self-worth.

The fight and the struggle of Jelinek and Morrison remind me two most important feminists of their age who resemble very close to Jelinek and Morrison in the treatment of their subject. One of them is Marry Wollstonecraft, often characterized as the first feminist philosopher. *A Vindication of the Rights of Women* (1972) is one of the first works that can be called feminist. Wollstonecraft argued that women's education and upbringing is responsible for their limited expression and expectation. She advocated the need for women to speak out and tell their stories. And other name is Simone de Beauvoir who fiercely opposed to the image of women in home and in relation to men. She provided a new dimension to the feminism with the publication of *Le Deuxième Sexe* (*The Second Sex*) in 1949. By raising the question over the defined inferior position of women, she writes that "She is defined and differentiated with reference to man and not he with reference to her."[1] Analogous question is raised by Morrison and Jelinek by describing the sufferings and humiliations of women in most touching manner.

Through their outstanding linguistic abilities in their fiction, the above-stated novelists have attempted to portray the dilemmas, the rebellion, the ambitions of women when they have reached the crossroads, though their fiction brutally throws light on the fact that all religions and cultures expect woman to maintain the traditional gender roles heavily loaded against women. To assume that sex signified power in flat, in varying relation of metaphor will always entail a blindness, not to the rhetorical and pyrotechnic but to such historical categories as class and race, before we can fully achieve and use our initiative group of the leverage that sexual seems to offer on the relations of oppressions, we need more and more different, more complicated, more daring application of our present understanding of what it may mean for one thing to signify others.

While going through the works of these noble brains, I could measure the anger, disappointment and rage they have expressed through their books and articles. If we throw a glance on literature we may conclude that male authors view the problems prevailing in society from the male angle and their literature dignifies the woman as a matchless domestic creature. Morrison's consciousness is the consciousness of victimization. It is an apprehension that one is victim because one is female and stereotyped as a female gender and similar is the approach of Austrian Noble winner Elfriede Jelinek. Her heroines are a study in a female psyche alienated due to lack of compassionate relationship.

Through her every word Jelinek puts a sarcastic question mark on this male-dominated society that if woman is such an undignified creature in their dictionary, if they are so emotionless in all their responses towards her every need and wound, if men are so boastful of their manhood on the account of their sperm factory; then why they require women in every walk of their life? Alexithymia and inequality in power distribution is prevailing in our society since ages. It has been my endeavor to survey these writer's attempts to bring out gender, race, class and power issues in their respective patriarchies through their works. These laureates not only unfold a radical feminist vision but also interrogate the binaries of male/female, black/white, power/powerless, domination/surrender and so on.

Jelinek's fictional works each within the framework of its own problem complex presents a merciless world where the reader is confronted with the locked down system of male/female, assault and submission, hunter and prey. "The sex may be largely joyless and unhygienic, in keeping with Jelinek's theme that power and male aggression are the driving force in relationships, but it was explicit enough to leave the Cannes audience speechless."[2]

She further adds that such psychological damages that every society generally inflicts upon the second sex, results in horrible outcomes. What men can do; women can do better. And when it comes to be free, women fall dangerously. Writing about sexuality is still hurtful to men, it could mean women talking about their husbands' shortcomings or writing about being bored with them sexually, mentally or spiritually. These novelists portray the nasty side of India's rich and gorgeous, describing the shocking sex scenes of her heroines and negating the men for their sex-centred life provides the proper shape to her novels. They write about women who like herself, flee marriages because they are bored. Acrid, morbid, hedonist, tart, amazon, firebrand, explosive, misanthropist are but a few non-sufficing attributes to these two authors, I have picked up for my analysis. Their themes are brutally open in exposing, particularly a woman, to every kind of exploitation, degradation, and violence.

The Bluest Eye articulates Morrison's concern for black community, which then manifests itself in a concern for world in general. Morrison has claimed that "love or its absence" is one of her central themes: under the name of love "[P]eople do all sorts of things.... The violence is a distortion of what, perhaps, we want to do."[3] The novel picturises the victimization of a small black girl Pecola. Pecola is obsessed with a myth of physical beauty and as a result plunges into a world of madness. Her self-hate makes her vulnerable to abuse not only from her family but also from the community. Pecola's life is devoid of love, full of brutality and ugliness. She is a character with totally defenceless approach having no sense of self. Ugliness becomes all-pervasive in her character. She is able to suppress all her emotions and senses; she is able to hide behind ugliness but she in not able to keep away from seeing the ugliness that surrounds her in her home.

Toni Morrison describes *The Bluest Eye* as a novel "about one's dependency on the world for identification, self value and feeling of worth". The voice of patriarchy shatters her realm, ruins the world of relationships and finally produces conditions of isolation, psychic derangement and silence in Pecola's life. The brutal patriarchal encounter removes Pecola from the sense that granted distinctions between self and other, between appropriateness and the forbidden just as her father was removed in the early phase of his life. She remains as cultureless entity in the patriarchal society when she tries to achieve Oedipal love for her father. She is left to collect the garbage of life by seeking a pathetic regression to the previous generation.

Morrison mirrors the models of conformity that systems of capitalism inflict and create by reflections emanating from the passions of the non-conforming. Pecola is destroyed by being raped and impregnated by her father Cholly. This disaster shatters the cohesiveness of her self, violates her reflective image and transforms her existence in a big contaminated other. Cholly's sense of self is just a matter of light over darkness, power over powerless, male over female and the father over daughter.

Morrison through *Beloved* expanded the themes of telling stories untold; the thoughts took the form of the writing in the memory of the millions of lives lost during slavery. The plot revolves around an ex-slave Sethe who would rather kill her own children than risk that they be re-enslaved. She has been depicted as a pathetic figure who is raped by whites and her femininity is torn into pieces. The worst part of this barbarism is the stealing of her milk which was the right of her daughter. A character that is shown as the worthless mud in the wall of the society runs as a contemporary female gender norm.

In Jazz, Violet the wife disfigures the face of Dorcas, the mistress of her husband. A female is the foe of a female and both females are the subjects of sexual pleasures for the male society. On the first hand, a wife has to fit herself in the role of a faithful spouse, so she has to bear the violence of her husband and on the other hand, she has to save the ideal definition of woman.

Wonderful, Wonderful Times by Elfriede Jelinek is the story of four alienated students—two male, two female. The protagonist Anna is a desperate figure physically abused by his father devoid of confidence and utter physical beauty. She concludes with her experiences of life that power is enjoyed by male not by females. She reveals that the power in her house lies with men and not with women. She tries to liberate herself from her given fate and restore her self-respect. She is also a subjugating figure who bears the brutality of male dominating society. She is perfectly fit in a domestic setting and denies the possibility of being a rebellion character.

Lust by Jelinek is an attack on Austrian culture where the silence and the physical muteness of a woman rarely find any space for expression. Lust is a pornographic description of sexuality, aggression and abuse. She wonderfully depicts that a woman owns nothing more than the "mute kingdom of her body". The man's demand for power, control on violence and the female submission reflects the power structure of the society. "He roasts his hefty sausages in her oven, in its flaky pastry case of hair and skin and his articulated penis roars to a standstill in the lay by of his wife."[4] Gertie, the wife of Hermann is used as a property and she is not asked ever how she feels about the ways Hermann does with her the nasty sex. She has to tolerate the marital rape by her husband almost twice a day and every night, which is nothing but a sexual abuse for a female. She is an object for sexual gratification only and wants to liberate herself from that brutality during which Hermann pour his juices into her nastily. She indulges herself in an extra-marital love affair with a belief that this time she would be loved for being an important individual and not only a physical body. But dreams shatter when Michael, a student who rescues her from her barbaric husband also represents power of male society only. The vigorous use of her physical entity proves again that he is after all a man. Love is again as distant from sex as it was earlier. The relation becomes a love less horror. Once again, the norms of gender discourse picturises her as a stereotyped female. The myth of love and defence of woman's sexuality again faces the reality.

The novel *Women as Lovers* is similar in the nature to the audio play what happened after Nora left her husband or the pillars of the society. This novel depicts those whom with Jelinek empathizes most in the society: women without their own identity. The poor ordinary women are economically dependent on the lowest rung of the social ladder; find themselves in the shadow of their men and watch themselves through men's eyes. The gender norms for the women society in Jelinek's writings define that women give birth to children, dress and cook them, gratify their men's needs and live in a glass show case of feminity without the capacity to engage themselves in transforming world.

In an aggressive tone, the novel *Greed* portrays the social dimensions in which the woman is used as an attire to be used and thrown into the gutter, to be exploited both sexually and socially. Kurt Janisch, the typical of Jelinek's men, the policeman, symbol of patriarchal society, is violent, insatiable and possess a greed for domination. Kurt, who goes about sex with Gertie, only wants to get hold of her property; this is the ultimate object of her greed, and the novel superimposes the image of the house with the image of the body.

He prostitutes himself to every woman in the vicinity and beyond, in the hope that they will hand over their property to him one day. He looks at female genitalia in the way as if these doors are permanently open for him. Sex is furtive and base—"you give each other a good licking"—and love is a common foible, which, for women at least, involve a dangerous loss of selfhood. What women want from their men is neither gentle nor soft nor reasonable—it is just true.

The novel *Women as Lovers* was published in 1975. The book presents a group of young characters uncritically adopting the shallow, money-driven conventions that, as Jelinek sees it, regulate sex and marriage in provincial Australia. Jelinek has unremittingly established her genius throughout this work of fiction, she doesn't even spare a moment to satirise the hypocrisy that is as evident in today's world as sunshine itself. She has truly brought out the ignominious life of the married women in her native nation. However, this description applies equally well to nearly all the geographical boundaries across the globe.

> "life seems meaningless without him, even with him life doesn't seem to be very meaningful, at any rate more meaningful than her work in the brassiere factory."
>
> "come back, heinz! I love you, and I need you."[5]

These heart-wringing cries symbolize the helpless love of Brigitte, who is perhaps the self-proclaimed spokesperson of the instigator herself. Jelinek has drained the lion's share of her privileged acumens to produce this one scintilla of a line—wherein she exhibits her earnest yearnings for the man she loves. Her effort is still more commendable in the light of the horrible state of affairs that enshroud her co-protagonist's entire being. Jelinek has illustrated that she does have those unique sparks in her creations that trigger-off a high voltage response for her uneasy stimuli. She has dared to take her soul to these people who are marginalized and downtrodden; and thus, like a thermometer, taken a bit of the oppressive heat that those poor souls face everyday and every night. The passion, the fervour, the authenticity with which she has blasted-off the prevalent assertions that women can never be a part of literary texts is commendable.

The author, in her agonised recitation of the sorry expeditions of the protagonists, has discovered the possibility of authentic identity of women and projects the women characters through the balanced perception. Through her writings in the most oppressive moods, the esteemed instigator has stated that a woman is merely an object of cosmopolitan ridicule and her entire existence is confined to provide sexual gratification only. Thus, the belief that "a woman's claim to the rights of creation means first to create self"[6] itself lays emphasis on finding a separate entity in which a woman has to build herself up psychologically even before for right is placed before the society. The question of self is more of a matter of understanding than fulfilment. Jelinek's portrayal of women is an antagonising set of the social as well as political values. She has attained popularity not only for writing literature with female protagonists but also for projecting the true woman who, de facto, remains in the background. This implies that an ideal woman is not the woman whom she has described, but the woman as it is, and ought to be. The serious issue is that in the projection of mind, soul or the physical entity a 'being'; the inner self is never represented. The reality claims that a human being is divided into so many sleeves among whom it becomes troublesome to say as to which self must be the real one.

In *Lust*, Jelinek has illustrated the debacles, the fiascos and their aftermath that run the life of the bleakest creature that ever treaded this Planet. Gertie, the timorous yet audacious, protagonist of the oeuvre is the unfortunate spouse of Hermann, who "...sings, plays, yells, fucks". Everyday sun rises, with it; raise the hardships of hers that can alone suffice to bring even the Satan to ignominy. Hermann is merely a lesser mortal who is "just a fart in hurricane", and has got just one philosophy to take care of: "it doesn't take long to make merry". Gertie is analogous to a receptor antenna that is bound to the receiver's appalling frequencies that are the habitual springs of inexcusable treatments, whose description even one may regard as grisly. The badly bruised Gertie, then one day, "bares her soul and her bosom with words", to Michael, who didn't go 'astray' when it came to rescue her from her regular butcher. That was a day when her esteemed, yet undermined feminism, was put to the extreme batteries. A thoroughly battered soul, amalgamated with a dilapidated physical realm, better known as Gertie, surrendered all that she had to her saviour. And this pristine operation should not be considered from the point of view of her perfidy, but rather by perceiving that a soul as pure as crystal rain, was asked to emanate from a chunk of charcoal. However, there is still no respite for this poor soul Gertie as Michael, too, is another brute of the same genre as that of Hermann. Devastated and shattered Gertie is left to cry for herself.

> When she bends down she has to spread her legs. Now he can cop hold of her whole fig tree with one hand and set his fingers angrily a-roving. Oh and while she's at it with her legs apart like that she can stand over him and piss him in his mouth.[7]

The signature approach of Elfriede Jelinek towards one of the nuts and bolts of all living beings, humans and brutes alike, sex—has been more of deference as an art than anything else. She is truly well-verse at this elucidation of hers—for she doesn't consider it forbidden to air her revered analysis regarding this audacious subject. She has very artistically depicted the terrible music that scores of her contemporary women have to face everyday. They are taken as wives only for one principle cause: sexual gratification. These wretched, pathetic, dismal creatures are perhaps deserted by the Almighty also—for they are simply forsaken in His kind Kingdom, with nothing to help their undermined souls, that renders them subjugated.

> The woman is passive as a toilet, for the man to do his business in. He shoves her head into the bathtub and, his hand clawing her hair, threatens that as you make your bed, so you must cry on it, that's love. No, cries the woman. She isn't crying for love.[8]

These sorry tales determine the diluted nerves and murky equations that they have to face day-in and day-out. The protagonist of this novel is no different, at least in the terms of the ghastly courtesies that are always at her disposal because of her husband. Her spouse "is as puffed-up as a pig's bladder, he sings, plays, yells, fucks". Murkier become all the dimensions of one's life when one has a spouse who is so focused with the vision of one's life! Almost instantaneously, one is strained by an unnatural stimulus to think if for such a fanatically determined spouse, the one at the receiving end is a woman! A meek woman, that is, very politely, the meekest creature Almighty ever created. Sorry tales trail....

Throughout the length and breadth of this opus of hers, Jelinek has portrayed that Gertie is as "passive as a toilet, for the man to do his business in". Alarms emblazon her morbid-sounding wails, yet she is desperate to vent her agony out. And she discovers Michael the most suitable candidate for the same, after her entire revered someone who only yells razes feminine-self. Jelinek has astonishingly verified the pinnacle of her scholarly insight in this mesmerizing sonata to illustrate Gertie's affliction and her pining and yearnings for freedom; freedom from regular rapist, who happens to be her spouse also. Marital rape is but one instance of Gertie's abuse, she is pressed to pose the ultimate ridicule of her crushed subsistence in more ways than one. "The woman has to crook and angle her legs like a frog so that her husband, the examining magistrate, can look into the matter closely."[9] Not only this, she is forced to oblige him in all the ways she is ordered to, viz.

> He stares at her cleft. This is familiar territory now. When she looks away, because she cannot bear his scrutiny and the groping, pinching hands that examine her, he hits her. He wants to see and do everything. He has a right to. There are details you can't see, and, in the event of there being a next time, a flashlight would come handy.[10]

Aforesaid arguments sponsor a useful and a pretty obvious inference that there are only two distinct ways in which one can dehumanise a woman to such extremes that her entire subsistence, including her feminism is all razed. And these ways are superseded by everything else—they are pornography and marital rape. However, there does exist a subtle distinction between the two; whereas pornography is more centred on the grounds of financial and/or sexual securities, marital rape sabotages the entire being of a woman for merely ego-satisfaction of a sadist. Such a sadist is under a two-way reprimand from the Almighty—for the culprit is not only inflicting pain on someone's physical domains, but also, he is viciously piercing her tender spirits.

These oppressed women suffer both the physical violence to which they are exposed with their men and the powerlessness, which they choose for themselves in their womanly role. Her idiosyncrasy regarding the dismal, rather wretched environment in which her protagonists dwell, questions the reader in his very face: how do you feel now and how would you have felt had the very same things happened to your mother or your sister or your daughter? This one question is found zeroing-in on the reader's subconscious psyche and Jelinek's feminism makes one ponder over the "in attendance" conditions of the women, globally. What if we're cooling our heels in our homes and excusing ourselves from any such botheration, these issues are, nevertheless, staring at us fixatedly. The immaculate polarity of authority distribution has been marring the configuration of our civilised society since time immemorial; it is so damn wrong, yet no one sees it. Men consistently need some poor soul to exercise their authority on: this satisfies their ego; and women are the most suitable candidates for the purpose—for they are timid, or worse, they can be made timid (by slashing their integrity first as an individual, followed by blasting-off their feminine subsistence).

Beyond doubt the power structure is reflected most clearly in Elfriede Jelinek through sexuality, she is never afraid to present the race, sex, betrayals, social and political bluff. The horrendous and shocking nature of violence against women and the power practices of male-organized structure of the society through the gender, specifications make an attack on the darkly satirical critique of the society.

The power of the language is not only used for communication. It is to protest, to project and to create a personality. Language is functional. It is a way of life; it is the identity and individuality of a speaking subject. Jelinek uses language as a means of expression to unsettle the arrogant domain of abusive language. Jelinek's predicament is all the more touching as the female protagonist of *Lust*. Gertie longs for the human touch, sensitivity and companionship of her husband. She fervently longs for his affection and feels that Hermann knew nothing that concerns her.

> The man compacts, loaded, fresh from the factory. Waiting to unload. He has been fermenting in his bottle and he wants to uncork the fizz. Tonight, that's right we almost forgot, how could we, tonight is the legally appointed time for the transaction. And the woman waits with her absorbent cloth to soak up everything the man has produced during the day.[11]

This instance gives an idea of Gertie's psychological and emotional alienation from her mate. Through her writings in the most oppressive moods, the esteemed instigator has stabbed that a woman is merely an object of cosmopolitan ridicule and her entire existence is confined to provide sexual gratification only. That's why her texts lay emphasis on finding a separate entity in which a woman has to build herself up psychologically even before get placed in the society. The question of self is more a matter of understanding than fulfilment. To quote, Shobha De in one of her novels, where she portrays the hypocrisy and alexithymia of men in every culture. She says,

> Women who stray are called assorted charming names. 'Bitch' is one of them. Then they are 'slut', 'whore', 'nympho' and 'challu'. Men who do the same become heroes to their less adventurous contemporaries.[12]

Simone de Beauvoir argued in *The Second Sex* that in a patriarchy, women have been constructed, as man's "other", denied the right of her own subjectivity. "She is the incidental, the inessential as opposed to the essential. He is the subject, he is the absolute—she is the other." In all her novels Jelinek raises the question over the debased position of women and she applies the language as a tool of criticism against the abusive male society. It may appear strange that at one point she makes a fight to restore women's dignity and at another point she portrays their pornographic sufferings. The answer lies in the efforts of revealing the painful history of the brutality against women in postwar Austria. The real sufferings are portrayed on paper and compel the readers to feel similar anguish and loss.

Gertie also feels the same rejection as her husband's ignorance serves as a cruel repressive force on her sensitive temperament. Her self-esteem undergoes severe battering, for director sees nothing in her to respect, he knows only one thing—how to derive maximum pleasure of her body. What emerges as a close study of Elfriede Jelinek's novel is an understanding of the sufferings of women, which result from uneven power-division in marriages.

> A court of no appeal, she is flooded and shat full him, she has to get up and the last of her clothes fall on the floor and she fetches a sponge to clean the Man, that irreconcilable enemy of her sex, of himself and the slime that she has caused to emit.[13]

This mammoth male ego, the desire to own and control, spoils the very base of her marriage and carries her on an extramarital affair. She falls in the same unfertile attempt to be loved and graced by Michael who is more fatal to Gertie because of his dual personality. Outwardly, he may appear as a man of clear principles but inwardly he too is merciless examiner. Elfriede Jelinek's exploration of female subjugation in patriarchal family structures takes on a larger dimension than the inner psychological world portrayed by Toni Morrison. She constantly focuses on the network of male dominance, power of male repressive forces and its effect on woman. The agony of a woman forced to confirm to a socially prescribed image is best conveyed in the words of Indian English poetess Kamala Das, the poetess who has fiercely rejected being fitted into any mould:

> Dress in Sarees, be girl,
> be wife, they said. Be embroiderers, be cook,
> be a quarreler with servants. Fit in, oh,
> Belong, cried the categorizers.[14]

Silence has always been referred as the most desirable virtue for women. They were punished for their claim to their subjectivity. Women were given their part to play either directly, through pressure or by rituals and laws. It was the patriarchal society in which the female existence was submerged beneath the masculine authority. The mainstream literature that scaled women against financial bequeaths, came out with a subjugated yellow-bellied conclusion of the instability of both. Their mobility created the possibility of loss, so both once won over, need to be confined. Deprivation of full human status of women in society made them treated as an object of possession. The theme of Daniel Dafoe's *Roxana* also sites maid and mistress on the same ladder. Male-authored texts define the qualities of good women as accepting the restrictions and disappointments with their loving submissiveness to their husbands and fathers despite their cruelty towards them. Now the question arises for how long woman has been the object of possessions and uses and abuses in the world. Thus, we can conclude that the themes of Jelinek and Morrison as quite useful in the analysis of subjectivity, especially those of which are beginning to note the importance of analyzing gender in relation to discourses and practice of marginalization, namely those generated with respect to the intersection of class, race, ethnicity, sexuality and nation. Toni Morrison's approach in interpreting feminine pain and their negative sexuality and Elfriede Jelinek's nudity of male oppressive powers is quite innovative. What they have in common, I believe, is that they both reclaim woman's identity and experience in a holistic way. They both present and represent feminism as the centre not as marginals. Their subjective approach crosses the limits of localization and touches the spirit of universalization.

NOTES

1. Beauvoir, Simone de. *The Second Sex*. Trans. H.M. Parshley. London: Vintage, 1997: 66.
2. Jelinek, Elfriede. "A woman of mad passion and mixed metaphors." *The Sunday Times*, October 10, 2004.
3. 'The Seams Can't Show', An Interview With Toni Morrison by Jane Bakerman, *Black American Literature Forum*, 60.
4. Jelinek, Elfriede. *Lust* (London: Serpent's Tail, 1992), 35.

5. Jelinek, Elfriede. *Women as Lovers* (London: Serpent's Tail, 1994), 24.
6. *Ibid.*
7. Jelinek, Elfriede. *Lust* (London: Serpent's Tail, 1992), 35.
8. *Ibid.*, 33.
9. *Ibid.*, 65.
10. *Ibid.*, 102.
11. *Ibid.*, 104.
12. de Beauvoir, Simone. *The Second Sex,* tran. H.M. Parshley 1953; Harmonds Worth: Penguin, 1983: 726.
13. Das, Kamala. *An Introduction: Indian Poetry in English.* (ed.) Makarand Paranjape, Madras: Macmillan, 1993.
14. Woolf, Virginia. *A Room of One's Own* (ed.) Mary Eagleton, Feminist Literary Theory, London: Basil Blackwell, 1986.

24

Problematizing Social Issues from Human Rights Perspectives: A Critique of Mahasweta Devi's *The Glory of Sri Sri Ganesh*

Koyal Chakrabarty

Socialists and activists like Arundhati Roy, Mahasweta Devi, Gopinath Mohanty and the like take up their stands through their pens in depicting the real 'public scenario'. If scrutinized well, at one level, this artistic concern manifests itself through the exploration and postulation of Human Rights in literature.

As a writer and human activist, the canon of contribution that Mahasweta Devi has provided the readers, is vastly inspirational. She is one of the most prolific Bengali writers of modern times that talk about the alarming condition of the Dalits in the Indian villages of interior Bihar and Bengal. Her receiving of the Padma Shri award in 1986, Jnanpith Award in 1996, Magsaysay Award for Literature in 1997 and the Officier des Arts et des Lettres in 2003 and her several times nomination for the Noble Prize for Literature, not only prove her as a great writer, but being a hardcore social activist, Mahasweta Devi's writing gives voice to the silent and her social activism arises hope in despair.

A large part of Mahasweta Devi's writing is inspired by the status of the tribal communities of Bengal and Bihar. Her work is a valuable documentation of these communities that have been marginalized and yet they remain forgotten to a great extent in the developmental process. Mahasweta Devi translates her perception of society through the lives of her well-etched characters as they journey through the trajectory of cruelness of life, struggling to maintain their dignity amidst the indifference they face along the way. Her writings reflect a lot of her own work as a social activist with the Nomadic tribes, non-tribal poor and people generally isolated by mainstream society. Her corrosive humour and cryptic style are brain hammering in nature, as she takes on issues of agrarian land relations, inter-caste violence, so-called rural development and discusses the position of women in rural India. Her style eludes a sense of compassion for human suffering and vulnerability, but at the same time she depicts the strength and courage of the human spirit which rises against all odds through her powerful and effective characterization and new historic revelations. The plot of *The Glory of Sri Sri Ganesh* tells us of the lives of the "Lachhimas, the Rukmanis, the Mohors and the Haroas—as a contrast to the lives of their all-powerful Rajput Zamindars—the Medinis and Ganeshes, who despite all odds and ends of a crippled existence rises in a revolt in the end for the upkeep of their identity and make their voices heard."[1]

The Glory of Sri Sri Ganesh presents the miserable hard-hitting lives of the low caste class where we are petrified to read about their tragic existence; this gives the novel its realistic flavour. Caste as an institution and ideological structure has served as the striving force for communal authority in India. But with the unequal division of wealth and property among the merchant class in the pre-independent era, when the merchant class had enough money and a voice to make their presence, the norms of social equation started changing slowly. Now the Brahmins who were the head of the Hindu caste system, were respectable and authoritative only in the religious and social spheres but the major economic rise and control went into the hands of the Kshatriyas and Vaishyas as they gradually took over the position of the Feudal lords in the villages having huge shares of land and low caste tenants to work for them. This transformation was simple because with the initiation of the land distribution and settlement schemes introduced by the British, much of the land holdings were automatically transferred to the people working directly or indirectly for the company by dint of favoritism and personal pleas. As a result of it, the existing Zamindars who were the original Feudal Lords, of the land, were now added with a handful number of newly born rich landlords, irrespective of their caste or status. The society continued with the existence of both the Brahmins and the rich landlords at its head, which added to the natural doom of the Dalits all the more.

The Glory of Sri Sri Ganesh reproduces the torments in the lives of the male and female Dalit/tribes pressed below the ruthless domination of their maliks (Feudal Lords). It is due to their grinding poverty that the Dalits/tribes lose their voice, identity, confidence and the power to revolt. What lies before them, as the ultimate reality is that they are the bonded labourers or *gotis* of the Zamindars to whom they owe their lives and labour for borrowing a meagre sum of money for some dire cause. The novel pleas for the space and free play of human rights in the lives of the downtrodden and thus, satirizes the existence of the concept of human rights on the whole both nationally and internationally.

Mahasweta Devi once in her interview in 2002 angrily exclaims,

> I have been going through the "Universal Declaration of Human Rights" and questioning myself, which article is really true for India from Articles 1-30? None. In India, the society is caste and class divided. Casteism is not the only curse. Indian society is thoroughly indifferent to the word "tribe". Then comes the ultimate truth as it exists. For India's millions of deprived ones living either below the poverty line, or on the fringe of it, the word "human rights" is non-existent. Right to have a living, proper housing, drinking water, education, electricity, health facilities, communication, right over the land, they are denied everything. And they are the people whose poverty is really a big capital for the country's ruling powers. Their poverty, depravity of their lives,

> the non-development of their areas, form this capital. Showing this, the ruling powers make big projects and get money.... Whatever I say here, is born of three decades of day-to-day experience of India's poor. And, amongst them, India's tribals share a worse fate. Their's is a faceless existence. They are in India from ancient times, for thousands of years, yet the mainstream India has continually refused to recognize them. In the tribal society there is no caste division, no dowry system, divorce and widow remarriage is socially sanctioned. They are, after centuries of oppression and neglect, still so civilized![2]

The Glory of Sri Sri Ganesh largely underscores the human rights problems, both social and economic. The major issues that *The Glory of Sri Sri Ganesh* as representations of society mainly highlights are social, political, economic and ethical in nature. The prominent and dominant concerns that the novel explores are the social evils of poverty, casteism and untouchability, class division and economic inequality, illiteracy, child-labour, pitiful living conditions, abuse of human dignity, exploitation of women and the repression of the fundamental and human rights by the high-class society and its establishments, including the government machinery. Human rights concerns tend to take shape in literature through different characters and vicarious events in the lives of the characters, which focus on the compromise between the appearance and reality of Dalit/tribal existence in the presence of a just and concerned legal system in India.

If one deciphers the novel *The Glory of Sri Sri Ganesh*, one can easily empathize the stings of pain present in the lives of the protagonists. The novel is not a tragedy in proper, but is vivid delineation of excruciating pain. The demonstration of the trauma that the characters in the novel endure with, is an easy premise to conclude that there is a major human rights abuse in the Dalit/tribal society. From the very beginning, the novel lets the readers taste the taste of grinding misery existent in the lives of the Dalit/tribal. The characters of the novel suffer the intolerable pangs of poverty and wretchedness. The major problem that affects them is the problem of caste and class.

Mahasweta Devi aptly sketches the picture of Barha village in north Bihar where the socio-economic demography is quite similar to the contemporary socio-political economic scenario of the then agrarian Bihar. Before understanding the caste-class relationship as projected in the novel, *The Glory of Sri Sri Ganesh*, we must analyze the inherent complexities embedded in the contemporary agrarian setup. According to Ashok Rudra, class relations are relations of productions but not all relations of production define classes; they define various 'social groups'. But only such social groups constitute classes as are subject to contradictions of interest arising from the way they are related to the means of production. The term 'agrarian class structure' means the arrangement of groups or classes determined by access, or denial of access, to land, the principal means of production. The differential access to land, which governs how one class relates to another, is the basis of relations of production, or in general terms, of class relations. Anand Chakravarti argues that agrarian class relations in Bihar are embedded in caste because whether a person controls land or not is conditioned by that person's caste status.

Mahasweta Devi in her novel explains the demographics of Barha village thus:

> the schedule caste was both marginal and necessary they were marginal. The mainstream was the Rajputs. They were necessary they did all the work that the people of the mainstream needed. Because the village was very much a creation of Rajputs like Medini Singh, nine-tenths of the land in the village was under their control. The rest, the majority, farmed the lands of the minority. The conditions governing this farming were also of various types. Generally, most of the cultivators were 'purchased' or *kharidi ryots*. Almost all the maliks had once been in the private armies of the local Rajas who often made the *kharidi* subjects farm their land.... No one had descendants of these slaves whether bonded labour was abolished. So the present-day owners benefited. These

> people cultivated the land and were paid in grains. Even a good year would not yield enough for them to eat. In years of drought-poor harvest-flood, the rule of debt repayment was a thumb impression in the malik's ledger. They had to give him the lion share of the crop plus, if necessary, free labour. In this manner they were mortgaged, caught in the snare of the all-powerful ledger in the malik's *katcheri.* They were *kharidi banda, 'Bought subjects'*.... In places like Barha village the head were former *sipahis* of the former raja's, the prevailing laws were those created by their one-time masters.... One village, nine malik families, the rest *kharidi* subjects. The bhangis, hajams, dhobis and other such indispensable groups did the jobs assigned to their castes...the malik didn't mind giving out land for sharecropping. Because when these sharecroppers have nothing left to eat after they have paid the malik his share, they take a loan. And get bonded. Repaying the interest on loans, almost every one of them has lost his own piece of land, and they had learned that in order to survive to stay alive it was best to share crop or serve the malik.[3]

In *The Glory of Sri Sri Ganesh* again we find a new situation when the land labourers pass through a crisis period every year. As they are employed for six months only and the other six months unemployed and are in dire need of a second profession, Ganesh retorts:

> The sharecroppers and the *kharidi* subjects have always tilled their land, and also given free labour. They've always borrowed money by mortgaging their land and they still do. When the debts piled up and we see that even free labour or crops were not enough to pay off the loans, then we maliks took over their land we still do. He had nothing when he lost the land, but he remained the malik's field labourer. Why? Why does he still stay on? For us. Otherwise we'd have to get migrant labourers to work the fields. That's why we didn't let them out of our grasp. Or else we'd have to take the adivasis or low caste *acchuts* from other villages. The

> adivasis used to live here once. We evicted them and took control. And even then, we never loosened our hold on the landless labourers. They will starve for six months? They've always done that. It's nothing new. Why should I worry about it this year? Look, among my subjects there are four ganju families' field labourers now. And this year I shall be forced to evict twelve to fourteen ganju families. I'm supposed to be the worst man in the village. So during the years of Baba's illness, I didn't deduct anything towards repayment of loans. Gave them their share of the crop. Now I have checked the accounts and found that taking interest and principal together, two hundred, two fifty, three hundred rupees are outstanding against each fellow's name. Think of that. Twelve to fourteen families do not own even four acres of land but if I take they will become my field labourers. I shan't let them go and I'm not going to allow them to take permits and collect firewood either.[4]

Ganesh reminds us of Shylock who too stands out as a heartless being in the matter of extortion of money. Ganesh's above speech brings out several critical issues present in the economy of Bihar in manifolds. First, it becomes clear that the Rajputs like Ganesh extorts labour and land cunningly from their subjects. Second, they buy them as commodities through guiles and unfair means. Third, they take advantage of their poverty and helplessness and first take their land as mortgage in lieu of a small sum of money and then add interests after interest on the principal amount which they cannot pay and the result of which the land gets automatically annexed and then they serve him as bonded labourers or *kharidi* subjects or field labourers for the entire cropping season. His stone-hearted nature prevents him from feeling a minimum sympathy for them and he rejoices in the idea that with the lack of occupation and cropping for the later half of the year, the labourers will be bonded to him and this will give him another opportunity for exploitation and another round of credit which will again be the source of their perennial slavery. The fourth point is even more critical. It depicts the different layers of imperialism imbedded in Indian villages. Here in the matter of exploitation and shrewdness Ganesh seems to take the top position. He boldly asserts his power and astute sense. He is proud and defiant in declaring that his Rajput forefathers have evicted the Adivasis or the tribal people of the area forcefully and illegally and captured their entire area thereby having a total control over the land resources and the people by coercive means. The Adivasis are the victims of three-fold marginalization. They are first marginalized because they belonged to the backward sect; the government has not done much for them.

Another issue that the novel explores is the problem of land alienation as faced by the Dalit/tribals. Marx, in his early writing especially in his economic and philosophic manuscripts, discusses the concept of alienation as 'estranged labour'.

A further additional issue that the novel highlights is the merged existence of the local administration and the Feudal Lords in the villages. India from its time of independence and before has been corrupted heavily from every layer of administration. Mahasweta Devi proves through different events that the Maliks and the dominant-class Zamindars influence the establishment agencies of the government, the Panchayat, the police, the forest department, lawyers, the SDO and other representatives of the bureaucracy. The effects of red-tapism and corruption pay hard on the poor and the powerless, Indian administration is no exception to this.

In the novel, we see how not only the rich but also the kinsmen exploit the poor and suck out their money and labour. Chakravarti explains that in 1979, just two years before the publication of the novel *The Glory of Sri Sri Ganesh*, the Maliks were the dominant class in Bihar, controlling about 79 per cent of the land. They wielded three, interrelated or overlapping, forms of power in the community, which was a consequence of the blending of class and caste dominance: social, economic and coercive. These elements of power together may be called as "the culture of exploitation"—the complex norms upheld by Maliks, which governed the relationship between them and the subordinate population. The term 'social power' is used to define the capacity of Maliks to assert their common interests as a collective. These interests were both material such as exercising economic control over the labours employed, as well as non-material such as maintaining the 'honour' of the caste, which is inextricably bound up ensuring the perpetuation of Bhumihar dominance in the community. The social power wielded by the Maliks was reinforced by instrumental links with officials holding key positions in the executive arm of the state, including the police, revenue, and the labour and development administration, through whose connivance or active support they ensured that their interests were upheld. Indeed, there was a close connection between the social power of Maliks and state power. In other words, state power in Bihar by being appropriated by village-based elites, is actually embodied in structures of power at the grassroots. The exercise of economic power, the second element underlying their class position was derived from their pre-eminent control over land which gave them the capacity to exploit hired labourers and perpetuate relation of dependence with pliant tenants.

When Ganesh is threatened that the SDO may arrest him for blighting the forest to fire and putting an end to the Dusads and Bhangis, he shouts in anger: "What will the SDO do? The court? Won't they need money for the elections? Sure, we'll give money.... Tell me who is more important to them—Ganesh Singh, who owns lakhs, or that Harijan, Abhay Mahato? I'll see that he dies first. Who'll protest? The *acchuts*? I burn the bhangi *toli,* ousted them, got Rukmini pregnant, she died what could any of them do? Ramrup you don't just inherit land, you hang on to it—through power."[5] It is a pity that the administration would be silent to all this. The novel also satirizes the Sangh or the Gandhi mission and the rich NGOs that come to help the downtrodden only to bring more harm to them.

The task of relating human suffering in literature and human rights remains incredibly complex as the entire process engages a telling and showing method but the remedy lies in the hands of the people and society. "The Left legalists now tell that unless the politics of human rights remains vigilantly self-reflexive, a politics organized around publicizing pain constitutes a further degradation of subaltern selves into a species of sub-civilized non-agency."[6] This study through the representation of certain instances from Mahasweta Devi's translated Indian fiction has brought into focus how realistic literature as an art form can depict the society and its people amidst the social, economic, cultural and political trajectories and thus acts as a measure-stick determining the status of human rights enjoyed by them. This work is a veritable outcome of a research that human rights concepts and literature are inevitable inter-disciplinary interfaces that inform and complement each other as critical scaffoldings.

NOTES

1. Devi, Mahasweta. *The Glory of Sri Sri Ganesh*. Tr. Ipsita Chanda. Calcutta: Seagull Books, 2003: 23.
2. Devi, Mahasweta. "Year of Birth-1871, Mahasweta Devi on India's Devotified Tribes." *India Together*. Interview by Mahasweta Devi in March 2002.
3. Devi, Mahasweta. *The Glory of Sri Sri Ganesh*. 39-40.
4. *Ibid*., 130.
5. *Ibid*., 137.
6. Baxi, Upendra. *The Future of Human Rights*. Third Edition. New Delhi: Oxford University Press, 2008.

25

The Inheritance of Loss: An Insight into the Internal and External Conflict of Class, Race and Culture

Reshu Shukla

Kiran Desai's *The Inheritance of Loss* is the book rewarded with the Man Booker Prize in 2006. The novel is a detailed description of contemporary issues introduced with globalization and advancement followed by the growing impressions of economic differences, multiculturalism, fanaticism and rationalism as the most dominant survival threats of the time. It weaves the story of people, from different backgrounds, struggling with social parameters under the stigmatic impression of caste, class, culture and nationality. The novel reflects post-globalization-consequences, which though has made remarkable changes at the world spectrum in different aspects yet has more ironically affected the part of society identified as middle class, sectioned furthermore as upper middle class and lower middle class. The novelist has amazingly succeeded to put forth the bleak side of changes progressively taking place in technical, economical, social, cultural and ethical front at all levels across the geographical boundaries.

The Inheritance of Loss is a realistic and highly impressive novel known particularly for its poignant narration and deals with multi-dimensional and multi-locational survival issues of people. One set of story is running in Kalimpong, located in the northern part of India near Darjeeling while the other in America where people from different countries have come to earn their livelihood. The theme is set in the mid-1980s and the main characters are Sai, a young Indian girl; her grandfather, a retired judge and a Cambridge-educated Anglicize man; a cook, an old north-Indian poor man; Biju, cook's son working in American kitchens; Gyan, Sai's Math tutor, a Nepali man; Lola and Noni, Sai's neighbors.

Sai, a seventeen-year-old girl comes to live with her grandfather after the death of her parents in an accident. We identify her as protagonist who is made to face sudden changes when she is brought to Kalimpong from an Anglican convent from Dehradun. This makes her life different in many ways. Sai has been grown-up in an environment full of Western cultures and etiquettes. This is clearly exhibited in her attitude which is more like Westerners. She feels Indian culture and environment uneasy and takes everything with a strange eye. Living in a family comprising of the two old male members except her, Sai tries to confide to her own world which she has created out of her loneliness to live her imaginations. As the novelist narrates, "Sai walking to the kitchen, caught a glimpse of herself being smothered and reached forward to imprint her lips upon the surface, a perfectly formed film star kiss. "Hello," she said half to herself and half to someone else." As a result the first encounter of a teenage girl with a man of her own age instigates her feminine energies towards a romantic relationship. Sai starts a love relationship with her Maths tutor, Gyan. However, this courtship reaches to a sadistic end due to cultural and social differences between the two, but this adds a beautiful chapter to the novel which, except it, holds an intense pressure of all kinds.

There are three members in the house, named Cho Oyu. It is a big house built long ago by a Scotsman in a pattern of some monument, though now is breaking down with "the gamy mouse stench of a smell place...the ceiling had a reach of a public monument and the rooms were spacious in the old manner of wealth, windows placed for snow views". Sai lives in this big house with her grandfather, the retired old judge. He is a highly educated man from Cambridge University presently living his days after retirement. This retirement for him is not from work only but also from the power, position and aura he used to live with then as an officer. He has lost his social position and recognition with the passes of time due to the political and economic instabilities in the country of the time as reflected in novel. The judge has taken responsibility of rearing up his granddaughter, who has lost her parents in an accident. One of the strongest reasons of taking the responsibility of his granddaughter is his guilt for not having paid his responsibilities towards his wife due to so-called Englishness. As we see his sheer negligence for his wife Nimmi whom he considered throughout an illiterate, ill-mannered Indian woman unwilling to adapt to his Western etiquettes. The judge feels relieved from his repentance by taking care of Sai. We see him as a rigid and dissatisfied man irritated out of everything happening around. This is his firmness (engrossed by the past power) which despite life's ups and downs resulting into lower manages to sustain his attitude of so-called "sahib". His irritation for bakery man, who has gone to attend a wedding without supplying to them their monthly order, expresses the same—"How dare he go for a wedding? Is that the way to run a business? The fool." Further he shifts his anger towards the poor cook "Why can't the cook make something?" This gives a glimpse of the position and power he lived for a long span contrasting to his newly introduced poverty and unrest aroused out of his existing insecurities of all kinds. Also we can see his rigidness to class differences though is mild yet is clearly exhibited in his attitude. The way judge passes orders to his servants and anybody around expresses his culminating thrust for power and feel of high position lived in past. We see him facing discomfort in settling down with his own family and wife after he returns back from England completing his education there. Though he was not satisfied and never felt dignified in the foreign land in all his graduation years, yet he expects to be treated like a Westerner, a man with more refined etiquettes then anybody around, as he thinks. Throughout the novel, he seems holding his lordliness forcefully and gives a clear impression of as superiority driven man who takes his high origin and English knowledge as a matter of great pride.

A contrast to judge's persona, Desai has created the character of the cook who is a representative of the class deprived of the fundamental needs of mankind. He is "A poverty-stricken man growing into an ancient at fast-forward." There is something with Desai's description as it becomes picturesque with the progression of the story. Readers, in a while, become part of the narration; it seems as real as taking place before one's eye. She further describes the cook's stature as a "Compressed childhood, lingering old age. A generation between him and the judge." Clearly exhibited "...age in his temperament, his kettle, his clothes, his kitchen, his voice, his face, in the undisturbed dirt, the undisturbed settled smell of a lifetime of cooking, smoke, and kerosene." The cook has subdued a kind of bitterness for his work which he has accumulated out of his miserable life conditions. Though he seldom feels satisfied with his salary and position, yet dares not quitting the job scared of a queue waiting to replace him. This shows the depth of insecurity, a gift of poverty and scarcities. Admitting his miseries, he murmurs, "No thanks to me for anything...see what I have to deal with and I am not young and healthy anymore.... Terrible to be a poverty-stricken man, terrible, terrible, terrible...."

So, realistically Desai has created the picture of a servant, a class paradoxically set against any definition of development and advancement. This class has seldom shown any mark of development in position and survival in any age, rather ironically has always been pushed far more behind from any impression of so-called globalization in order to sustain the class differences by the dominating classes. This difference is convincingly expressed "...something about their closeness being exposed in the end as fake, their friendship composed of shallow things conducted in a broken language, for she was an English-speaker and he was a Hindi-speaker." Undoubtedly it is one of the most realistic narrations close to contemporary issues of the time.

The cook originally belongs to the northern part of India and has settled down in Kalimpong for his own survival as well as to make his son financially sound whom he has sent to America to earn name and money. He always introduces his son with utmost proud behind we see his culminating thrust for self-security and respect. We see Biju working in various kitchens in New York City and changing his job frequently struggling with everyday issues of survival in Western country as an outsider. Through his letters he connects the entire story taking place in India with America and its globalization contrasting with colonization and immigration.

"All the way in America, Biju had spent his early days standing at a counter along with a row of men." Among these strange people Biju feels nostalgic and struggles for survival in a way or the other "The spirit of these men he worked with amazed Biju, terrified him, overjoyed him, then terrified him again."

All his days in America Biju continuously feels being victim of differences common with both the cultures, Indian as well as Western. Their approach looking at the low class or whatever you name it is the same. In India, he faced dissimilarities in the name of cast, class and background which forced him to search his identity away from his homeland. He goes to America to escape from the class system, his lower cast origin with expectations that he will be treated well in a highly advanced and developed country that according to him will be grown above from small discrimination of class and cast. However, the experiences in a foreign land acquainted him with same rejection, criticism and ignorance in more humiliating way. His everyday struggle with new set of people, working environment and owner make him feel no change in frequent changes except those modified faces of different colours and backgrounds, however the thinking, attitude, differences and complexes remain the same as the owners wife says, "He smells," The statement is enough to assess his struggle there. Elaborating her statement, she voices her thoughts further, "At least they might have something in common with them like religion and skin colour...."

Biju realizes soon that he is trapped within the economic enslavement in America; the term suitable for immigrants. Despite his tough time in the United States, Biju does not abandon his Indian identity, we see him rejecting a tempting suggestion of his co-worker to visit the prostitute to show his manliness while Biju takes it all "dirty". This further blends Indian culture with advancement in a beautiful manner irrespective to all imbalances.

Biju returns to his country with a comprehensive understanding of the two cultures which preserve negativity, distrust and hatred for lower class and strongly deny to their presence as equal human. He has lived the narrowness of thought and life at marginality in his own country, so as America for him shrank into the underground society where no advancement reaches to enhance the status of slaves who are mend to be treated as second citizen.

So as feels Gyan, a Nepali young man and Sai's Maths tutor turned lover. He joins Gorkha movement and gives a different direction to the story. At one point, his presence contributes in painting the most colourful and hopeful side of the story relieving it from in a sadistic thread. Their love blossoms amidst prevailing pressures and turmoil in country as we read, "Eating momos dipped in chutney, Gyan said: "You'r my momo." Said Sai "No you'r mine." On the other, he connects the story with a contemporary burning issue that holds all distress growing in the time. He lives two states of mind one preserves a heart-full of soft emotions and the other is of a restless Nepali graduate frustrated with his unemployment and identity survival blaring with nationality issues. Though he loves Sai intensively, yet he hates her English culture and way of living in highly anglicized way. He burst out his feelings on Christmas celebration saying "Don't you have any pride? Trying to be so westernized. They don't need you!!!! Go there see if they will welcome you with open arms. You will be trying to clean their toilets and even then they won't want you."

Their love story ends with Gyan's joining of Gorkha movement. Gyan overwhelmed by his passionate involvement in the movement convinces himself: "Sai was not miraculous; she was an uninspiring person, a reflection of all the contradictions around her."

Desai has influentially narrated the crucial Gorkha movement of the time connecting it to the main plot maintaining entire sensitivity involved and the vague of pursuance by the young Nepali boys and their demand of separate land for Gorkhas. The novel covers many chapters to discuss the issue in many consequences and keeps our attention captivated with growing national, social and economic pressure high. As characters discuss:

"They have a point," said Noni, "maybe not their whole point, but I'd say half to three-quarters of their point."

"Nonsense." Lola waved her sister's opinion away. "They've been plotting this a long while. Dream come true. All kinds of atrocities will go on—then they skip merrily over the border to hide in Nepal. Very convenient."

"But you have to take it from their point of view," said Noni. "First the Neps were thrown out of Assam and then Meghalaya, then there's the King of Bhutan growing against."

"Illegal immigration," said Lola. "You saw that letter they sent to the queen of England? Gorbachev and Regan? Apartheid, genocide, looking after Pakistan, forgetting us, colonial subjugation, vivisected Nepal...."

The discussion between Lola and Noni has perfectly put forth the seriousness of the subject from both the sides Indian as well as Gorkhas. However, the seriousness of a mature woman and vague of emotion of a young woman have also been expressed beautifully. Lola, a divorcee and a mother of a young girl, is mature enough to take the seriousness of the demand and their outcomes. Whereas Noni, as described in the novel, is a young girl confined to her dreams neglecting her age and feelings reaches to a prolonged repent of letting her days gone. It seems "Life has passed her by and in those days, things had to happen fast for a girl, or they didn't happen at all." Sharing her restlessness with Sai she says, "Listen to me, if you get a chance in life, take it. Look at me, I should have thought about the future when I was young. Instead only when it was too late, I realize what I should have done long ago."

We observe identity, insecurity and survival issues as continued struggle of characters facing contradictory imbalances of life in different occurrences in novel irrespective of their age, gender and background (educational, financial, social and national). They become victims of social disparities as whole. We see colour difference with immigrant Biju, a poor Indian boy who migrates from his own country with the aspiration to earn money and dignity for himself as well as for his father who has lived all his life in services of others for the minimum gain. There are impressions of stiff class system. The cook represents the class born to serve others and live on leftover. Reflections of superciliousness and hypocrisy as governing attribute in people who belong to the elite class of society. The temperament of judge echoes the same at various occasions in novel. The severity of culture differences responsible for ending affectionate relations of innocent lovers (Sai and Gyan) due to overpowered vague of emotion and intensifying social unrest. The presence of Lola and Noni in the novel adds the angle of growing insecurity of survival for lone woman in society so realistically.

The discrepancies, spreading its giant wings, seem crunching the hopes and dreams of characters ending in their hopeless withdrawal from ambitions and a desertion of their aspirations of being identified, respected, loved and independent (financially, socially and morally). What binds these seemingly disparate characters is a feel of insecurity present in both the class whether it's highly educated and empowered elite class or uneducated and suppressed low class.

Desai, according to me, is one of those writers who are blessed with the skill to deal with an extensively sensitive subject in an outstanding humorous style and deliver the topic weaving poignant stories in the miseries of characters contradictorily set to face various life conditions and succeeds in dragging reader's attention towards the seriousness of the subject abruptly. Almost in every work of Kiran Desai we observe her narration raises above all human weakness and aspirations and reaches to an ironic self-fulfillment in the midst of all disparities. We notice the same trait in the present novel as we see all struggles pacing down some or the other way and life remains continue with all. Like her first novel *Hullabaloo*, the entire clamor gets quiet at the end and novel reaches to its end with aspiration continues.

WORKS CITED

Desai, Kiran. *The Inheritance of Loss*. New Delhi: Penguin, 2006. Available at http://www.amazon.com

Indra Mohan, T.M.J. "The Literature of Diaspora: A Synoptic View", *The Atlantic Critical Review*, Vol. 5, Number 4 (Oct.-Dec., 2006).

Wikipedia Kiran Desai. "The Inheritance of Loss". http://www.themanbookerprize.com/perspective/quanda/40